A GRAND TOUR JOURNAL
1820-1822

For the publication of this volume we are most grateful to Angus's two daughters Kate and Emma for granting permission for their father's work to be published here; to Alan Sutton and Jasper Hadman at Fonthill Media for bringing it to publication; to Dr Ralph Walter for his kind assistance; to Alexandra Mayson, one of Angus's last doctoral students, for transcribing the poem about Venice; to Dr Charles Doyle for his editorial eye; to Clare Bates for photographing artwork in the Derby Collection; and to Melissa James at Knowsley Hall for creating the map. Our sincerest thanks must go to our curator, Dr Stephen Lloyd, who found the previously overlooked manuscripts in one of the library cupboards and encouraged me to pursue their publication. Stephen also helped me choose the illustrations of key sites visited by Stanley across Europe, and completed the final draft of the unfinished text and introduction that Angus was working on before he died.

I have been fascinated to follow the various routes of these European travel journals, whether travelling by car, train or aeroplane in the footsteps of the young Edward Stanley, revisiting some of the places he himself reached by horseback, carriage or on foot. I have formed a sense of a young man who enjoyed a privileged childhood at Knowsley, where he was exposed to the outstanding collection of Old Master paintings formed by the 10th earl of Derby during the 1720s, including sixteenth- and seventeenth-century pictures by Bassano, Rubens, Snyders, Rembrandt, Ribera, Castiglione and Salvator Rosa. This elite upbringing was followed by a traditional education in the Classics at Eton College and Christ Church, Oxford.

Such an intellectual training prepared Stanley well for the aesthetic and historical impact of the many art collections, buildings and classical sites that he visited across Europe. His academic prowess and poetic sensibility developed further on his exposure to European society, history and culture, alongside random interactions with a wide range of people on his daily forays across cities, towns and the countryside. He expressed strong opinions with youthful naivety on manners, style and taste, for instance appreciating the classical collection of the Villa Melzi d'Eril at Bellagio on Lake Como, while criticising the 'vulgar' neo-classical taste of the owner of the nearby Villa Sommariva, on the other side of the same lake at Cadenabbia. Likewise, the confident young Stanley preferred the austere classicism of the Danish sculptor Bertel Thorvaldsen in Rome to his Venetian rival Antonio Canova, the 'sad pilferer' of neo-classicism, despite Canova being the most celebrated sculptor in Europe.

To illustrate these journals we have chosen images of oil paintings, watercolours, drawings and prints by artists who had either lived abroad or travelled to study art and architecture, the various landscapes or the classical sites. Some of these works were created by artists such as

Preface

While preparing a new survey in 2018 of the contents of the Derby Collection's library cupboards and archival muniment rooms at the Stanley family's ancestral seat of Knowsley Hall, our curator, Dr Stephen Lloyd, discovered a bundle of hitherto overlooked small notebooks, filled with neat but energetic handwriting from the early nineteenth century. Stephen was delighted to establish that these manuscripts had been written by the Hon. Edward Geoffrey Stanley (1799-1869), who was titled Lord Stanley after the death of his grandfather in 1834. On the death of his father in 1851 Stanley became the 14th earl of Derby, the future three-times prime minister in 1852, 1858-59 and 1866-68.

It soon became clear that five of these little notebooks contained Stanley's previously unknown European Grand Tour travel diaries, begun after his arrival at Florence in December 1820 and completed upon his return to England in July 1822. Also surviving is an additional sixth volume comprised of Stanley's technical notes from the ten lectures given by his guide Antonio Nibby about ancient Rome's most prominent surviving classical sites and buildings. That volume is neither transcribed nor printed here.

As this European travel journal was not previously known to Professor Angus Hawkins, author of the definitive two-volume biography *The Forgotten Prime Minister* (OUP: Oxford, 2007-8), my husband and I decided to invite Angus to prepare a scholarly transcription and edition of these journals for publication. He was almost able to complete this, together with footnotes and an introduction, during the first year of the global Covid-19 pandemic, before his untimely death in December 2020. We present this publication as a legacy to the memory of Angus, who presented stimulating papers on aspects of the 14th earl to two academic symposia held at Knowsley Hall during 2004 and 2013.

Contents

Preface by Caroline Derby   7

Introduction by Angus Hawkins   11

Stanley's Itinerary   19

Map of Stanley's Route   24

Volume 1: Florence—Rome:
      16 December 1820 to 9 March 1821   25

Volume 2: Rome—Naples:
      10 March to 27 May 1821   67

Volume 3: Naples—Venice—Tyrol—Switzerland:
      27 May to 18 September 1821   93

Volume 4: Milan—Naples:
      19 September 1821 to 5 May 1822   131

Volume 5: Bologna—England:
      5 May to 29 July 1822   171

'Venice' by Edward Stanley, transcribed by Alexandra Mayson   195

Index   203

Fonthill Media Language Policy

Fonthill Media publishes in the international English language market. One language edition is published worldwide. As there are minor differences in spelling and presentation, especially with regard to American English and British English, a policy is necessary to define which form of English to use. The Fonthill Policy is to use the form of English native to the author.

www.fonthillmedia.com
office@fonthillmedia.com

First published in the United Kingdom
and the United States of America 2022

British Library Cataloguing in Publication Data:
A catalogue record for this book is available from the British Library

ISBN 978-1-78155-890-4

Typeset in Sabon LT Std by Palimpsest Book Production Ltd, Falkirk, Stirlingshire
Printed and bound in England

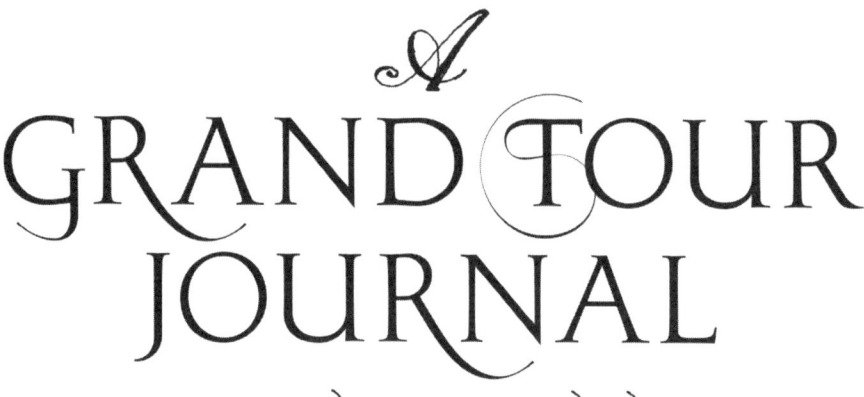

A GRAND TOUR JOURNAL

1820-1822

THE AWAKENING OF THE MAN

EDWARD GEOFFREY STANLEY

EDITED WITH AN INTRODUCTION AND NOTES BY
ANGUS HAWKINS

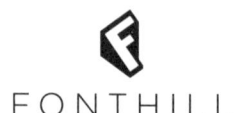

FONTHILL

Canaletto and Vernet in the eighteenth century, during the best known phase of the European cultural phenomenon known as the Grand Tour, which had its origins in the seventeenth century. However, we have also selected watercolours and drawings by J. M. W. Turner and Edward Lear, who made repeated lengthy visits across Europe during the early and mid-nineteenth century.

It is tantalising to note that Edward Lear dedicated the second book of his lavish two-volume *Illustrated Excursions in Italy* (London, 1846) to the future 14th earl. That long tour by Lear around central Italy had been part-funded by the artist's great early patron, the 13th earl of Derby, an eminent zoologist, to whom Lear dedicated the first volume in the 1846 publication. Tales of Edward Geoffrey Stanley's adventurous journeys through the extremely rough terrain of the spectacular Abruzzi mountains in 1821-22 may well have inspired Edward Lear to travel through and sketch many of the same rugged landscapes during the late 1830s and early 1840s.

Much has been made of Stanley being the only English prime minister to spend a night in jail after an altercation with a local official in the town of Benevento, not far from Naples. His reflections on this incident reveal his innate self-belief and expectation that he should be treated with fairness, despite being incarcerated at such a young age in a foreign country. The episode demonstrates Stanley's strength of character and also the courage that he would show later in life as a politician.

The fifth volume of the travel journals concludes with Stanley's draft of a long poem of 180 lines. It is a profound meditation on the fall of Venice, then under the control of the Austrian Empire. In this poem, Stanley exhibits an early abhorrence to the use of enslaved human beings, in this case on the Venetian galleys:

> Oh, arise the sacred spark! Your ancient fame
> Speaks with the voices of a thousand years,
> Bids you your Island boon of Freedom claim—
> Oppression's slavery's wrongs demand your tears—
> Your tears!—Yes, mourn as injured nations should
> Your country's insults! Mourn in tears of blood.

William Wilberforce's leadership of the campaign for the abolition of the transatlantic slave trade in 1807 is rightly celebrated, but also worthy of recognition is Stanley's key contribution as colonial secretary in 1833-34 to push through parliament the act to abolish slavery within the British Empire, especially across the Caribbean colonies.

We plan to follow up this volume of Stanley's European Grand Tour journal with the re-publication next year of Stanley's second set of travel diaries, which he wrote during his extensive tour of North America in 1824-25.[1] I am grateful to Andrew O'Shaughnessy, the former Saunders director of the Robert H. Smith International Center for Jefferson Studies at Monticello and professor of history at the University of Virginia, who has agreed to prepare a scholarly edition and write a new introduction to these journals.

Stanley's tour to eastern Canada and across the young United States of America included travelling through the Deep South and the plantations worked by enslaved Africans. It was this experience that truly laid the foundations of Stanley's political career, which was later manifested during his term as secretary of state for the colonies (1833-34), and culminated in his three terms as prime minister. However, the young future 14th earl's decisive exposure to a range of North American societies in colonial Canada and the newly independent USA was built upon his recent intensive travelling across Italy, over the Alps and through Germany a few years earlier. The impact of that first formative Grand Tour was summed up by Angus Hawkins:

> Both the refined and robust facets of Stanley's character were revealed during his Italian journey. Proud of his family and status, often haughty in manner, both boisterous and intelligent, his self-assurance cloaked a literary sensitivity and evangelical belief familiar only to his intimates. Never quick to compliment others, the combative Stanley expected deference as the natural acknowledgement of his birthright and abilities. He returned to England with a strengthened resolve to embark upon a political career.[2]

Carine Derby

The Countess of Derby

---

1   In 1930, the 17th earl of Derby commissioned a little-known transcription of these North American diaries. Only fifty copies were privately printed, and these were mostly presented to family and friends, with only a few being given to public libraries on both sides of the Atlantic.

2   Angus Hawkins, *The Forgotten Prime Minister: The 14th Earl of Derby, Volume I, Ascent, 1799-1851*, OUP: Oxford, 2007, p. 29.

Introduction

Late one evening in January 1821, twenty-one-year-old Edward Stanley wandered alone through Rome's darkened Forum. He was fresh out of Christ Church, Oxford, where he had studied the works of Horace, Virgil, Juvenal, Tacitus and other Classical writers, building on a passion that had taken root in his early schooldays at Eton. That moonlit evening he pondered the melancholy contrast between the long-past cultural glory and pre-eminence of the powerful and proud city of ancient Rome and the desolate ruins he now surveyed. He sensed a silent sombre mockery haunting the scene where glorious celebrations of martial triumph had once taken place. In October 1764, in contemplation of this same sight, the historian Edward Gibbon had conceived his great work *The Decline and Fall of the Roman Empire*. Stanley was moved by the same spectacle of shadowy ruins, and that night back at his lodgings, he reflected on his thoughts in a poem.

> Oh Rome! in this thy solitude thou art
> Bitterly eloquent, in all thy pride
> Of full blown pow'r, thou could'st not touch the heart
> With such deep feeling, as when by the side
> Of these ruined monuments of art
> We stand, and back by the resistless tide
> Of memory borne, recall thine ages past,
> And see what now thou art, and dream what then thou wast.

Edward Stanley had begun composing poems as a boy of nine, and at Christ Church he had won the prestigious Chancellor's Prize for his Latin verse. He possessed a talent that, according to his tutor, marked him out as 'a clever promising young man'. Later in life he published translations of Horace and Catullus and of the Greek poet Anacreon. He also translated the French verse of Millevoye, the Italian verse of Metastasio, Filicaja and Manzoni, and the German verse of Schiller. Most well known, however, is his two-volume English translation in blank verse of Homer's *Iliad*, which was published in 1864 to critical acclaim.

Stanley was exceptional not only for his talent, but also for his birth. Upon the death of his father in 1851, he became the 14th earl of Derby. This earldom had been granted to his forebear by Henry VII in 1485 with extensive property in Lancashire, north Wales, the Isle of Man and Ireland. It was one of the most prominent of all the English peerages. At Knowsley Hall, the Derbys' imposing family seat outside Liverpool, there were family portraits memorialising the Derby lineage hanging alongside paintings by Rembrandt, Rubens, Castiglione, Ribera and Van Dyck.

Edward Stanley's grandfather, the 12th earl of Derby (d. 1834), epitomised the high ideals and earthly pursuits of Regency Whiggery, while his father, the 13th earl, devoted himself to his passion for zoology. The 13th earl became president of both the Linnaean and Zoological Societies, and amassed the largest collection of birds and exotic animals in Great Britain. He employed the young Edward Lear to illustrate his specimens. Stanley's mother, meanwhile, the evangelical Lady Stanley, educated her son in the importance of faith and the Christian responsibilities of wealth and privilege.

Stanley's birth and abilities marked him out for a career in politics. In July 1822 he became MP for the 'pocket borough' of Stockbridge, a constituency controlled by the wealthy Whig peer Lord Grosvenor. In the mid-1830s, convinced that the Whig party had succumbed to the taint of radicalism, Stanley transferred his loyalty to the Conservatives, although he always insisted that he retained his Whig principles.

In his long career, Stanley served as chief secretary of Ireland, colonial secretary, and prime minister three times, forming governments in 1852, 1858 and 1866. His principal political achievements included the reformation of school education in Ireland, the abolition of slavery in the British Empire, and in 1867, the framing of the Second Reform Act which extended the male electorate. It was a career of distinction. Stanley was the first man to become prime minister three times, and as leader of the Conservative party from 1846 to 1868, he remains the longest serving party leader in the history of British politics.

In December 1820, at twenty-one years old, Stanley began an extensive tour of continental Europe. By the time of his return to England twenty months later in July 1822, he had visited Florence, Rome, Naples, Venice, Bologna, Innsbruck, Salzburg, Munich, Zurich, Lucerne, Berne, Lake Como, Milan, Augsburg, Frankfurt and Brussels. In a travel journal he recorded his social life, his visits to historical sites, his viewings of art collections, his comments on architecture, his admiration of landscapes and his impressions of foreign societies. He was energetic, enthusiastic and discerning. The bridge of Augustus in Umbria gave him 'a stupendous idea of Roman grandeur'; the charm of the towns crowning the Tuscan hills struck him with the same delight that he felt when gazing at one of Poussin's paintings; the waterfall at Terni, which dropped 370 feet into an abyss of spray, was 'awfully magnificent'; while the ceremonies of the Italian Catholic Church he judged to be a blend of mummery, superstition and bigotry, with little religion. Sights and experiences like these influenced him for the rest of his life.

The victory against Napoleon at Waterloo in 1815 had opened the door to a new and exhilarating age of freedom of travel for the English. The lure of continental Europe, particularly Italy, was powerful, and armed with Joseph Forsyth's *Remarks on Antiquities* (1813), Revd John Eustace's *A Classical Tour* (1815), and later, with travel chronicles such as Charlotte Eaton's *Rome in the Nineteenth Century* (1820), the rich and culturally curious sallied forth. Theirs was the opportunity to gaze upon the imposing remains of past civilisations; to admire the flowering of Renaissance art and the works of the Masters that followed; to experience the customs and behaviours of other nations; to develop interests in collecting and connoisseurship; to refine aesthetic tastes; and to contemplate the rise and fall of civilisations. It was, in many ways, a revival of the eighteenth-century Grand Tour, the cultural education of the British nobility; but more than that, it was also the chance to experience new and emerging cultural sensibilities. Romanticism in art and literature shaped fresh responses to sights, landscapes and art, and many of the great artists and writers of the age were drawn to Italy.

J. M. W. Turner's sketchbooks from his tour of Italy in 1819 capture his immediate and vivid response to the light, colour and beauty of the country; his large oil paintings of Italy, which he completed on his return, immediately went on public exhibition. John Keats travelled to Rome in November 1820 suffering from tuberculosis and never returned; his fellow poet Percy Bysshe Shelley called the city 'the paradise of exiles'. Shelley wrote *Prometheus Unbound* in 1819 sitting among the ruins of the Baths of Caracalla, while the previous year his friend Lord Byron published the fourth canto of *Childe Harold's Pilgrimage*, an autobiographical journey through Italy. Byron especially became an inspirational and charismatic ideal for ambitious young men looking to project a brooding creative genius through sartorial flamboyance, subversive disdain for authority, passionate bisexuality, and heroic melancholy. In 1823 he left Genoa to fight in the Greek War of Independence, where he died eight months later.

The Romantic response to Italy drew attention to aspects of its culture and geography less prominent in the experience of those who had undertaken the eighteenth-century Grand Tour. For Byron, Italy evoked infinite sorrow and the beauty of the past. The grandeur of nature and the solitude of the soul embedded in the landscape suffused his writing. The fourth canto of *Childe Harold's Pilgrimage* was a poetic commentary on the pageant of Italian history. In the supplementary notes of the first edition, Byron's admiring travelling companion John Hobhouse gave evocative descriptions of the landscapes that had inspired Byron's poetic muse.

It was difference and variety that caught the Romantic imagination. The people of Italy, Byron observed, were entirely apart from the English, the French and the Germans. They were at once temperate and profligate, serious in their character and buffoons in their amusement, driven by passions both sudden and durable. They were at their best in carnivals, balls and masquerades. It was local particularities that struck the French novelist Stendhal when he published his *Rome, Naples et Florence* in 1819. Rather than one civilisation, Italy possessed seven or eight centres of civilisation, each with its own distinct character.

Stanley's tour occurred towards the end of the period when continental travel was only possible on horseback or by horse-drawn carriage. This brought the traveller into direct contact with Italians of all classes and communities (and occasionally exposed him to the threat of brigands). In his many interactions with Italians, Stanley encountered everything from generous hospitality, puzzled incomprehension, cringing servility and open hostility. The political uncertainties prevailing in Italy at the time—with revolutions occurring in Naples in 1820 and in Piedmont in 1821—posed further hazards. In May 1821 Stanley was arrested in Benevento, where political tensions were high, and thrown into one of 'the most filthy holes in the world'. He thereby acquired the dubious distinction of being the only British prime minister to have been incarcerated in a Neapolitan gaol.

The influence of Romanticism gradually reshaped the geography of interest for English travellers. From the 1820s, Romantic sensibilities for the dramatically sublime encouraged excursions to the Alps and the landscapes of Switzerland. Here the awesome and majestic power of nature offered the visceral thrill of gazing upon forces beyond the human. On a summer's day in June 1821, Stanley gazed at the valley of Lauterbrunn in the canton of Bern, surrounded by the snow-covered peaks of the Schilthorn, the Bietenhorn and the Jungfrau. He thought it 'the most beautiful and romantic valley we have seen ... bold and beautiful'. Crossing the high alpine pass of Simplon, he found the landscape 'wonderful and the scenery magnificent'.

During the Grand Tour of the eighteenth century and up to the early 1820s, Florence, Rome and Naples were the well-established places to see and be seen. In these cities, wealthy English communities enjoyed a social life built around their own exclusive entertainments and hospitality; Stanley records an intense round of engagements among this transplanted English elite. (Social occasions that included Italians almost always retained a very English flavour and identity.) Venice, on the other hand, was regarded as a city of silence and decay, marginal to the fashionable lodgings and entertainments of Florence, Rome and Naples. In June 1821 Stanley left the city 'without regret', and it was only from the 1830s that interest and taste began to suggest that Venice was worthy of admiration. Appreciation was then accelerated by John Ruskin's first visit in 1835 and his publication of *The Seven Lamps of Architecture* (1846) and *The Stones of Venice* (1849).

In such an intense social climate, romantic entanglements between young bachelors and unmarried daughters were a frequent occurrence. Mothers could often be found scoping out eligible suitors for their daughters at social engagements. Stanley himself was a highly eligible young bachelor and was caught up in romantic imbroglios on two occasions during his tour.

In September 1821, while at Geneva, Stanley got to know the duke and duchess of Leeds and their twenty-year-old daughter, Lady Charlotte Osborne. Stanley played tennis with the duke, considered the duchess 'a very nice good-humoured woman', and found Lady Charlotte 'charming'. In Naples, from November 1821 to early February 1822, Stanley joined them frequently in their opera box and for 'agreeable' dinners at which he often found himself placed next to Lady Charlotte. However, his friendship with the family ended abruptly on 17 February 1822 when, at the end of an opera performance, the duchess declared: 'I said nothing during the opera, but I hate having people in my box all night.' Stanley was mortified. He replied: 'I am only sorry your Grace did not tell me so earlier. I have now the honour of wishing you a good evening.' He rushed out of the box, found his carriage, and when he got home was violently ill. He determined to leave Naples immediately, interpreting the duchess's speech to say, 'I do not approve of your attentions to Lady C. if you mean nothing'.

Back in Rome in March 1822, Stanley met Mrs Mary Patten Bold, a wealthy widow who had inherited Bold Hall in Warrington, Lancashire, approximately 20 miles from Knowsley Hall. She was travelling with her three unmarried daughters, Mary, the eldest at twenty-seven, Frances or 'Fanny' and Anna Maria. Stanley dined with the Bolds and accompanied them on riding excursions through the countryside around Rome.

At the same time, Stanley befriended Lord Clare, who had been the object of Byron's infatuation at Harrow, and the Hon. Ferdinand St John, a son of Lord Bolingbroke. St John introduced Stanley to his friend Prince Sapieha, a twenty-five-year-old Polish aristocrat. They all socialised with Mrs Bold and her daughters and a complex set of relationships developed. While St John fell in love with Fanny Bold, Clare and Sapieha had romantic interest in Mary, and Stanley clearly enjoyed her company too.

The group met at Narni, Bologna and Venice, and at Venice in May 1822, Stanley learnt from Mary that she had engaged herself to Prince Sapieha. The confidential nature of this conversation suggests the closeness of their relationship. Stanley told Mary that he regarded Sapieha highly, but soon afterwards Sapieha became jealous of Stanley's friendship with her. Meanwhile, a deeply upset St John was informed that there was no prospect of him marrying Fanny. Stanley left Venice on 24 May with much sadness; he had liked the family, 'especially Miss Bold'.

Stanley's tour from 1820 to 1822 came at a point of transition. It was the last time that cities such as Florence, Rome and Naples were to be the leisurely preserve of English aristocrats and the exceptionally wealthy. Stanley was acutely conscious of his social status and often recorded in his journal his distaste at meeting Englishmen and women not of the elite who had already begun to visit these destinations. In Rome in January 1821 he noted: 'a bad set of English here . . . A party of them went a few nights ago to eat Beefsteaks and drink Porter by moonlight in the Coliseum! These are the men of taste who travel in Italy! These are the people who give an idea of our national character!' Then in October at the Uffizi Gallery in Florence he found 'an execrable crew of English', and the next month in Naples he observed: 'There was a bad set of English here and too many of them.'

From the 1830s the social composition of British travellers to Italy and Switzerland had begun to change with the wholesale arrival of the affluent middle class traveller. The flourishing of handbooks for travellers, giving detailed advice on where to stay, where to eat, and the best routes from one place of interest to another, supplied a growing demand. *Murray's Handbooks for Travellers* began its publication in 1836, and by the 1860s English editions of the German *Baedeker Guides* provided detailed information on destinations all over Europe. Charles Dickens's *Pictures from Italy* (1846) and Edward Lear's handsomely illustrated books *Views in Rome and Its Environs* (1841) and *Excursions in Italy* (1846) also stimulated popular interest in experiencing what previously had been the preserve of the privileged few. In addition, the rapid development of the railway system from the 1840s revolutionised travel throughout Europe, providing a safer, faster, cheaper and more reliable means of visiting continental destinations. Italians blamed the growing number of English travellers for driving up the cost of everything.

In his journal, Stanley conveyed both a sense of Italy as the cradle of civilisation and refined aesthetic taste—though this did not prevent him criticising some of the art he saw—and a Romantic sensibility of the stirring beauty of landscape and climate. Naturally, given his education at Eton and Oxford, he travelled with a copy of Horace in his pocket. He attended Antonio Nibby's scholarly lectures on the Classical ruins of Rome, and declared, upon visiting the studio of the sculptor Bertel Thorvaldsen in Rome, that Thorvaldsen's work was superior to that of the leading contemporary Roman sculptor Antonio Canova. He diligently examined paintings, sculptures and architecture, but found scenes of natural beauty equally inspiring. With the fourth canto of Byron's *Childe Harold's Pilgrimage* as his literary companion, he surveyed Lake Thrasimene: 'Nothing could be more beautiful,' he recorded. And it was a nocturnal walk through the ruins of Rome's Forum that stirred his meditation on the melancholic beauty of desolation.

Stanley's Itinerary

December 1820 to July 1822

December 1820

16th Florence

26th Lucca

29th Livorno and Pisa

January 1821

1st   Florence

4th   Perugia

7th   Spoleto

9th   Narni

10th Rome

April 1821

6th   Palestrina

7th   Tivoli

9th   Vicovaro

10th Subiaco

11th Vicovaro

13th Tivoli

Then returns to Rome

30th Albano

May 1821
1st   Frascati

2nd   Velletri

4th   Naples

19th Eboli

20th Naples

31st Benevento

June 1821
3rd   Naples

14th Capua

15th Terracina

16th Rome

17th Spoleto

18th Macerata

19th Lareto—Ancona—Fano—Pesaro

20th Bologna

22nd Padua

24th Mestre—Venice

30th Bassano

July 1821
1st   Primolano—Trento

2nd   Bolzano—Brixen

3rd   Innsbruck

6th   St Johann

7th   Salzburg

10th Wasserburg

11th Munich

15th Augsburg

17th Memmingen

18th Lindau

19th Constance

20th Schaffhausen

22nd Zurich

25th Zug

26th Arth

27th Einsiedein

28th Zug—Lucerne

August 1821

1st Stansstadt

2nd Grafenort—Buochs

3rd Wassen—Andermatt

5th Meiringen

6th Brienz—Giessbach

7th Grindelwald

9th Stechelberg—Interlaken

11th Thun

13th Berne

15th Bienne

16th Sonceboz—Aix-de-Fond—Neuchâtel

17th Neuveville—Neuchâtel

18th Yverdon

19th Lausanne

22nd Bex—St Maurice

23rd Aigle

24th Lausanne—Geneva

September 1821

12th Thonon—St Maurice

13th Sion

14th Brig—Artars—Simplon

15th Domodossola—Baveno—Feriolo—Laveno

16th Isola Bella—Pallanza

17th Bellinzona—Laveno

20th Varese—Valganna—Ponte Tresa—Lugano

21st Como

23rd Cadenabbia

25th Torno—Caddenabbia

26th Rezzonico

27th Lecco—Caddenabbia
28th Como—Milan

October 1821
16th Pavia—Novi
17th Campo Morone—Genoa
20th Sestri
21st La Spezia—Prato—Florence

November 1821
1st   Siena—Rome
3rd   Velletri
4th   Sant' Agata
5th   Naples

January 1822
14th Capua—Sant' Agata
15th Portella—Terracina—Cisterna
22nd Portici
26th Naples

February 1822
22nd Rome

May 1822
2nd   Tivoli
3rd   Vicovaro—Carsoli
4th   Colli—Rocca di Cerra—Razzano
5th   Celano—Carcolo—Rocca di Mezzo—L'Aquila
6th   Rieti
7th   Terni
10th Macerata
12th Forlì
13th Bologna
17th Ferrara
18th Padua
19th Venice

25th Padua

26th Verona

29th Trento

30th Brixen

31st Innsbruck

June 1822

1st   Wallersee

3rd   Munich

11th Augsburg

12th Ulm

13th Stuttgart

15th Karlsruhe

16th Strasbourg

18th Karlsruhe—Heidelberg

19th Mannheim

20th Frankfurt

21st Mainz/Mayence

22nd Bingen—St Goar—Boppard

23rd Koblenz—Cologne

24th Aix-la-Chapelle/Aachen

26th Liège—Namur

27th Brussels

July 1822

2nd   Ypres

3rd   Calais

5th   Canterbury

6th   London

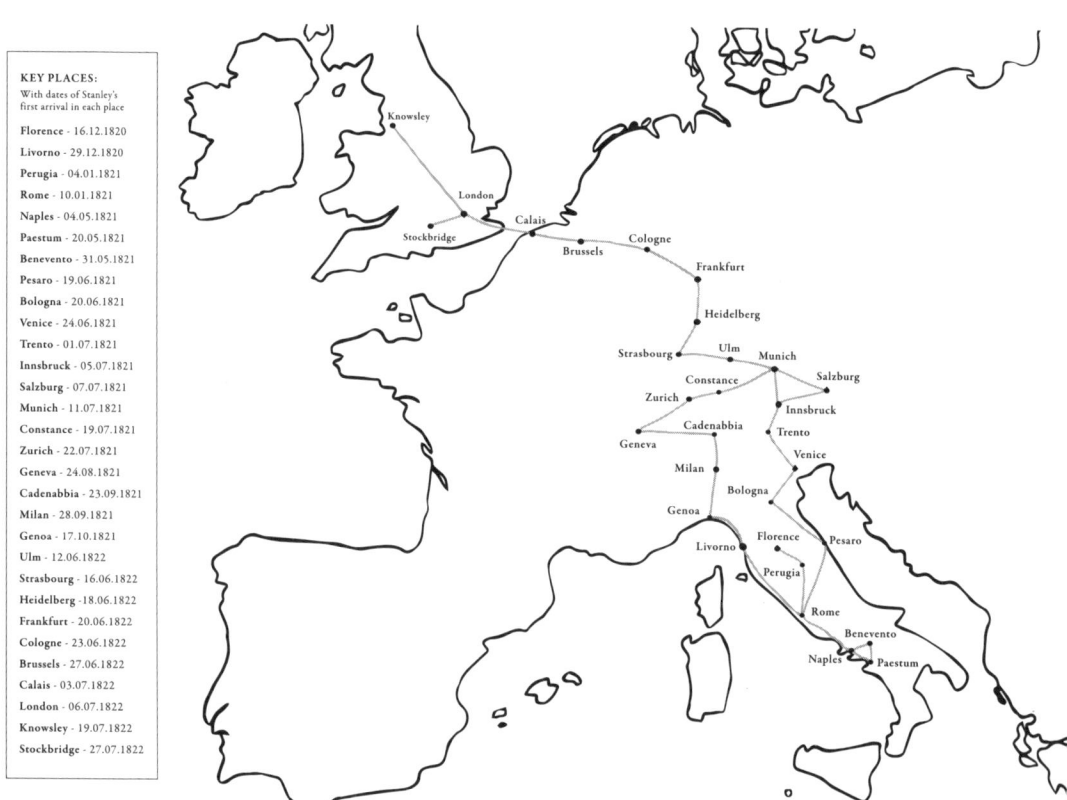

KEY PLACES:
With dates of Stanley's
first arrival in each place

Florence - 16.12.1820
Livorno - 29.12.1820
Perugia - 04.01.1821
Rome - 10.01.1821
Naples - 04.05.1821
Paestum - 20.05.1821
Benevento - 31.05.1821
Pesaro - 19.06.1821
Bologna - 20.06.1821
Venice - 24.06.1821
Trento - 01.07.1821
Innsbruck - 05.07.1821
Salzburg - 07.07.1821
Munich - 11.07.1821
Constance - 19.07.1821
Zurich - 22.07.1821
Geneva - 24.08.1821
Cadenabbia - 23.09.1821
Milan - 28.09.1821
Genoa - 17.10.1821
Ulm - 12.06.1822
Strasbourg - 16.06.1822
Heidelberg - 18.06.1822
Frankfurt - 20.06.1822
Cologne - 23.06.1822
Brussels - 27.06.1822
Calais - 03.07.1822
London - 06.07.1822
Knowsley - 19.07.1822
Stockbridge - 27.07.1822

Selected places visited by the Hon. Edward Geoffrey Stanley on his European
Grand Tour from December 1820 (Florence) to July 1822 (Knowsley).

VOLUME 1

Florence—Rome

16 December 1820 to 9 March 1821

Introduction to 'My Journal'

Yesterday arrived a letter for George,[1] containing nearly the following words. 'I promise myself much amusement from your Journals, for though Edward only speaks of <u>one</u>, I cannot imagine him such a <u>slug</u> as to have taken no permanent note of what interests him.' To say the truth, I have already several times found the want of some 'permanent note' to which I might refer to refresh my memory: and if it wants refreshing already, how much more necessary, as well as amusing, it will be hereafter to have the means of doing so, when the recollections of what we see here become less vivid, and more confused. Lady Alvanley[2] told me the other day that she has at this moment a book in which is recorded the way in which every day of her life has been passed for forty-eight years: mentioning even where she dined, who were her party, what was the tone of conversation, and a thousand minutiae of no interest in themselves, but which acquire one by the lapse of time: and she declared that

---

1   Edmund George Hornby (1799-1865), Stanley's first cousin, who was known as George in the family to distinguish him from his father Edmund Hornby (1773-1857), the Whig MP for Preston, Lancashire, from 1812 to 1826. George became the Whig MP for Warrington, where the Hornby family lived at Orford Hall from 1832 to 1835. The Hornby family and the Stanleys were closely inter-related. George Hornby's mother was Edward Stanley's aunt, Lady Charlotte Stanley; she married George's father Edmund Hornby in 1796. Edward Stanley's mother was Charlotte Hornby (1776-1817), George Hornby's aunt, and she married Edward's father, the 13th earl of Derby, in 1798.

2   Anne-Dorothea, Lady Alvanley, née Bootle-Wilbraham (1757-1825), was the sister of Lord Skelmersdale. She married Lord Alvanley in 1784, and he predeceased her in 1804. She became Stanley's aunt by marriage when he married her niece Emma Bootle-Wilbraham in 1825.

she had no greater amusement than looking over her Journal. I do not intend to be quite so particular, but I shall put down all that takes my fancy, and probably much more than will be worth remembering.

December 1820

From this day December 16 1820, I begin my Journal. I could not have chosen a worse. Like all last week, it has been almost constant rain, and I have therefore hardly stirred out of the House. Dined at home with George and Corbett, and went to Madame Albany's in the evening.[3] Of course a large party (Saturday) and did not speak even to her. Talked all evening to the Ardens and Tiesenhausens[4]—avoided being presented to Bill Pigott[5] who was between them and engaged myself to Madame Hitroff's for tomorrow.[6] No news in the English papers.

December 17. Rain again. We are leading a very heathenish life in Florence. There is no Chapel, and though service is performed in a room at Lord Burghersh's,[7] there is no possibility of getting a seat. I have only been once. Never went out all day except to the newsroom, where I found a terrible set of English and no news. I went in the evening to the Cocomero[8] to hear an Improvisatore, but was much disappointed. We came too late to hear what was his subject, but his Verses, as far as I could follow them, seemed very commonplace, and his rhymes infamous e.g. *lagrime* and *anime—fiori* and *ore*, etc. He was received with but little applause, though the theatre was very full. But this seems usually the case in the

---

3   Madame Albany was Louisa Stolberg (1752-1824), the widow of Prince Charles Edward Stuart (1720-1788), 'the Young Pretender', whom she married in 1772. She was subsequently styled the countess of Albany. She lived in the Palazzo Gianfigliazzi, Florence.
4   Of German Baltic origin, the von Tiesenhausens were a noble family associated with the Russian court.
5   Possibly William Pigott (1773-1838).
6   Madame Elise Hitroff (also transliterated as Khitrovo) (1783-1839) was the widow of Count Ferdinand von Tiesenhausen, who was killed at the battle of Austerlitz. His heroic action became the inspiration for the character of Andrey Bolkonsky in Tolstoy's *War and Peace*. In 1811 she married Major-General Nikolay Hitroff, who was appointed Russian *chargé d'affaires* in Florence in 1815. Major-General Hitroff died in 1819. Madame Hitroff eventually returned from Italy to St Petersburg in 1826.
7   Lord Burghersh (1784-1859) was the eldest son of the earl of Westmoreland. In the Peninsular War he served as *aide-de-camp* to the duke of Wellington. In 1811 he married Priscilla Wellesley-Pole (1793-1879), the favourite niece of the duke of Wellington and an accomplished linguist and artist. He succeeded his father as 11th earl of Westmoreland in 1841.
8   The Teatro Cocomero, the oldest theatre in Florence where comedy and tragedy were usually acted, was on Via del Cocomero, now renamed Via Ricasoli. In 1860 the Teatro Cocomero was renamed the Teatro Niccolini.

Italian Theatres where I have been, and must be a great discouragement to an actor. The Improvisatore declaimed in a sort of recitative, very slow. Avenue leading to it composed of magnificent ilex and cypresses. For the front, *vid* G's Book. I went afterwards to see the Palazzo Vecchio, or palace of the first of the Medicis:[9] I was disappointed on the whole, though the great room is very fair, 90 feet by 37 (I must be wrong, *passi* more likely), but this ill lit, and one does not see to advantage the frescoes and statutes with which it is ornamented, among which an unfinished Victory by Michelangelo.[10]

Remarked, in coming along the quay from the Ponte alle Grazie, a marble slab in the wall with this inscription: (I quote from memory)

> Ossa Equi Caroli Capelli Legate Veneti
>   Non ingratus herus, sonipes memorande sepulchrum
> Hoc tibi pro meritis, hoc monimenta dedit.
> Obsessa urbe M.D.XXX.III.

It was expected that the K. of Naples would be here today and the royal carriages went out to meet him, but he did not come.[11] His wife, it is said, stays here while he goes on to the Conference with the Allied Sovereigns.[12] English papers of today dull to a degree.

20th. Fine day, but mist on the hills. Corbett and I set out for a walk: went up to Fiesole. Sent a little boy from thence with an excuse to Thelluson, which amused George.[13] Agreed to go on with Corbett from Fiesole to the Pratolino.[14] A beautiful country, but horrible road, being the bed of a torrent for the first mile. Met an old peasant in the bottom. Walked with him some way, and found him very communicative, and

---

9   The Palazzo Vecchio was originally built in 1298.

10   The Salone del Cinquecento, measuring about 170 feet in length and 85 feet in breadth, had a carved gilded ceiling with pictures hung in deep compartments. Michelangelo (1475-1564), called during his lifetime 'Il Divino', was the pre-eminent Italian Renaissance master of sculpture, painting and architecture.

11   Ferdinand (1751-1825) became Ferdinand IV of Naples in 1759. When the kingdoms of Sicily and Naples were merged in 1816, he became Ferdinand I, king of the Two Sicilies. He married his second wife, Lucia Migliacco, in 1814.

12   In December 1820, in the wake of the uprising in Naples demanding liberal reforms to the constitution, King Ferdinand was invited by Austria, Russia and Prussia to the final days of the Congress of Troppau. He was then invited to the Congress of Laibach, which took place between 16 January and 12 May 1821. At the Congress of Troppau, Austria, Russia and Prussia agreed with King Ferdinand that Austrian troops would march into Naples 'to restore order' and reinstate the unreformed monarchy.

13   William Thellusson (1798-1839) succeeded his brother as 3rd Baron Rendlesham in 1832.

14   The Villa di Pratolino, 7 miles north of Florence, was designed by Bernardo Buontalenti and built by Francesco de' Medici between 1569 and 1581. The estate was known for its gardens, but by the early nineteenth century it had fallen into decay.

very much astonished that there were no olives in England *ne sulle montagne ne nelle pianure* [neither on the mountains nor the lowlands]. The olive and vine *raccolta* [harvests] have been very good this year, and he was in high glee. He described to me the process of the pressing, which is with a horse in the plains, and by water in the mountains. Mem. Though he did not tell me, the system of farming is here not by leases, but from year to year, and the landlord and farmer share the crop equally: the farmer being tied to having only a certain number of bearing branches on each tree. They generally stay a long while on the property, and become almost feudal retainers. All improvements are done by the landlord. So much for a mem. Our old man refused to take money at parting, and directed us to the Pratolino. This is a very pretty country house with fine trees and gardens quite *à l'Anglais*. But it is utterly ruined and when we were there they were employed in clearing away the rubbish and fallen stones. There is a gigantic statue of Appennino by Giambologna, but I own I did not admire it.[15] The view, however, was superb, looking down a wide mountain valley, closed by the beautiful hill of Fiesoli, on one side of which, though beyond, is seen the town of Florence, and the plain of the Arno, backed by gigantic Apennines of all shapes and tints. The sun was nearly setting and the rich red light on the hills contrasted strongly with deep black masses of shade, formed a splendid *coup d'oeil*. Coming home the sky after sunset seemed in a perfect blaze of all colours, blue, orange, green and bright red. They sunk at last into the latter, which as we both remarked continued fading and suddenly flashing up again more than once. At length coming down a hill, an instantaneous flash of light made us both start, and turning around we saw the perspective of the road closed up by the brightest and most splendid full moon I ever saw, by whose light we arrived in Florence about ½ past six. George went to Lady Alvanley's.

21st. Saw nothing worth notice today except the Palazzo Corsini, and even in this there is nothing very remarkable. Went to Lady Alvanley's in the evening.

22nd. Fine morning, but turned out cold and raw. Walk with George and Corbett to the Pratolino. Went to Madame Hitroff's, but she was not in.

23rd. Went to the Palazzo Strozzi.[16] There are not many good pictures and it is not worth the trouble of getting a ticket, except from curiosity to see

---

15   Giambologna (1529-1608) was a Flemish sculptor living in Italy.
16   First built in 1489 by Filippo Strozzi.

Benvenuti's picture of Bonaparte.[17] Very cold: walked in the Corsini and I met Madame Hitroff, and very near starved walking with them. To go there tomorrow. Letters from Henry and Charles this morning.[18] All good accounts and amused me much. Dined at home, went afterwards to Mad. Albany, very full and I thought dull: went afterwards Mad. Corsi and played whist till 12 o'clock. Engaged to dine tomorrow at Lord Rendlesham's.[19] Just as we were sitting down to dinner we were startled by the firing of cannon, and found on enquiry that it was in honour of the arrival of the old King of Naples, who was just entering the town, after being nearly sunk on his passage by the Vengeur running foul of a frigate.[20] He only stays till Tuesday and then goes on to accept the Invitation to Troppau.[21] There is some talk of a Ball at the Palace on Sunday next, but Ld. Burghersh has promised to let me know if there is, that I may be presented. The ceremony, however, is very simple and one does not even go in Court dress.

24th. Cold winter day. Went to make the tour of the churches. Visited the Santo Spirito, Carmine, Santa Maria Novella and Santa Croce.[22] All fine churches, but particularly the last which is magnificent and full of monuments of great men. Among others Michelangelo, Alfieri and two Galileo's, the Architect and the Astronomer.[23] The monument of Michelangelo struck me as particularly beautiful, though the three figures, Sculpture, Painting and Architecture are hardly sufficiently distinct. That of Alfieri erected by the Countess of Albany struck me as heavy and devoid of grace.[24] There are several other very beautiful monuments, and

---

17   The painter Pietro Benvenuti (1769-1844) was director of the Florentine Academy of Fine Arts.

18   Stanley's younger brothers, Henry (1803-1875) and Charles James Fox (1808-1884), who was named after the leading Whig politician Charles James Fox (1749-1806).

19   John Thellusson, 2nd Baron Rendlesham (1785-1832).

20   The *Vengeur*, an English ship of 74 guns, was carrying the king to Leghorn.

21   In November 1820, at the Congress of Troppau, Austria, Russia and Prussia signed the Troppau Protocol, agreeing to joint action in suppressing the revolution in Naples. King Ferdinand was invited to attend towards the end of the congress.

22   The Santo Spirito was an Augustinian foundation dating from 1250. The Church of Santa Maria del Carmine contains the fresco *The Life of Saint Peter*, which was painted by three artists—Masolino, his pupil Masaccio, and finally, Filippino Lippi—over a fifty-year period. The Church of Santa Maria Novella, first constructed by the Dominicans, has a striking marble façade and contains some of the most important works of art in Florence. Santa Croce is considered the largest Franciscan church in the world and also contains the tombs of Machiavelli and Leon Battista Alberti.

23   Vittorio Alfieri (1749-1803), dramatist and poet, was considered to be the founder of Italian tragedy. The 'Architect' was Alessandro Galilei (1691-1737), and the 'Astronomer' was Galileo Galilei (1564-1642). Because of his heresy, Galileo Galilei was initially banned by the Pope from being laid in the main body of the church, but a monument was finally erected to him in 1737.

24   Antonio Canova was commissioned by the countess of Albany to provide Alfieri's monument. The countess and Alfieri had lived together in Florence for much of her later life,

a remarkably fussy private Chapel to the left of the grand altar as you go in. When we went to the Chapel we found them engaged in preparing for the celebration of Christmas, by dressing up a number of dolls representing the holy family and on a stage in a niche of the church, and boys were employed in bringing grass to fill up the manger!!

Dined at Lord Rendlesham's and had a pleasant dinner, though nobody there but Thellusson and his wife.[25] Went afterwards to Madame Hitroff's and found some vulgar English. Staid, however, until 12 and then went out with them to the Church of the Annunciation to hear the celebration of Christmas Eve. The Church quite full and guarded by soldiers inside. A great deal of mummery and no devotion. The holy doll was well handled by the Priests, and by abundance of ceremony. I left the Hitroffs soon and got close to the grand altar. Staid till about two, and then came home, but was kept awake by bell ringing all night.

Monday 25th. Settled the packing off of my books for England. A miserably cold day and a sort of sleet falling. Shall not stir from my fireside where I am comfortably established. I doubt our going to Lucca tomorrow. There is a Ball at Lord Burghersh's on Thursday, but that alone would not stop us.

Thursday 28th. I have not had time to keep up my journal regularly for the last two days. I must make it up as I can. On Monday we dined at the Sykes's and went nowhere in the evening.

Tuesday 26th. Dark cloudy morning and very cold. We determined, however, not to delay our journey and about ten the sky cleared and it became a beautifully clear day. We set out about 12, Corbett , George and I together, and the two servants in our *calèche* [light carriage with a folding hood]. After crossing the plain of the Arno we entered on the mountainous country about Prato, the first post, from whence to Lucca the country is delightful. The road is very good and the ground charmingly tumbled: with hills of all shapes and sizes, houses well sprinkled about, and covered not only with the sombre grey of the olive, but with birch or oak intermingled. This continued I should think to Lucca, but we did not arrive there till after dark and drove to the Pelicano. The Inn was very good, but their stock of provisions lamentably small. Indeed, the shops were shut, it being festival, and it was with great difficulty and after waiting two hours that we got our dinner. Lucca is however quite

---

following her separation from Prince Charles Edward Stuart.

25   Ann-Sophia, née Tatnall, who married Lord Rendlesham in 1816.

a summer place and in winter there is no travelling. George had a bad headache all day and went to bed early.

Wednesday 27th. Took a *Laquais-de-place* [guide] and went first to the Cathedral [Duomo di San Martino], a handsome building enough outside, but the inside which is Gothic is magnificently fine. There some large round arches broken into three pointed ones, the pillars of which are perfectly beautiful for grace and lightness. There are also some *alto relievos* on the outside, very old and seemed good. The Church of St Michele [San Michele in Foro] which we also visited, has a very handsome façade, consisting of five rows of arches one above the other, and diminishing, though it struck me not enough, towards the top. We were told that the interior of the Palace [Palazzo Ducale] was very beautiful and that there were some very fine pictures, but as the Arch Duchess was there we could not gain admittance. The exterior is respectable and very well for a Sovereign of Lucca. In the Cathedral we saw the Sermon beginning. The Bishop, a very old man and very infirm being seated in his throne, the preacher began.[26] It was evidently for the day from his exordium, but we did not stay long. His voice was very strong and I could follow him perfectly, but it was very harsh and unpleasant and he used a great deal of action. We went afterwards to see the Marchese Buonvisi's collection of pictures.[27] There are not many good ones, though some good Poussins,[28] but all in a lamentable state, except a very good dead Christ on his Mother's lap by old Ferrari.[29] We just took a turn on the ramparts, which will be a beautiful promenade, but great part of it is only just planted.

Left Lucca about ½ past 12. Travelled through a very pretty country as long as we were in the Duchy of Lucca; and particularly admired the situation of the little village and fortress of Laiano, placed on and occupying the whole of a steep rock in the plain, and backed by mountains. I saw other towns and a fort also stand beautifully just before we reach the borders of Lucca. They have been in ruins, however, since the time when, as our postilion told us with some pride, *La repubblica di Lucca faceva la guerra contro della Toscana* ['The republic of Lucca waged war against Tuscany']. At the recommendation of the same postilion, a sharp intelligent fellow, we took a little detour and went by the Baths of Pisa. This, however, does not repay the trouble of it, at least in winter, but in

---

26 Filipo Sardi (1736-1826), archbishop of Lucca from 1789 to 1826. He was eighty-five years old in 1821.
27 The Buonvisis were a very wealthy and long-established family of bankers and merchants in Lucca.
28 The French painter Nicolas Poussin (1594-1665).
29 Francesco Ferrari (1634-1708).

summer I dare say it is pretty. It will, however, in two or three months lie in the direct road between Lucca and Pisa, as they are now engaged in making a new one which by crossing the mountains will shorten the distance by one half. They will, however, thus miss some beautiful scenery which I am glad therefore we have seen. N.B. Any one who wishes to see it should go from Lucca to Pisa, and not from Pisa to Lucca, as he would then miss much of the view. Arrived at Pisa, we drove to the Tre Donzelle, where by the way is written in flaming letters 'the three Damsels', but the waiters at the Damsels were saucy and the rooms dear, the Pelicano is filthy to a degree, and the Croce di Malta not much better. So we determined, having made a tour of the Inns, to go on to Livorno. On going out of town we were stopped by a crowd, occasioned by a postilion having run over a woman and killed her. The postilion was gone on to Livorno and ours told us *Oh Signor! Non ne so niente* ['Oh sir! I don't know anything']. Country to Livorno flat and ugly, particularly under the influence of a wet day. Tired horses, late at Leghorn. Went to the Globe—found the Inn bad and dear, and the waiter intolerably impertinent, who finished by telling us that they could do very well without us. Accordingly immediately after dinner we took our baggage on our shoulders and sallied forth in a very wet night to the Aquila Nera where we found better and cheaper rooms and the people civil to a degree. The waiter, on our going, said he never had seen three such 'Capitani'.

Thursday 28th. Wet day. Wrote to Lady D. did not go out till very late. Saw the Cathedral and a manufactory of Coral, with the simplicity of which I was much surprised. Went to the Opera in the evening, *Matrimonio segreto*,[30] wretchedly acted, and the ballet, *I viti Indiani* quite infamous.

29th. Cold raw day, some little sleet in the morning. Went out, however, to see the town, which is certainly a fine town, though all is for use and nothing for show. Went first to the English Cemetery. Several prettyish monuments, but general effect spoiled by their being crowded together. Very melancholy, almost the first monument we saw was a plain stone raised to the memory of poor Mrs Barnett!—Horner—Smollett.[31] A very neat monument to Mr Gwillyum.[32] Went afterwards to the Dutch Cemetery, which is laid out very neatly as a garden with rows of flat

---

30   *Il Matrimonio segreto* (*The Secret Marriage*) was a two-act opera by the Italian composer
     Domenico Cimerosa (1749-1801), first performed in 1792.
31   Elizabeth Catherine Barnett (1765-1820), daughter of William Markham (1719-1807),
     archbishop of York; Francis Horner (1778-1817), Scottish MP who died in Pisa; Tobias
     Smollett (1721-1771), Scottish writer who died in Livorno.
32   A son of Robert Gwillyum of Atherton Hall, Lancashire.

plain gravestones for walks. Nothing like a monument to be seen. Walked along the Quay and round the very fine Pier, but the day was cloudy and very cold which prevented our enjoying the view from there or from the *Maison de Force*. Saw several of the Galley slaves there and heard some extraordinary cases. One of a Baker who in a jealous fit flung his wife into his oven and baked her to death. He is confined for 30 years, and is within a month of his release. Two for ravishing and murdering an English family and one for the same crime on his own sister. Went in the afternoon to see the Depot for Oils, a good vaulted building, which holds 2,400 barrels, and where merchants deposit it at 3 Sous a month. Went afterwards to the Jewish Synagogue, said to be the finest in the world, and was much disappointed. The service, indeed, seems much more reason as to manner than the Catholic. It is a sort of recitative, where all the congregation join at times, but they all have their books and seem attentive. Some Jewish schools amused me, but they hollered to the very utmost pitch of their voices and very near deafened us. Our *Laquais-de-place* said it was all the same and we came away in a quarter of an hour.

Saturday 29th. Came in Corbett's carriage, wretched day, sleet and snow, to Pisa. Cleared up as we came and was fair, though bitter cold, all day. Not much to see in the town, and I should be very sorry to live in it. Brought a letter of recommendation which was admirable from our landlord at Leghorn to the Majter of the Pelican, whose Inn I find we wronged. It is not dirty inside, and we are very well here. Visited the Leaning Tower, the Cathedral, very rich and handsome, and I have little doubt that the work they call Egyptian in it was taken from Hadrian's palace which stood on the same spot, and some fragments of which remain in the Campo Santo. Several fine Andrea del Sartos,[33] much silver, marble, mosaic, Lapis Lazuli, and antiques, etc. When the French were here they made their ransom the plate of the altar at 18,000 Scudi. The Baptistery unfinished, but very beautiful, as are the Arches of the Campo Santo, and an Antiquarian would spend ages here. But, except these and the Lung' Arno,[34] there is nothing to see; and all this may be done in two or three hours. Went to see a collection of dresses and figures, with a model representing the Game defending the Bridge at Pisa, which it is said is a remnant of the Olympic Games![35] This model is at the House of

---

33   The Florentine painter Andrea del Sarto (1486-1530).
34   The streets lining the River Arno.
35   A traditional contest called the Gioco del Ponte held annually in Pisa on the bridge over the Arno. Two teams, the Tramontana and the Mezzogiorno, compete to push a large carriage over to the opposing end of the bridge.

the Chevalier Primi and is curious. Lady Charlotte Campbell here.[36] Her daughter is to be married directly.[37] Return tomorrow to Florence and well satisfied with our excursion, though the weather has been villainous.

Sunday 30th. Weather very clear and bright, but intensely cold. So much so that little waterfalls are entirely congealed and hang in icicles or rather sheets of ice. The country between Pisa and Florence is very pretty, very thickly inhabited, and in some parts also with ups and downs—a very rare occurrence in the Italian plains. Arrived at Florence about seven. Dined and went to bed. In the course of the day passed one more of the 28 Imperial villas. An ugly square house with a square tower at each corner, and nothing remarkable in the appearance of it.

January 1821

January 1st 1821. Beautifully clear frosty morning and the Lung' Arno exceedingly gay, being covered with holiday folks in their best dresses. By the way the luxury in which the *contadine* or peasant women indulge in point of dress is very great. While at Pisa we saw a very poor looking woman bargaining for some heavy drop earrings and from curiosity told our *Laquais-de-place* to see what she paid for them. He came back and told us she had agreed for 10 Sous/100 Pauls/or nearly £2.10 of English money, and he added that besides an enormous Cross at their breast they have often earrings so large and heavy as to tear out the ear, and that to lessen the weight they often tie them by a string to the hair. I have since repeatedly seen this. This is one of the great feasts, which occur every other day *per la disgrazia de negozianti* ['to the misfortune of shopkeepers'] as my Bookseller tells me. Today all the world go about leaving cards and wishing each other a happy new year. Lord B's Chasseur had the impudence to come to wish me one. We wished him the same and Good Morning!! Our waiters, however, earned their 10 Pauls by a beautiful bouquet to each of us of Jonquils, Rous, Orange flowers, etc.

Walked to the Caraggi,[38] the favourite villa of Lorenzo, but *il Padrone* was gone down to Florence and we could not see the inside. It has been very extensive, but is now split into several farm houses and the ornamental gardens converted into olive grounds. A beautiful view from the

---

36   The novelist Lady Charlotte Campbell (1775-1861), daughter of the 5th duke of Argyll, who had been a lady-in-waiting to Caroline of Brunswick, princess of Wales.

37   In Florence, February 1821, Lady Charlotte Campbell's daughter Harriet married Lord Tullamore (1801-1851). He succeeded as the 2nd earl of Charleville in 1835.

38   The Villa Careggi, where Lorenzo de' Medici died in 1492. The villa was subsequently owned by the grand dukes of Tuscany until 1780.

hill above. Returned to Florence in rain and went to the Opera in the evening—very bad.

Tuesday 2nd. Visited the Laurentian Library beautifully arranged with reading desks and a list at the end of each desk.[39] All the books chained down. The Riccardi Palace. Fine Library and magnificent allegorical ceiling by Luca Giordano,[40] but very unequal. Some pretty painting of Cupid flowers etc. in a large mirror. Visited with Corbett for the last time to the Tribuna,[41] and staid some time. Went into all the rooms but the Sala de Frati, which we mean to visit tomorrow early.

Wednesday 3rd. Went with Corbett to the Sala de Frati, but I think on the whole I was disappointed with it. Went next to the Palais Pitti. I think nothing struck me so much as the Judith, but I wish I had been here oftener. Once or twice is not sufficient. To see and admire pictures I am sure you should go often and see little at a time; otherwise the eye and mind are both fatigued and become indifferent. The rest of this wet 'soft' day was taken up in having P. P. C. Had the mystery of the Ball cleared up. Lord B. had sent one of his attaches and either he or the waiter blundered the matter. Went to the Opera, into Lady Sykes's box, and talked too fast to see the first act of the opera acted last. Not uncommon.

Thursday 4th. Received a letter from Lady Derby to George. Our letters have been admirably managed, for we have lost none, and hear by this that there are some waiting at Rome. Set out very pleasant day and arrived late at Arezzo. Found a tolerable Inn, the Albergo Reale.

Friday 5th. Set out next morning in very good time, but were stopped two stages on by a battle with the postilion, who first tried to cheat us and then abused us. I pulled out a pistol in answer to a great stone which I saw ready to fly, and it was comical to see the people get one behind another in awful expectation, while my antagonist and I stood watching each other. Fought our way out and went to the Prefect, whom we found a comfortable Grocer looking man, and a great fool. We humbugged him at first, and bullied him afterwards—the last plan much the best. Retired victorious, after a delay of an hour and a half which brought us late to Perugia.

---

39   The Laurentian Library held over 9,000 manuscripts and was judged by many to be the most important library in Italy.

40   The painter and printmaker Luca Giordano (1634-1705).

41   An octagonal gallery in the Uffizi, which was completed by Cosimo de' Medici II in 1610. It contained the sculptures *The Venus de' Medici* and *The Wrestlers*, as well as paintings by Michelangelo, Raphael, Titian, Veronese and others.

I cannot conceive what people mean by saying the road is ugly. The country is rich, great variety of hill and valley, some timber trees, and a good deal of brush wood. Altogether from Florence to Perugia, with the exception of from Arezzo to Castiglione (our perfect town), very beautiful. Set out from a fair Inn at Perugia (the Post) about half past eight. Town charmingly situated from whatever side you see it. Indeed, I have remarked this of all the Italian towns that I have seen in this part. They all crown the summit of some eminence greater or smaller, and the absence of smoke and beauty of outline gives quite the effect of Poussin's pictures. By the way, nothing can be more beautiful than the plain of Thrasimene in our yesterday's journey, and one sees at once how Flaminius suffered himself to be entrapped and how thorough was the snare into which he fell.[42] The best guide for this scenery, and it is a perfect one, is a note to the *4th Canto of Childe Harold*.[43] We passed with this in our hand and could not mistake its directions. By the way, we are changing the road, but not materially. Another quarrel today at Foligno and forced to take four horses. A lovely May day, tomorrow to rain at night.

Sunday 7th. We find ourselves so well here that we mean to explore the environs of Spoleto if weather allows, but it is very threatening. Our Inn is the Speranza, very comfortable, though we are in a large room, through which all the family pass to their rooms. Everything, however, is clean and people very civil. When I talk of good Inns I only speak of for single men, for Ladies I have no doubt many I have been at would be far from pleasant. But I am very agreeably disappointed in Italian Inns in general. They are much better in essentials than Scotch Inns or than the worst sort of English, though brick floors, no carpets, rafters, etc. give an uncomfortable appearance. Those, however, who condemn them at once judge too hastily and therefore unjustly. N.B. The worst looking Inns often the best.

Monday 8th. After writing the above, we went out with our Guide to see everything in the town worth seeing. The first thing we went to, which indeed we saw out of our own windows, is the Aqueduct [Ponte delle Torre], which crosses a deep valley between two steep hills, upon

---

42   At the battle of Thrasimene (217 BC), the Carthaginian general Hannibal routed a Roman army commanded by Gaius Flaminius. Of 35,000 Roman troops, only 10,000 returned to Rome. The rest were either killed in battle, drowned in the lake as they tried to escape, or taken prisoner. Flaminius himself was killed in the battle.

43   A note supplied by John Hobhouse (1786-1869), Byron's travelling companion, on pages 176-182 of the first edition of *Childe Harold's Pilgrimage. Canto the Fourth* (London, 1818) gives a vivid and detailed description of the battle scene, the topography and the details of the conflict.

a very high range of nine arches. The arches are, however, too high for beauty and seem to be so for strength, for they seem to have given way, and to have been supported by second arches about half way up. We went to what is called the Temple of Drusus, certainly an old vaulted Roman building, but dark and difficult to distinguish objects. Ponte Sanguinario, celebrated for an ancient massacre of, it is said, 1,200 martyrs in the early years of Christianity.[44] The Bridge or rather two arches of it have just been discovered, within two years, in laying the foundations of a new Bridge. This seems to have led to the Temple of Concord [the Crocifisso], which is still very perfect, almost all the pillars still remaining, though several of them are embedded in the walls of a modern Chapel, which we wished burnt to the ground together with the wretched mendicant Monks. Went back by the Porta di Fuga, where an inscription over the ancient gate celebrates the repulsion of Hannibal after the victory of Thrasimene.[45] Two pictures in the Chapel [Church of San Domenico], the other in the Palazzo Muncipale, of Raphael and Pietro Peruggino,[46] but one as bad as the other, and the latter very much damaged. Called on the Ispettore della Posta to settle our numbers of horses, who called on us in the evening accompanied by his men, to one of whom George offered a 10 Paul piece which he rejected with horror, and we found afterwards that he was a student and a gentleman. Corbett and I took a tremendous walk or rather scramble over the Hills. Our Guide, who by the way was glad to be excused herding us, was a rank Napoleonist and very amusing. He fancies Bonaparte will come back again. Very good Inn the Achora della Speranza. Recommended to the Fortuna at Terni.

Set out early in the morning, mizzling rain—cleared up towards eleven, and after breakfasting at Terni walked to the Cascade [Cascata delle Marmore].[47] I should advise those who can only see it from one point to go above, but if they can take both, to go by the lower road, very beautiful, and return by the upper, the Fuga del Velino above the Cascade. The view of the first fall of 370 feet, boiling and raging from the abyss below, and the smoke or spray which flies near half a mile, are all awfully magnificent. But the fall has been described so often that it is absurd to describe it, or rather attempt it, and all painting is yet more ridiculous.[48] George rode a donkey which had had the honour of carrying Marie

---

44   Legend has it that Lucrezia Borgia used to meet her lovers on the bridge.

45   Following the battle of Thrasimene, Hannibal's army was repulsed at Spoleto.

46   The painter Pietro Perugino (*c.* 1446/52-1523) was the teacher of Raphael (1483-1520).

47   The road from Spoleto to Terni ascended steeply over the Pass of Monte Somma, rising to 3,786 feet above sea level, before descending into Terni.

48   Byron gave an extended poetic description of the waterfalls at Terni in the fourth canto of *Childe Harold's Pilgrimage*.

Louise.[49] Our Guide, a good intelligent fellow and very civil, took us on our return to see an oil mill—a curious process, and this being a great oil country one sees it to advantage. The *reccolta* has for 5 years been very bad and the people are in uneasy mind. In good years the processing lasts for 4 or even five months. 70 mills are at work at the rate of 70 Somma/47 lbs each a day. He described it as a very animated scene—masters, servants, all at work at the oil, and wages so high that children can earn a Paul a day. The first grinding of the olives is performed in a circular trough, by a large millstone set upright and turned by water, having a sort of iron hook attached to the middle of it which sweeps the trough and draws the olives within the action of the stone. The olives, reduced to a consistency like chocolate ground, are then placed in a sort of basket of rushes, and there are placed vats with a strong screw pressure upon them, and with a little hole in the bottom of the vats like the entrance of a beehive, where the oil slowly runs out into reservoirs placed below. The refuse is subjected three times to this process and then kept for fuel, but never given to cattle, and my question amused the man much. Saw the Temple of the Sun, but it is whitewashed and modernised into a Chapel,[50] and we saw no vestiges of antiquity in the interior. The Inn here, with every appearance against it, is really comfortable, very civil people, very good eating and very clean beds. Our sitting room is indeed a public one, but we have had nobody here but a little priest with a consumptive, who George says must die soon, and it is next to the kitchen with no door between, but these are secondary considerations. There has been in our hearing a great dispute between the waiter and the daughter of the house whether we were English or Spanish: which was at last ingeniously decided by the waiter who on my asking the Italian of snuffers, asked me the English name for them. I had not my wits enough about me to say I did not understand English. Had enough of my walk and shall go to bed early.

Tuesday 9th. After a bad night occasioned by beds which though hard gave way and left your feet in the clouds and your head on the ground, we set out about nine on a beautiful May morning, crossed a fine plain and arrived at Narni about half-past 10. The town stands well on the slope of a hill, in ascending which we got out and were immediately accosted by a man who told us he would show us Augustus' Bridge, which was much handsomer than the Cascade at Terni. George was all for going on, Corbett for stopping, and I joined the latter opinion, though

---

49   Marie Louise (1791-1847), the Austrian archduchess, was duchess of Parma from 1814
      until her death.
50   The twelfth-century Church of San Salvatore was built on the reputed site of the Roman
      Temple of the Sun.

without any expectations being raised very high. When, however, we came down to the Bridge we all exclaimed in raptures that we had seen nothing so fine in Italy.[51] This Bridge gives me a stupendous idea of Roman grandeur as exhibited in a provincial town; it crosses the river and a deep valley, joining two fine craggy rocks or almost mountains half way up. It has consisted of four arches, one of which is still entire: the pillars of the others are standing, but the arches are gone. The magnificence of the design is inconceivable and only equalled by the grandeur and the solidity of the execution. Through the remaining arch is a beautiful view of a very fine hill crowned with a church and a village, and the hills on the sides and background covered for miles and miles with Ilex, the spontaneous produce of the soil in every part. George took a sketch of the Bridge, which we shall certainly visit on our return if we go that road.

Leaving Narni the country soon becomes more open, and you get a view of an enormous plain, only broken apparently by the bold ridge of Mt Soracte[52], metamorphosed into Sant 'Oreste - a new saint in a Christian Calendar. I must not forget to observe that we saw at Narni a prison [the old castle] where 200 persons are confined, accused of being Carbonari;[53] in fact, Italian radicals, or, as our *Cicerone* informs us, *Masoni.* Whether this has any connexion with the Free Masons or not I do not know. These unhappy people, among whom is a Hungarian Baron, have been bandied about from prison to prison for two years, are now shut up in one much too small, in dungeons underground, where several have died already, and all this without any trial having taken place. So much for Papal justice! We slept this night at Nepi in a small bad Inn, but we wished to get into Rome by daylight.[54] Left all remains of pretty country at Otricoli.[55] Passed today through Civita Castellana, the modern Fabrium, a poor mean town, but I dare say was strong.

---

51 The Ponte d'Augusto, a ruined Roman bridge, is regarded as one of Umbria's most famous landmarks. The arches of the bridge rise over 60 feet and were described by Roman writers as the tallest known. J. M. W. Turner made several sketches of the bridge during his Italian travels, and in 1826 Camille Corot painted a much-admired view of it. *The Murray Guide for Central Italy* (London, 1843) noted 'nothing can be imagined grander in its general effect or more striking in its details than this magnificent ruin and the picturesque scenery by which it is surrounded.'

52 Rising to 2,000 feet above sea level, Monte Soratte was praised by Horace in *Odes* I.9 and Byron in the fourth canto of *Childe Harold's Pilgrimage*.

53 The Carbonari were members of a secret revolutionary republican society that was active throughout Italy. They sought liberal reforms and instigated the Neapolitan uprising in 1820.

54 The small, picturesque town of Nepi, set on the edge of a deep glen, had just one inn, La Posta.

55 After Otricoli, the road to Rome leaves the Apennines and drops down to the plains of the Tiber.

Wednesday 10th. Entered today on the desolate unvaried waste of the *Campagna*.[56] This is not, as it seems, a dead flat, but a succession of little hills, where you fondly hope on arriving at the summit of each to find some object to relieve the eternal dullness and melancholy air of desolation, and are constantly disappointed. No signs of habitation and but very little of cultivation, the region, in short, of dreariness and solitude. The only object of <u>any</u> interest, and that one of disgust, was the recurrence at every other mile of high poles with human arms, legs, etc. suspended, black, shrivelled, and waving in the wind. Such is the ancient Latium, the populous *fauxbourgs* of Rome, in its greatness!

The first view of Rome on entering this way by the Porta del Popolo disappoints you much, and all we have yet seen of the modern town is wretched to a degree. Established for the present in Jenny's Hotel, comfortable but dear. But had procured us a *lascia passare* [pass or permit] at the gate, a precaution which saves much trouble. We find almost all the Florence set at Rome, but with great additions and I think society will be good. Very much disappointed in the first view of St Peter's. The dome cannot be seen well and the building appears flat and lumpish, but I have not yet been in, so I must not judge hastily, particularly against the wonder of the World.

D. of Hamilton here, a great joy to me.[57] Sir James Maitland arrived from Naples, and it is said Sir W. à Court[58]—a thousand rumours afloat.[59] Letters arrived from Mary and Charlotte.[60] What a comfort letters are abroad!

Thursday 11th. A close unwholesome day, passed the whole day in hunting over the town for lodgings, but have not found any yet. Found leisure, however, to renew our visit to St Peter's. Let nobody judge of St Peter's by the outside. We went in and were, as Gray says, struck dumb with astonishment.[61] The immensity, the magnificence and the proportions are striking to the last degree. Yet I prefer the Gothic style for a Cathedral, and we all made the remark that St Peter's did not strike us with the

---

56 The extensive, undulating tract of land between the Apennine Mountains and the shores of the Mediterranean.

57 Alexander Hamilton-Douglas, 10th duke of Hamilton (1767-1852), Whig politician and art collector, succeeded to the title in 1819. He was ambassador to St Petersburg from 1806 to 1807 and grand master of the freemasons of Scotland.

58 Sir William à Court (1779-1868) was appointed British envoy to Naples in 1814 and British envoy to Spain in 1822. He was created 1st Baron Heytesbury in 1828.

59 The rumours were regarding events in the kingdom of the Two Sicilies.

60 Stanley's aunt, Lady Mary Stanley, daughter of the 12th earl of Derby, and Stanley's sister, Lady Charlotte Stanley (1801-1853).

61 A quote from a letter dated 2 April 1740 by the poet Thomas Gray (1716-1771) to his mother. *The Letters of Thomas Gray*, Vol. I (London, 1817), p. 68.

awe inspired by the pillared aisles of a Gothic Church. To have an idea of the size of St Peter's, go into one of the cross aisles; look along it. You fancy yourself in a very fine Cathedral. Then walk into the main body of the Church and compare the two. Talking of St Peter's, I advise nobody to take Eustace as a guide in Italy.[62] He praises everything indiscriminately, and the reality disappoints the expectations he has raised. The remarks on him in the notes to the 4th Canto of *Childe Harold* are very just.[63] Went to the opera in the evening. Opera fair—the ballet would have disgraced dancers at a fair, and was much in their style.

A bad set of English here, though some good, but it is said there are above 1,500 in all. A party of them went a few nights ago to eat <u>Beefsteaks and drink Porter by moonlight in the Coliseum</u>! These are the men of taste who travel in Italy! These are the people who give an idea of our national character!

Friday 12th. Still a close oppressive day. No wonder we have been complaining all the time of oppression, the Sirocco has been blowing for near a month! Went with Corbett to the top of St Peter's: the view would be superb, but the fog was thick over the distance. Went, like many other fools, into the ball, and came down again, for one sees nothing from it! The ascent to the Cross is forbidden by order of the government, and the ladder covered over.

Dined at home. Fine moonlight night, walked down to the Coliseum. The Forum, which you cross degraded to the Campo Vaccino,[64] is a sad scene of desolation, and makes one very melancholy—broken pillars, ruined arches in every direction, and you walk over ground swelling with heaps of rubbish, it is said 14 feet over the level of the ancient pavement. I own the first view of the Coliseum disappointed me, but I came down upon it from the wrong side, that the one where the building is lowest, and seeing it for the first time by night I am convinced you do not perceive the effect of the size. The loneliness however of the place, only disturbed by the sentinels challenge, the partial light, the remnants of buildings scattered all around, have an awful melancholy effect, and we both came home *recru* [exhausted] and *distrait* [preoccupied]. In short, I left George and marched on about half a mile quite forgetting him. When we are settled, however, we must begin examining in earnest. Mr Aylmer, a friend of George's, is here. We dine there on Sunday. He has

---

62 The Revd John Chetwode Eustace, author of *A Classical Tour of Italy* (London, 1815).

63 On page 233 of the first edition of the fourth canto of Byron's *Childe Harold's Pilgrimage*, Hobhouse observes that while Eustace might adorn a library, *A Classical Tour of Italy* is of little or no use to the traveller.

64 Literally 'the cattle field', the local name for the area between the Capitoline Hill and the Colosseum.

been here two winters, and says he has much more to see, having been employed in visiting Antiquities two hours every day. Hit with a poeticising mania, of which here are the effects:

'Tis past—the living all are left behind,
Before us, and around us are the dead—
The beauty of desolation! o'er the mind
An awful melancholy shade is spread,
A tide of rushing feelings undefined,
Mysterious terrors, almost holy dread,
 As slow we pace, and mutely gaze on this,
The ancient City's Tomb—the worse than wilderness!
                    2
Six airy pillars yet, sublime and high,
One massy frieze, unshattered still, uprear
Cutting with clear sharp line the midnight sky,
Full on th' admiring gaze—What once was here?
They stand to mark the sport of destiny—
They stand to mark a ruined City's bier—
'Mid wrecks of war, 'mid scenes of rage and blood,
They stand to mark where once the fane of Concord stood.
                    3
Say now, what may yon Arch of Triumph mean?
Darkly magnificent in gathering gloom
It stands in solemn mockery of the scene,
Like blazon'd scutcheons on a Monarch's tomb;
And shows the Passenger where once has been
The populous mart, the gath'ring place of Rome,
Imperial City! And was this thy Throne,
Once thronged with swarms of life deserted now and lone!
                    4
On that proud hill, where laurelled victors trod,
And led the martial pomp, the captive line,
Up to the Temple of the Thundering God:
On that proud hill there stands no Thunderer's shrine,
No victims bleed upon the holy sod;
No listening Senates wait the Augur's sign;
No gorgeous temple now the summit crowns,
No steep Tarpeian Rock in savage grandeur frowns
                    5
And thou sad plain, with ruin girdled round
Where are thy halls of pride, thy pomp of state?
Of all the glories that thy surface crowned

One pillar stands forlorn and desolate:
Thou canst but shew in many a swelling mound
The sepulchre of all that once was great;
Thou canst but boast that all which dazzles now
In shapeless ruin lost shall yet be such as thou?

6

Where winds, 'mid nameless heaps, yon heaving road
Whose is yon lowbrowed arch, yon half sunk grate?
Around is many a mighty relic strewed,
The wild grass waves above its ruined state.
Is this then all that ages have bestowed
On him, the pride of Rome, the good, the great,
The conquering Titus? Him the appointed Rod
Of vengeance long fore—doomed by an insulted God?

7

Aye start indeed—these where yon pale moon gleams,
Where yon cold flood of liquid radiance falls,
Silvering the grey stone with her shadowy beams,
And the wild tangled shrubs—those shattered walls
Were once the Coliseum! Sunk it seems,—
But greatness, sunken so, the more enthrals;
Hark for the applauding shout by murder bought
That rings th' Arena round. Yet hark! What hear'st thou? Nought?

8

Nought but the but the flickering bat's short peevish squeak
Or challenge of the wakeful Sentinel:
Thyself thou canst not, dar'st not move, breathe, speak,
Though with deep thoughts thy labouring bosom swell;
Nought is now heard the sacred calm to break
Save when at times the far St Peter's bell
Soothing the ear of the night, with solemn sound,
Floats on the air which sleeps in loneliness around.

9

Oh Rome! In this thy solitude thou art
Bitterly eloquent, in all thy pride
Of full blown power, thou couldst not touch the heart
With such deep feeling, as when by the side
Of these thy ruined monuments of art
We stand, and back by the resistless tide
Of memory borne, recall thine ages past,
And see what now thou art, and dream what then thou wast.

Saturday 13th. Writing three days after I do not remember that we did anything but find lodgings which we think will suit us. Dined with the Aylmers, very nice people, and <u>very</u> civil. Wrong, this was on Sunday.

Sunday 14th. Went to the Vatican, but did not pass above two hours there. Of course only walked through, amazed with the <u>extent</u> and arrangement. Shall go very often.

Monday 15th. Went up, after leaving cards etc, to the Capitol, the Piazza a cruel disappointment, though the house of Aurelius is magnificent. But there is nothing which recalls <u>old</u> Rome—fine view of the City—and a very clear day. Thence to the Ponte Rotto, tried to get up stream in a boat, but failed. Drove to S. Pietro in Montorio, the spot where S. Peter was crucified. Fine general view and modern Rome looks well.

   Went to a magnificent Ball at Torlonia's. D. of Bracciano got the property and took the title of the real Simon Pure, and pleases the English well.[65] His house is splendid and everybody was there. Saw the Hitroffs again to my great delight. Dolly tells us she is certainly going to be married to Ficquelmont.[66] That it was settled the Friday before she left Florence and she is to be married on the 24th April. Presented to Madame Blacas.[67] Madame Appony very nice and not at all Italian.[68] Consalvi— very civil old man—Duchess of Devonshire[69]—Mr Howard, a Catholic, no trouble too great for any relation of Ld. Derby's, and most exceedingly kind he has been. D. of Hamilton makes great promises of any little help he can be of, etc. etc. Very well amused—staid a good while.

16th. Visits again—what a bore they are! The Pantheon very fine, because perfectly simple and on a great scale, beautiful proportions, and the flood of light from the circular aperture in the roof more than could be conceived. Canova studio.[70] He is certainly a very fine sculptor, but a sad pilferer, his statues are very many complete copies in attitude and

---

65   The wealthy banker Giovanni Torlonia (1754-1829) was given the title duke of Bracciano by the Pope in 1794. He acquired the palazzo in 1820. 'The real Simon Pure' alludes to a character impersonated by another in the play *A Bold Stroke for a Wife* (1718) by Susannah Centlivre.

66   Dorothea 'Dolly' von Tiesenhausen (1804-1863) married the diplomat Count Charles-Louis de Ficquelmont, Austrian ambassador to Tuscany and Lucca, when she was seventeen. In 1821 Ficquelmont was appointed Austrian ambassador to Naples.

67   Henrietta Blacas, wife of the French ambassador to the Holy See. The comte de Blacas headed the French delegation at the Congress of Laibach.

68   The Italian-born wife of Count Antal Apponyi (1782-1852), the Austrian ambassador to Rome.

69   Elizabeth, née Hervey (1758-1848), widow of the 5th duke of Devonshire, whom she had married in 1809. She was his second wife.

70   The celebrated Venetian sculptor Antonio Canova (1757-1822), who moved to Rome in 1780.

expression. I think the one that pleased me most was an Endymion now in progress for the D. of Devonshire.[71] Almost all the statues of the models we saw are in England. There is a beautiful Nymph, his last model, not yet begun. His friezes and many of them excellent. He is just now shut up as he has something on hand he wishes to finish. So says Prince Lapouquin. Dined with the Aylmers, went to the Opera in the evening.

17th. Went early to see a nun take her veil. Very well to <u>have</u> seen, but for the comfort of those who have not, very little <u>to</u> see. In the Church, where there is a great deal of mummery, is a little grate, through which you get a peep at the nuns. After the end of the ceremony in the church she advances to the grate and you see her distinctly for a little while, but our nun was neither young nor handsome and not the least interesting. The end of the ceremony, investing with the veil, is performed within the Chapel and not seen. No gentlemen admitted. Some ladies are with difficulty.

A visit from Ld, Colchester—a queer old man, but good humoured and obliging.[72] I wish he would not stay so long in a morning. Went today with the Aylmers to the Palazzo Sciarra, a younger branch of the Colonna family. A small but good collection of pictures. Two good little Claudes, four Guercinos, two Boths very good,[73] and a Leonardo da Vinci reckoned the finest in the Collection, and several other good ones. Thence to Mr Gibson's and two or three churches—nothing particular. Ball at Mr Canning's did not stay late, but before it went to the Duchess de Fiano—nice woman, speaks beautiful Italian, good lesson.[74] Bad Ball at Mr Canning's.

18th. Early in the morning to St. Peter's to see the ceremony of the anniversary of the establishment of the Papal Chair. Fine ceremony, but no religion. Cardinal Fontana very good face.[75] Pope a fine old man, but worn since last year. Very strong voice and hair black at 80![76] Cardinal Fesch, do not like him, but spoken well of here. Introduced to a Mr Gradwell, a Lancashire man, President of English College here.[77]

71 The 6th duke of Devonshire (1790-1858), who succeeded to the title in 1811.
72 The sixty-three-year-old Lord Colchester (1757-1829) had served as speaker of the House of Commons for fifteen years.
73 The French painter Claude Gelleé (1604-1682), known as Lorrain, who settled in Rome in 1628; the Bolognese painter and draftsman Giovanni Francesco Barbieri (1591-1666), known as Il Guercino; and the Dutch painter Jan Dirksz Both (1610-1652).
74 The duchess was married to Marco Ludovisi Ottoboni, 4th duke of Fiano (1777-1830).
75 Cardinal Fontana (1750-1822).
76 Pope Pius VII (1742-1823), who was elected to the Holy See in 1800.
77 Richard Gradwell (1777-1833) was appointed rector of the English College in 1818.

All civility, nothing like being known as a Friend of the Catholics in England.[78] Went to the Vatican—rooms of Raphaels, St. Peter in prison the most perfect light and shade that can be conceived, taken in for a moment fancied it a transparency. Dined with the Aylmers, stupid dinner. Mr and Mrs Hutchenson, do not like either, dine with them on Tuesday. Opera, Madame Appony's box, none but the Hitroffs and the intended of Catherine—do not like him.[79]

19th. Disappointed with the Doria palace. Some fine pictures in the Gallery, a splendid Claude or two, and a Salvator Rosa[80]—superb—but the rooms trash. Fine pictures in the Rospigliosi. Disappointed too with the Villa Borghese. What shall I be with the Princess? going there directly.[81] Disappointed again, the P. herself a nice woman, very agreeable manners, and pretty enough, young looking and a good figure, but the party was dull and formal to a degree. I was very black and sulky. Went to Lady Ellenborough's[82]—her daughter cannot sing, but she won't believe it. This, however, better than the other, but a moderate day altogether.

Hear Col. Brown has been very near murdered at Milan.[83] Sorry for it [is] sure to raise a thousand idle stories against the Queen.[84] A mad servant heard of, in a drunken fit bit off young Mr Howard's thumb, and knocked his Mother down. Dine there on Monday—expect amusement.

20th. As we dressed for the Princess's last night Canova called. I am just come home from calling on him, being the fourth interchange of cards without effect. I want very much to know him and will do it. Everybody speaks well of him. He is now engaged in building at his private expense a very handsome Church in his native town, and gives to the Academy the whole of the fortune he receives as Marchese d'Ischia. Mr Gibson tells me his kindness to him and to all the young Artists under him knows

---

78 As Whigs, Stanley's father, Lord Stanley, and grandfather, the 12th earl of Derby, were supporters of Catholic Emancipation.
79 Catherine von Tiesenhausen (1803-1888), older sister of 'Dolly' von Tiesenhausen. At the age of nine, Catherine was made a maid of honour to the Russian empress.
80 Salvator Rosa (1615-1673).
81 A masked ball given by Princess Pauline at the Palazzo Borghese.
82 Anne, née Towry (1768-1843), widow of Edward Law, 1st Baron Ellenborough (d. 1818), whom she married in 1789.
83 On his accession, King George IV sought a divorce from his estranged wife Queen Caroline. She was put on trial in the House of Lords in August 1820, accused of adultery with her servant Bartolomeo Pergami. She had the support of Whigs and radicals, and vociferous popular support, while on the other side Colonel Henry Brown had come to the fore in support of George IV's case of infidelity against her. On 8 January 1821 in Milan, Brown was attacked and severely wounded by a group of assailants armed with knives.
84 Rumours spread that Brown's attackers were former servants or partisans of Queen Caroline.

no bounds. Such a man is worth knowing, more especially when he is the first sculptor of the age.

We went this morning to the Mellini Villa a charming situation and certainly a very fine view of the town. But, with all the advantages of a splendid sky not as fine as it is reported. There is too much flat between it and the town, and the inequalities of ground in the City itself are lost from its superior height. Called on Mr Gradwell, not at home. Went to the Coliseum and on the way went to the top of the supposed Temple of Peace, which by the way is no Temple. But, from the top of it is the finest view I have seen of Rome. More rich and more varied than any I had seen elsewhere. But we had a splendid evening to see it and the lights and shades were really superb. Found oranges, anemones and jonquils growing among the rubbish on the top, the oranges in a garden belonging to the Convent through which you enter.[85] An artist on the top taking a view and a very beautiful one of the Forum. Dined with the Aylmers. Nobody there but Sir R Vyvyan.[86] Mr A. is a very sensible and well informed man, and I like him better every day I see him. Called this evening on Madame Appony, Madame Hitroff and Canova, none of them at home. No great fancy for Ld. Drummond, but we must go there—and directly too.

21st. I think the Ball was moderate, few foreigners and some very bad English. Two tables for play alone of which they were playing tolerably deep. Without this it is difficult to get into much Italian Society, or rather there is a good deal to which there is no other passport. But it is not worth it. Princess Cassia at the table looking like a skeleton, and Madame Mariscotti not much better, though she is a large handsome woman. Came home in good time, but kept awake all night by the noise of carriages, etc. This morning we went to the Capitol into the Palazzo dei Conservatori where there are some very beautiful pictures and not too many of them. Staid there, to our general astonishment, three hours in one side of the building. Went afterwards to the Church of Saint Antonino to see the horses blest, being a Sunday there was an excellent sight, rows of carriages, men on horseback all decorated with ribbons, all coming to receive the holy splash from the brush of the Priest and pay their money for the pictures of the Saint—men with little dogs in their arms and some even with sheep, all coming to be blest. Thousands of people all in their best clothes and some of the best figures that ever were seen. From thence we went to the Church of Santa Maria degli Angeli, a

---

85   In Italy a 'convento' is a religious community of women, while a community of men is a 'monastero'.

86   Sir Richard Vyvyan (1800-1879), a man of strong literary and scientific interests, became a Tory MP for Cornwall in 1825.

magnificent building in the form of a Greek Cross on the site of part of Diocletian's Baths. I think the handsomest Church I have seen. Returned by the Monte Pincio and Corso, the Hyde Park and Bond Street of Rome. Called in the evening on Madame Hitroff and Madame Fiano, but they were not at home. Madame H never is, which I am sorry for. Just received from Nibby *All' ornatissimo Signor Signor Stanley.*[87]

22nd. A fine day, though very cold. Our first object was the Borghese Gallery, the finest collection of paintings I have yet seen in Rome. There are four Albanos which are quite incomparable.[88] They are said to represent the four seasons, and of course went to Paris, a common test of merit here. From the Borghese we went through the Piazza Navona by the temple of Pallas, to the baths of Titus. These have been very well excavated by the French, whom we are almost wishing back again every day. It is said that antiquarians distinguish the additions made by Nero, and afterwards by Titus, to the original building, the house of Macenas. The frescos were as perfect in their colours as when first painted and some of the figures are very spirited and graceful. A work is in progress, but not completed, which will give drawings of all of them. From the baths we drove to the Church of St. John's latter end according to Lady B.[89] I own I was disappointed with it, though it is a fine building. The ruins of the little circular Temple of Minerva Media are fast falling to decay and a large fragment had fallen in about three weeks ago. It is a great pity for it is very graceful and beautiful. Was very near behaving ill at the Scala Santa when I saw two people going up on their knees, saying a prayer at each step.[90] The lady said hers fastest and beat the countryman easy. Dined at the Howard's, party very blue, but not much blue talking—two Misses Burgs, a Miss Fanshawe, Lord and Lady Colchester, Mr and Mrs Hamilton, Duchess of Devonshire and one or two more—pleasantish dinner.[91] Canova came in the evening—very civil and says Lady W. *c'est pas une femme, c'est un ange.* Forced to attend

---

87   Antonio Nibby (1792-1839), an Italian archaeologist and expert on the topography of Rome and its environs, published a study of Rome's walls in 1820. He was Stanley's lecturer and guide in Rome.

88   Francesco Albano (1578-1660).

89   This was presumably in reference to a joke about St John Lateran by Lady Burghersh, or perhaps a comical mispronunciation on her part.

90   The Santa Scala is a flight of twenty-eight steps in San Giovanni in Laterno, said to be those that Christ ascended in Pontius Pilate's house during his trial. The steps were supposedly brought from Jerusalem by St Helena, the mother of Constantine. They are climbed by the faithful on their knees while saying prayers.

91   The 'blue talking' was a political reference to the Tories, the blue party. The earls of Derby were traditionally strongly Whig in their politics. Miss Fanshawe was possibly the poet Catherine Maria Fanshawe (1765-1835). Lady Colchester was Elizabeth, née Gibbes, who married Lord Colchester in 1796.

the Duchess of Devonshire to the Opera: went afterwards to Lady Westmoreland—very much amused with her clever extraordinary manner.[92] She is furious about the Queen, and pushed all the people away to talk to us about her, which she did admirably.[93] Lord W. Russell there.[94] He is not bright in conversation. Came home late.

23rd. Went today to see the Farnese, Farnesina, Spada and Corsini Palaces. The former is built of the plunder of the Coliseum; there are some fine rooms and a beautiful fresco ceiling by Annibale Carracci and his two pupils Domenichino and Guido.[95] The Palace is fitting up for the reception of the King of Naples, on his expected return from the Congress at Laibach. In the Spada palace a poor collection of pictures and nothing interesting, excepting the supposed statue of Pompey, at whose base 'Great Caesar fell'; and this from not being ascertained loses much of its interest. In the Farinesina there are two rooms with beautiful frescoes, representing the Loves of Cupid and Psyche. The group of the three Graces, from which Giulio Romano[96] has copied his vile picture at Knowsley, is beautiful in colouring and being in this shape does not exhibit the long line of white cloud. The Corsini palace is very fine. The best gallery I think I have seen, excepting perplexing the Borghese. An Ecce Homo of Guercino is quite superb, but I must go again to this.[97] Went afterwards for the evening view of St. Peter's from the Villa Pamphilj Doria which is very fine and yet better in coming down to the Porta di Cavaleri. Dined at the Hutchinson's. Aylmers, Talbots,[98] Peel, Vyvyan, Drummond, Westerns, etc. going to the Duchess of Devonshire's. Hear no news. The Duchesses's a good house, but not for a Ball. I believe she had intended it to be a small party, and afterwards asked everybody. In consequence it was hot and crowded. I had an amusing scene. Looking at some caricatures, we were joined by a gentlemanlike foreigner, with whom I talked for some

---

92   Jane Huck-Saunders married the 10th earl of Westmoreland in 1800. She was his second wife.

93   In November 1820, to the king's fury, Lord Liverpool's government withdrew its Pains and Penalties Bill against Queen Caroline, anticipating that it would not pass in the Commons. Eight hundred petitions and nearly a million signatures were submitted to parliament supporting Queen Caroline's cause. As a Whig, Stanley was strongly sympathetic to the queen and highly critical of George IV's behaviour. Queen Caroline was barred from the king's coronation at Westminster Abbey in July 1821 and died shortly after on 7 August 1821.

94   Lord William Russell (1767-1840), Whig MP and uncle of Lord John Russell, the prime minister, stood down from the family's 'pocket borough' of Tavistock in 1819. In 1840 he was murdered in his sleep by his valet.

95   Annibale Carracci (1560-1609); Domenichino (1581-1641); Guido Reni (1575-1642).

96   Giulo Romano (1499-1546).

97   'Ecce homo', 'Behold the man': the words used by Pontius Pilate in the Gospel of St John when presenting Jesus Christ, wearing a crown of thorns, to the hostile crowd.

98   Sir George Talbot (1761-1850), who married Anna Preston in 1787.

time. Another came up and joined us in the conversation. After a little while, he asked my first friend to present him to me, upon which he was obliged to say, *mais monsieur je n'ai pas le plaisir de le connaître*: which made them both look so foolish that I could not help bursting out laughing, in which they joined, and I then relieved them by saying *Eh bien monsieur il faut dire que je me presente moi même*, which I did, and they then introduced each other, very near dropping with laughing. One of them was the Baron Reding, son of the Hanoverian Minister, and the other, I do not know his name, Chamberlain to the Prince of Denmark. Baron Reding asked me if I knew a Lord Stanley whose eldest son came of age a little while ago. Met the Duke of Hamilton and to dine there on Thursday. Quite delighted to find Madame Appony has got her gown, which we thought we had lost, by the Duchess of Hamilton;[99] how I do not understand.

24th. Met with Mr Aylmer and Mr Greenough[100] President of the Geological Society to the tomb of Cecilia Metella, wife of Crassus. An enormous circular pile of blocks of travestine which look as fresh and sharp as if they had been built yesterday. We looked as we came back into the Church of S. Lorenzo in Lucina, where there is a beautiful picture of a crucifixion by Guido. Sir R. Vyvyan and Mr Gibson dined with us. Went to the Academy of St. Luke, saw three students drawing from a model. Argentini—home.[101]

25th. Just returned from a delightful party at the Duke of Hamilton's. Early this morning arrived a note from Lady Westmoreland offering us her box at the [Teatro] Valle. Offered to Mrs Aylmer and Madame Hitroff, neither could take it—meant to go ourselves. Went with Mr Aylmer to see the statue side of the Capitol. The Gladiator a noble statue and beautiful expression. A Faun beautiful: and the Antinous, but a great deal only curious from being old. Disappointed on the whole. Went afterwards to the Villa Altieri, falling into ruin, but a noble view from the top of the house. Waited near an hour for our carriage to go to the Duke's; our rascally coachman too late. In consequence of which we found everybody sat down to dinner. Thousands of apologies and a lie about the carriage being broken down, but very well received. Found almost

---

99   The duchess of Hamilton was Susan-Euphemia, daughter of William Beckford. She married the future duke in 1810.

100 George Greenough (1778-1855), a pioneering geologist, became president of the Geological Society in 1811.

101 The Teatro Argentini was one of Rome's main theatres. The operas of Rossini, Cimerosa and, later, Verdi were premiered there.

all foreigners—Princess Borghese,[102] Mr and Madame de Hautmesnil,[103] Prince Piombino,[104] Cardinal Fesch,[105] two or three other foreigners, and a Mr and Mrs Halliburton. I was seated between Madame de Hautmesnil and the Princess Piombino[106] and talked French to the one, and boldly Italian to the other. Cardinal Fesch very civil. Princess Borghese whispered [to] Madame de H. that G was <u>very like somebody</u>. *Mais quelle organe! Quelle resemblance?* ['But what a mouth! What a resemblance?'] Madame de H. told George he ought to be much flattered. D. of H. exceedingly kind. Anything he could do, I had only to ask him—any day I liked to dine with him, any evening I liked to come. In short, everything that was obliging. The Duchess sang—and I, <u>even I myself</u>, could have listened till now. George cries a miracle and they laughed at me well. Did not go to the opera, but came straight home.

26th. We have been *a Laquais-de-Place Giro*, and I really think it is the best way to see things at first. Left some cards, and then looked into the Church of St. Carlos ai Catinari. There is a picture of Guido, but it is in a room without a window behind the great altar. To the Temple of Pudenzia, now a modern Church with some beautiful pillars imbedded in the vault. Thence to the Pyramid of C. Cestius, Monte Testaccio the Aventine; from a villa of Cardinal Ruffis there is a fine view of the town, the Temple of Vesta, and that of Fortuna Viulis close by, and both on the river. Why should not Horace allude to their two Temples, when he says v*idimus flavum Tiberini in dejectum monumenta Regum, Templa que Vesta.*[107] T. V. was built by Servius Tullius. They are both beautiful. A stupid dinner at Otway's,[108] goodish dinner at Pauline's[109]—<u>Miss Gordon</u>—Sir G. Talbot in the evening.

27th. There has been (I believe) an execution this morning. I went to see it, waited about an hour and came away. I since hear that the culprit was obstinate and after waiting till near 12 o'clock, instead of confessing and being first *convertitio*, which is necessary and then guillotined, he

---

102 Princess Pauline (1780-1825), sister of Napoleon, married Camillo Borghese, 6th prince of Sulmona, in 1803. Living at the Palazzo Borghese, she became estranged from her husband, who took up residence in Florence. Princess Pauline's subsequent lovers included the violin virtuoso Niccolò Paganini.
103 The Chevalier and Madame de Hautmesnil were companions of Princess Borghese. They also lived at the Palazzo Borghese.
104 Luigi Ludovisi, prince of Piombino (1767-1841).
105 Cardinal Joseph Fesch (1763-1839), an uncle of Napoleon, lived at the Palazzo Falconeri and the Palazzo D'Aste-Bonaparte, where Napoleon's mother, Maria Letizia Ramolino, known as Madame Mère, also lived.
106 Maddalena, princess of Piombino, née Odescalchi (1782-1846).
107 Horace, *Odes* I.
108 Robert Otway Cave (1796-1844), who became MP for Leicester in 1826.
109 Princess Pauline at the Palazzo Borghese.

astonished the attendants by requesting some <u>dinner</u>: which he had. He was to wait till four o'clock, and if he is not *convertitio* by then he is doomed by the Catholic religion to die and be dammed. The absurdity of it is that the Pope is kept fasting all day to pray for his Soul, but the moment that *l'esercita la Giustizia* [justice is exercised], the Pope goes to dinner. The man's crime was murdering a Priest, under these circumstances as told me by my *Laquais-de-place*. *Questo prete gli la dato la sua nipote per mogli. Egli è soldato, va alla a Guerra dojao tue anni torna a casa, trova due piccolo bambini che gli ha fatto questo Prete* ['On his going away as a soldier, the priest had had two babies by his wife']—and upon this he puts him to death. He seemed to sympathise with the culprit and indeed so did I. By the way, I was much amused by the same *Laquais-de-place* yesterday addressing my Coachman who asleep on his box, with a *Dormi Castactius, anima mea* ['Sleep Castactius, my soul']? We have today seen the splendid remains of the Palace of the Caesars and baths of Caracalla, but we must go there with an Antiquary. Dined at the Aylmers—Mr Greenough, Mr Gradwell, Mr Gibson. Called on the Duchess of Hamilton, not at home—went to Lady Drummond—did not stay late. Talk of there being a Carnival.

28th. Up very late; in consequence did not go to see a nun take the <u>white</u> veil. Went to the Vatican and St. Peter's. Dined at home alone and did not go out. Our coachman has just refused to send our carriage. I shall not pay him and we expect a lawsuit.

29th. A letter from Charlotte this morning, but no news in it.[110] Our coachman been here and the business quietly settled. We have been this morning to see the prettiest Villa in Europe, the Villa Paolina.[111] We had a ticket sent us and asked the Aylmers and the Miss Talbots to go. Beautifully furnished, with great appearance of plainness, but all in white muslin beautifully embroidered. Ladies in raptures. I saw Madame Mère in her carriage going there, and Pauline waiting opposite the Palazzo Rospigliosi.[112] Went afterwards with the Aylmers to the Circus of Caracalla which remains very distinctly marked out. As we returned walked home by the Rupe Tarpeia, which I was surprised to find so much <u>higher</u> than people represent it.[113] It is quite enough to break anybody's neck. Dined

---

110 Stanley's younger sister Charlotte, born in 1801.
111 Named after Princess Pauline Borghese, who bought the villa in 1809.
112 Madame Mère was Maria Letizia Bonaparte, née Ramolino (1750-1836), the mother of Napoleon. After 1815 she lived in the Palazzo D'Aste–Bonaparte with her younger brother Cardinal Joseph Fesch. Princess Pauline Borghese was Madame Mère's daughter.
113 The Rupe Tarpeia or Tarpian Rock is about 80 feet high. During the Roman Republic, people convicted of murder or treason were thrown off it to their deaths.

at home with Corbett and Peel. Called on Lady Westmoreland and Duchess of Devonshire, and Mr Hutchinson. Found the last at home. Found Mr Hamilton's craniologist quite wrong about George and me, except indeed that G *aimait beaucoup les femmes—plus que monsieur*: but he found out I was musical and G not, and that neither of us had any talent for mimicry—Gall and Spurzheim humbug![114]

30th. Went again to the Palais Borghese, then to the Orti Farnesia, from whence there are some beautiful points of view and curious baths called of Livia. Walked with Corbett to Cecilia Metella, Circus Caracalla and round by the Aqueduct—a long walk. Dined at home and went to bed tired—no news.

31st January 1821. Eleven PM!! Just returned from the Valle, been in Lady Ellenborough's box. She did not come till the end of all things. An excellent petite piece and beautiful acting. One woman very good in a Mrs Jordan part.[115] This morning there was to have been a review. We went to Madame Massimo's Villa to see it. Several other people there, but no review! And after some time spent there, the children's Dancing Master was announced, and a regular Ball began. I walked afterwards to look for sketches, but could not find any for walls. Dined at Sir W. Drummond: stupidish dinner.[116] Sir W. Gell,[117] Vyvyan, Malcolm, Mr Williams, George and I—not much talking and altogether dull. Many happy returns to Burgoyne and Mademoiselle Rose![118]

---

114 The German physiologists Franz Gall (1758-1828) and Johann Spurzheim (1776-1832) were leading proponents of phrenology, the reading of personality and behaviour from the external shape and contours of the skull.
115 The actress Dorothea (or Dorothy) Jordan (1761-1816) was known for her comedic roles. For twenty years she was the mistress of the duke of Clarence, later King William IV, with whom she had ten illegitimate children.
116 Sir William Drummond (1769-1828) was a diplomat, former MP and a poet. He died in Rome in 1828.
117 Sir William Gell (1777-1836) was an English archaeologist and fellow of the Royal Society. In 1804 he claimed to have identified the ancient site of Troy. He travelled to Italy in 1814 as one of Princess Caroline's chamberlains and gave evidence in her favour at her trial before the House of Lords in October 1820. Gell was a close friend of Sir William Drummond and a collaborator with the Italian archaeologist Antonio Nibby. He resided in Rome from 1820 until his death.
118 John Fox Burgoyne (1782-1871) was the illegitimate son of General John Burgoyne, who eloped with Lady Charlotte Stanley, daughter of the 12th earl of Derby. Following a reconciliation with Lord Derby, John Fox Burgoyne was brought up in the Knowsley household and subsequently pursued a successful military career. In 1821 he married Charlotte Rose.

February 1821

1st February. Went this morning to St. Peter's, but the review is postponed till Saturday. We therefore went over the Castle of St. Angelo. An immense mass of building, though it does not appear so from without. There is a good view of St Peter's from it, but not so good as I should have expected. Braschi Palace very indifferent. Barberini very good, small collection of good pictures and comfortable rooms. Thorvaldsen's studio—I was very much pleased with it.[119] A frieze of Alexander's triumphs for the Marchese Sommariva[120] at Como quite incomparable for genius, variety and originality. Of them I should say he has much more than Canova, but I do not like his single statues so well. More invitations to Lady Ellenborough: a <u>very small party</u> tomorrow night and dinner on Monday.

2nd. Fine day and I rode with Corbett. To say the truth I am beginning to tire of constant sightseeing and mean to take a little *relâche* [rest] before we begin with Nibby, which will not be long. Rode by the ruins of St. Agnese . A church built I believe by Constantine, but we did not examine them. Then along the road till we saw some immense remains on the right, which I since hear are the ruins of an ancient pratorium. Dined with Sir G. Talbot. Met General Church[121] and sat next to his Aide de Camp. He seems a fine determined character and has been so through the whole of the proceedings. Several persons offered to escort him from Naples here, but he refused saying he would expose nobody to unnecessary danger, that he and his two attendants were armed to the teeth and meant to sell their lives dearly. A horrible assassination has taken place on the frontiers. A school had been lately carried up into the mountains and all the boys ransomed but three. These the government sent to ransom, the money was paid, the children in the act of being restored, unfortunately three or four cuirassiers appeared, the brigands thought they were betrayed and murdered two of the children in the sight of their relatives, the third saved himself by clinging to the Chief

---

119   The Danish sculptor Bertel Thorvaldsen (1770-1844) lived and worked in Rome from 1797. His statue *Jason with the Golden Fleece*, finished in 1801, was much praised by Canova.

120   The Marchese Sommariva was the wife of the wealthy Count Giovanni Sommariva, whose villa at Tremezzo, Lake Como, housed a large art collection.

121   General Richard Church (1784-1873) was an Irishman who served in the British army from 1800 and then led Greek troops in the Greek War of Independence. In 1817 he entered the service of King Ferdinand I of the Two Sicilies and in 1820 he was appointed governor of Palermo and commander-in-chief of the troops in Sicily. He was briefly imprisoned in Naples on the outbreak of the revolution, but was released in January 1821 and made his way to Rome.

of the brigands who flung him off with '*Eh bien! Va-t-en donc*' ['Well! So go away']. Road to Naples very unsafe and the few English who go embark at Terrracina.[122] We went to Lady Westmoreland in the evening, who had a child's party to play at Cocomero and a very amusing scene it was. Staid there till 12 o'clock.

Saturday 3rd. Mad. Massimo's <u>famiglia</u> coming like that of all the great families one visits for their 5 Pauls. One <u>famiglia</u> come to Mr Aylmer because their master had dined in Mr A's house. It seems there is something in the wind, for the review this morning, after being twice put off, took place in consequence of sudden orders, in the Castle of S. Angelo, instead of the Piazza di San Pietro, and nobody was admitted. At the same time all the *forçats* [convicts sentenced to hard labour] at work in the city were marched in different divisions, and under strong guard. I believe a release or escape of these men is rather apprehended. They are here to the number 570, besides several hundreds at Civita Castellana and Narni and possibly other prisons which I do not know of. Rode again with Corbett. Dined at home and went to Madame Massimo's but too late. She was dressing to go to the Palazzo Lucciano, where I shall not go.

Sunday 4th. Wet mild day. George gone down to the Vatican. I have not been out—borrowed Livy and read the first book. Seen today a drunken man for the first time in Rome and he was followed by a great crowd, hooting and shouting, and very much astonished. Otway and Corbett dined here and have staid all evening.

Monday 5th. Went to Cardinal Fesch's pictures, but the Custode was engaged and a fellow was sent with us who knew none of them. There are some beautiful pictures there, but we staid no time and mean to go again. Wet day. Dined at Lady Ellenborough's—Locke, Cartwright, Mr Moore. Went with them to the Opera and came home.

Tuesday 6th. Clear day, but very cold with wind. Walked with Corbett, Ponte Molle[123] and Villa Mellini. Dined with the Aylmers, Lord Kinnaird.[124] Ball at Duchess of Devonshire's—too full and not very good. All sorts of reports tonight, but nothing known for certain. It is, however, very generally supposed that the Austrians will come down upon Naples.[125]

---

122 A port 47 miles south of Rome.
123 The Ponte Molle, crossing the Tiber north of the city, is now usually called the Milvio or Milvian Bridge.
124 Charles Kinnaird, 8th Baron Kinnaird (1780-1826).
125 On 6 February 1821, 60,000 Austrian troops crossed the River Po on their way to Naples.

Wednesday 7th. The Vatican. Very much disappointed with the Pauline and Sistine Chapels. The Last Judgement of Michelangelo is <u>of course</u> very fine. But it did not strike me. The grouping is noble, but the fresco is so spoilt by damp and time that it requires a painter's eye to see its excellence. The Library, however, is a noble establishment—the Gallery 500 Roman passi in length—the *Sala* a very fine room, and a good preparation for the Gallery. Dined with the Duke of Hamilton. Lady Westmoreland was to have dined—sent a message when we had waited an hour that she was coming directly, and ten minutes after that she should not dine, but would come after. Lord Kinnaird, Sir W. Drummond, Mr Milly. Several foreigners in the evening. Princess of Denmark, nice looking woman and pretty enough, but too shy for royalty—presented to her. Duchess delightful. Ld. Kinnaird played off Lady Westmoreland beautifully. The child the prettiest thing that ever was seen, but very like my sister Ellinor.[126] She will be spoilt.[127]

Thursday 8th. Cold raw day again with high N. wind. News arrived here by Carlo Forti of the mutiny of Parliament and that the restoration of the Queen's name to the Liturgy is lost by 310 to 209.[128] The Austrians are said to be at Florence and I think they will certainly be here, if the Neapolitans do not come first, which God forbid. It is said the Emperor of Russia has promised his protection to the Pope, and that he will be here for the Holy Week. Nobody thinks of leaving Rome, but the Pope. Meantime, 500 workmen are said to be employed on the fortifications of S. Angelo. 24 more Carbonari sent in there the day before yesterday. So much for today's report. Going to dine with the Aylmers. But a moderate dinner. Mr A. not well enough to dine. Went to the Opera— *Rosa Bianca e Rossa*[129]—could not make out the story and did not admire. Horrible story of Harvey Aston having gone off with Lady C. Harley and on being overtaken having taken laudanum and died.[130] I fear it is

---

126 Stanley's youngest sister, Lady Ellinor-Mary Stanley (1807-1887).
127 Lady Susan Hamilton-Douglas (1814-1889) was the duke's second child.
128 This was the defeat of a Whig Commons motion to restore Queen Caroline's name to the Anglican liturgy.
129 An opera by Simon Mayr, *La Rosa Bianca e la Rosa Rossa*.
130 Colonel Harvey Aston had married a Spanish woman named Margarita in Cadiz in 1813 while on service in the Peninsular War. The marriage proved disastrous, and in 1818 Aston brought an action of 'criminal conversation' against his wife and Captain Edward Elliot, a cousin of both Lord Minto and Lord Auckland. Aston won the case, but during the widely reported trial, numerous witnesses attested to his debauched character and constant soliciting of prostitutes. There was also a suggestion made that he had given his wife syphilis. Following the trial, Aston turned his attentions to Lady Charlotte Harley, daughter of the 5th earl of Oxford, a young woman famous for her beauty. Her mother, the countess of Oxford, was a lover of Byron, and it was rumoured that the poet had also seduced Lady Charlotte, to whom he dedicated the seventh printing of his *Childe Harold's*

quite certainly true. Hitroffs gone suddenly to Florence. Vichelman recalled
from thence. Baron Arnstein gone to join his regiment and expects to
find it at Florence. Ball at Mr Arbuthnot's, but I was not asked and did
not wish to go.

Friday 9th. Today Ercole Consalvi[131] is come out, declaring the approach
of Austrian troops, asserting perfect neutrality on the part of his Holiness,
but at the same time saying that though the geographical position of the
Papal Territories rendered it necessary that they should pass through
them, there was not the slightest necessity for them to pass through
Rome, and if they did he must regard them as unfriendly—and ends by
a severe menace against all disorder committed by his subjects. Tradesmen
sending in Bills in a fright, and the master of my new lodgings sends to
beg he may have my written agreement. I have no idea of moving and
I have taken lodgings for two months. We have been today at the [Palazzo
del] Quirinale, certainly a fine Palace and very well furnished—at least
the part which was fitted up for the reception of the Emperor and Empress
of Austria. The gardens are large, stiff and trim, but commanding a fine
view of the city. From thence we went to Torlonia's, where the Duke has
stuck up an inscription purporting only that Johannes Torlonia Bardemi
Dux furnished it, etc. The Palace is fine and the pictures good second
rate. Some fine Caravaggios though I do not like them.[132]   Down to St
Peter's—examined the mosaics. A beautiful copy of St Petronilla in the
Capitol and of the Transfiguration. People are all busy about the works
at the Castle Sant Angelo as they [have] been for some time, though not
with so much show. Apropos of St. Peter's, after seeing the original noble
design of Michelangelo or Bramante, I am not sure which, I quite join
in Forsyth's execration of the 'miserable plasterer from Como' who
ventured to alter and thereby spoilt it as he has done.[133] Dined at home,
went in the evening to Princess Borghese's, Sir G. Talbot, Lady
Westmoreland very amusing, and Lady Ellenborough's[134]—two first good,

Pilgrimage. Upon Colonel Aston's advances, Lady Charlotte's mother, the countess of
Oxford, promptly left England with her daughters for the Continent, to remove Lady
Charlotte from his influence. But Aston followed them to Genoa and eloped with Lady
Charlotte. The couple were pursued by the countess, and when she overtook them at
Alessandria, Aston killed himself with poison.

131   Cardinal Ercole Consalvi (1757-1824) was secretary of state for the Papal States and had
led the papal delegation at the Congress of Vienna.
132   Michelangelo Merisi da Caravaggio (1571-1610).
133   Stanley is referring to Joseph Forsyth (1763-1815) and his *Remarks on Antiquities, Arts
and Letters, During an Excursion in Italy in the years 1802 and 1803*, published in 1813.
134   Lady Anne, née Towry (1768-1843), who married the 1st earl of Ellenborough (d. 1818)
in 1789.

but obliged to come away too soon to go to others. Do not admire the Laws—eldest had temper—played at Chess and showed it.[135]

Saturday 10th. Fine mild day. Went with Mr Gibson to Canova's studio. My first opinion confirmed—not so much originality as Thorvaldsen and not much variety, but some of his statues magnificent—his Theseus for example, his Endymion and a Venreri the last room. Pleasant dinner—Mr and Mad. Falconeri, M. and Mad. Ponpi (Lucian's daughter), M. and Mad. Hautmesnil, D. of Hamilton, M. Cresentini,[136] George and I. Good ball at Lady Drummond's. Staid late.

Sunday 11th. Rode with Otway. Dined with Lady Westmoreland—very bad dinner, but a very amusing one. She is delightful. Went to call on Corbett who was ill and to the Opera. Lady Westmoreland coming away she took a fancy to go to the Coliseum. Malcolm and I attended—very amusing. Came home at <u>one</u>.

Monday 12th. Meeting at Peel's house about Bachelor's Ball. Not on the Committee, surprised, but glad. Went to St. Pietro in Vincoli. Noble Church and some good pictures—a fine statue of Moses by Michelangelo, though it struck me with defects. San Martino in Monti—too much gilding and frippery. Walked afterwards. Madame Appony's Ball very splendid and good. Staid till 2 o'clock.

Tuesday 13th. Occupied about the Bachelor's Ball, which has not advanced much. Dined at the Duke of Hamilton's. The Duchess very unwell, but dined with us, and quite delightful. I think much the pleasantest person in Rome. All sorts of rumours at night and an account that the Neapolitans were advancing, had advanced, were actually at Velletri. 250 horses pressed to remove the cannon from Fort S. Angelo to the gates towards Naples and everything prepared for the departure of the Pope (*malgrado lui* [despite him] as it is said) and all his ministers. About one a courier arrived with I suppose tranquillising news, for he did not set out. Streets all quiet, except a good many people about the Quirinal and bodies of four or five soldiers patrolling the streets. Disturbed in the night by guns firing about 2 in the morning, like a heavy cannonade for ¾ of an hour. I believe it was only trying the cannon, but this proof they are well frightened, though more I believe from within than without.

---

135 Law was the family name of the earls of Ellenborough.
136 The celebrated castrati singer Girolamo Crescentini (1762-1846).

Wednesday 14th. All a false alarm last night caused by the fright or folly of the Governor of Albano, who as I hear was frightened by Prince Poniatowski's shepherd, who had seen something moving which he took for an army and spread the alarm.[137] Guns removed today back again to their places and all quiet. Nothing to be seen round the walls where we have been. Seen some very clever pictures of a young French artist whose name is Robert—not at all French, very good, and quite unknown. Dined at Sir W. Drummond's, pleasant dinner enough—D. of Hamilton, Count Sommariva, Comte Mycielski.[138] The latter seems a particularly gentlemanlike well informed man and I was very much pleased with him. He talks of going to England next year and I should quite like to give him letters. In all present confusion it shows the character of the Romans that instead of talking or thinking about either Austrians or Neapolitans, everybody is engaged about a statue which was found the other day at Frascati, and which arrived today. Argentini—Lady Ellenborough Child's Ball, very select and very stupid. Played at Whist and shirked staying supper.

Thursday 15th. Dined at home: party Peel, Malcolm Otway, Sr. Hyppolite—latter a consummate coxcomb, but certainly a clever man and amusing. Opera.

Friday 16th. Rode with Otway to the Grotto of Eturia and saw the little Triumph of Bacchus above it. Dined with Lady Ellenborough. I had a tolerably pleasant dinner. George says it was very dull. Sir G. Talbot's in the evening—dullish.

Saturday 17th. Went to see French Artists pictures with Sr Hyppolite. Did not like any but Robert's, which I showed him. Should have bought a picture if Lord Kinnaird had not been beforehand with me and I think now I shall order one of him. Dined at the Aylmers—a large party and tolerably pleasant. Lady Drummond's in the evening.

Sunday 18th. Run out with Corbett in a carriage. He is still very unwell, but, I hope, getting better. Walked home taking a round over the *Campagna*—beautiful day—found some curious ruins which I shall go and look at again.

---

137 Charles, Prince Poniatowski (1754-1833) was a Polish nobleman who had moved to Italy after the Partitions of Poland.

138 Count Giovanni Battista Sommariva (1762-1826), secretary-general of the Cisalpine Republic under Napoleon, was very wealthy and became a prominent art collector and patron of Canova and Thorvaldsen. The Mycielskis were a Polish noble family associated with the Prussian Court.

Monday 19th. Showery day—an absurd Ercole came out regulating the size and nature of comfits to be thrown during the Carnival—and another somewhat more serious declaring symptoms of disaffection and hinting at rebellion in four towns. All a lie as I hear since, but evidently proves that the Cardinal [Consalvi] has been double dealing and I have little doubt that he sent for the Austrians to come within the town. His former declaration was contradictory and threatened them if they came within the walls, but their Commissariat are now engaged in converting Convents into barracks. Dined with Beckford.[139] Called from the Opera by Corbett being much worse. Left him I hope a good deal better.

Tuesday 20th. Wet day. Corbett better and I hope going on well, been with him all morning. Arrivals from Naples bring us news that the roads are undermined and ready to be blown up at a moment's warning. Dined at home—Opera—Lady Westmoreland's box—very amusing.

Wednesday 21st. Dined with Lady Westmoreland, Duchess de Fiano and her daughter, Count and Countess Ludolf,[140] Williams, Malcolm, G. and I. Good party in the evening. Saw in coming home numbers of carts loaded with bread, etc. for the Austrian army, going to Ponte Molle to meet them. Wrote to Henry today.[141]

Thursday 22nd. Corbett going on well. Walked with Mr Aylmer beyond the Ponte Molle,[142] all the world out in the false hopes of seeing the Austrian army, which will not be here for two days more. Courier who arrived today from Naples says that he is to be the last, and therefore all communication is now at an end. Dined with the Duke of Hamilton. Nobody there but Cresentini and old Cardinal Fesch. The Duchess more delightful than ever. If she was in health I should go there very often. The old Cardinal is a sad looking old fellow, and we agree that he talks bad French.

Friday 23rd. Nothing more heard of the Austrian troops, though it is imagined they are within a day's march of Rome. The Neapolitan *Guido di Guerra* is arrived here and it is worth remarking that it seems in a

---

139 William Beckford (1760-1844), art collector and author of the Gothic novel *Vathek* (1786). He was also the duke of Hamilton's father-in-law. Following his first visit to Italy in 1780-82, Beckford published *Dreams, Waking Thoughts, and Incidents, in a Series of Letters from Various Parts of Europe* (London, 1783). It contained picturesque and sensitive descriptions of Italy and revealed his developing sense of connoisseurship.

140 Count Joseph Ludolf had been, until recently, the Neapolitan ambassador to Constantinople. He was married to Countess Tekla Weyssenhoff.

141 Henry Stanley was one of Stanley's younger brothers, born in 1803.

142 Beyond the Ponte Molle lay the Farnesina Meadow or military parade ground.

covert way to call on all Italy. It is rather firm, but very bombastic. The roads are broken up and all is prepared for war. So they are at Terni, in the rear of the first division of Austrians, who are I think waiting for the remainder of their force. They seem to have run down with foolish confidence and to have found their error. Dined at home and went nowhere.

Saturday 24th. First day of the Carnival. Corbett a great deal better. I did not like his looks yesterday, but he is more animated today and getting on well. Went about two o'clock to the Capitol to see the Ceremony of the Jews doing homage to the Roman people for permission to live in the town.[143] There is nothing in the ceremony itself, but the peculiar circumstances of it make it interesting. Formerly the Jews were obliged on the first day of the Carnival to run barefoot (or naked I am not sure which) along the Corso. This has now been commuted for this ceremony of homage, and furnishing the flags and a small sum of money, the prize of the winning horse. They even make a considerable sum by letting the damask hangings which are suspended from every window, and of which they have the exclusive privilege. Their homage, however, is humiliating enough. The S. P. represented by two old men in robes covered with gold, who sitting in their chairs of state on raised steps, receive a deputation of the principal Jews, who prostrate themselves, then bow very low, and one of them giving a speech which to thank the Roman people for their clemency, and implore the continuance of it. But from the very Jewish accent and pronunciation I could not follow the Italian. The Senator then makes a short reply, without rising or moving a muscle of his face, but dropping out his words one by one with ridiculous dignity. The same farce is then created in the Sala dei Conservatori and all is over. Then follows the Corso with the absurdities of comfit throwing,[144] etc. practised, however, as far as I observed chiefly by the English. Very few masks, but the Carnival madness has not begun: and I think political events will make it dull this year—if indeed it is ever anything else. The horse race was not over till half past 5. Mycielsky, Williams, Aylmer and Peel at dinner. Went off well. After dinner called on the Duchess of Hamilton with Malcolm, found her in alone with the Duke, very agreeable, but did not stay as long as I should have liked. Valle to Lady Westmoreland's box and afterwards Argentini. Mantini for news. The first division of Austrians have halted I believe at Monte Rosa, and it is said will retire upon Frimont's division and all take the Abruzzo route, so that there

---

143 The Jewish ghetto in Rome was established in 1555 on the banks of the Tiber near the Isola Tiberina.

144 A sugar-coated seed or almond sweetmeat.

will be nothing on this side. The Neapolitans have made an attack on Terni, seized the Austrian stores and provisions, and returned to their strong position between that place and Rieti. The Austrian proclamation was here yesterday, but I could not get it except to look into in the street. It seems to lay great stress upon the <u>sect</u> of Carbonari.

Sunday 25th. Sat in my room till 2. Went down with Corbett to St Peter's. Spent the day there and walked back with him. He is much stronger and better, of which this is proof. Met among other people Abbé Gradwell, who tells me that the Church at the Quattro Fontane is built on the same space that is occupied by <u>one</u> of the pillars supporting the dome of St. Peter's and separating the middle from the side aisles. Several Austrian officers here. Everything portends negotiation if retreat on their part, but there is no news. Dined at home and went nowhere: began a letter to Maria.

Monday 26th. Stormy wet day, in spite of which the Carnival continued with some spirit and one cannot help entering into it, though one does not know why or what amuses one. Dined with Sir W. Drummond, Mycielski, Sir W. Gell, Beckford, Fairfield, G. and myself. Duchess of Hamilton's Ball in the evening. Pretty sight on the whole, but the Ball flattish. Staid, however, till quite the end. More reports of Austrians hoaxed this morning to the Ponte Molle, will never go again. Find that roads are <u>not</u> yet broken up and some English gone tonight to Naples. A letter from Louisa.[145]

Tuesday 27th. A letter from Fioravanti announcing the departure of my books from Leghorn, directed in the usual style *Al Illustrissimia Signor Padrone Colendissimo Il Signor* etc.[146] This is, however, rather beginning to wear out and the Romans like better than any other style *Al nobiluomo*, etc. Corso again. Dined at home and did not go to the masked Ball in the evening.

Wednesday 28th. Carnival improving, went to the end to see the horses come in, but could not get there for soldiers. Austrians arrived tonight. Reported different as to their numbers. They bivouacked tonight at the other side of the Ponte Molle.[147] Did not go to Mad. Appony's, which was as I expected full and crowded.

---

145 A younger sister of Stanley's, born in 1805. Louisa Stanley married Lieutenant-Colonel Samuel Long in April 1825, but died just eight months later in December 1825.
146 An elaborate form of address parodied by Giovanni Battista della Porta (1535-1615) in his comedy *Al Clarissimo Signor Luigi Bragadino dell'Illustrissimo Sig. Mio Colendissimo*.
147 On the Farnesina Meadow.

March 1821

Thursday 1st March. Rode to the Ponte Molle and saw the Austrians file off by the Villa Borghese and round the walls. The Cavalry are well mounted on stout horses, mostly Hungarian, but I do not admire their infantry. Found an officer who spoke good Italian and rode with him all round the city. It gave me quite a melancholy idea to think of the errand these troops were going on, and that one could not help wishing that the very troops we saw before our eyes might never return again. They, poor fellows, are mixed up of all nations, having 5 different languages among them besides German—Hungarian, Bohemian, Wallachian, Bessarabian, Transylvanian—and this is done that they may not converse with the natives and learn the truth of the story. The idea which is diligently impressed on them is that they are going against a troop of Brigands, the Carbonari, who rob and stiletto every rich man they meet in the streets. The Carnival in spite of rain went on tolerably well. I went to the end where the two sheets of sailcloth are hung across the street fastened at the four corners, with an interval of about seven or eight yards between them. A file of soldiers behind kept the people from going to the second and I saw one man in a ludicrous rage at being kept out of his own house. A little officer about four feet six directed these men. He was an old man, with little straight whiskers very well powdered, and two little sticks by way of legs, not unlike old Spiers at Eton.[148] He was alternate pale and red with fright and bustle, and his own soldiers could not help laughing when I laughed at him to them. Seventeen Riders were announced to start, and my little friend, not thinking the two sheets a sufficient security, got behind a doorpost, where he remained ensconced. At length we heard a tremendous clatter then a crash, and then through the second sheet we saw the first horse come <u>through</u> the middle of the first sheet, followed by about five others, and the grooms in their red caps rushed in to seize them. Such a scene ensued as I never saw. The horses, under the influence of blistered sides, squibs [small fireworks] fastened to them, and goads running in at every movement, added to the fright of finding themselves stopped after coming through the first sheet, were kicking furiously, the grooms swearing, hollering and jumping about with great agility to avoid the blows and catch them, and my little officer screaming to the top of his voice. When all were caught the second sheet was dropped and we were allowed to go. In the evening Graham dined with me. Went to the Festivo in

---

148 Spiers ran a shop, opposite the entrance to Weston's Yard at Eton, selling food and other provisions to the boys.

Domino[149]—too much crowd and rather dull. George said he had great fun and from his account I have no doubt he had, he was certainly well dressed, but I think I should have known him. Lady Ellenborough's supper—very stupid.

Friday March 2nd. *Relâche* at last, thank God, for I am tired—plenty of parties, however, tonight. Walked with Graham, who is gone mad about Antiquities. Lady Ellenborough's dinner dull and blue. Lady C. Linsday a clever woman.[150] Miss Berry's quite detestable I think and so vulgar! Cartwright, Sykes, Mr and Mrs Crawford. I do not admire her at all, very artificial and affected. Lady E. pressed me exceedingly to go with her to Princess of Denmark's, but I fought off. I have already behaved so ill I durst not, and to say the truth I have no inclination. Princess Borghese's amusing. Sir G. Talbot's in the evening, goodish party in a quiet way.

Saturday 3rd. Rode with Corbett who was out for the first time. Met the Austrian baggage at the Ponte Molle and suppose the troops will be in tonight. Corso very full, but I thought dullish. Dined at home. Beckford dined with us. The Festivo in the evening very crowded and not very good.

Sunday 4th. Hot oppressive day, another breathing from the Carnival, but a Ball at the Alibert *dopo mezza note* [after midnight], which they say will be good *pour la belle Société*. Walked with Graham, dined at home and had Graham, Graves, 2 Clives and Peel—noisy dinner and not very pleasant I thought. Argentini Festivo great amusement, knowing G's dress and being V's and C's confidant as to who he was. Lady W. very good. Today is arrived a flaming account from Pepe[151] *Prima battaglia prima Vittoria* [First battle, first Victory] announcing the rout of an Austrian force and five pieces of cannon taken. The truth of which is imagined to be that there has been a skirmish between some picquets and a little baggage has been taken, among which are 5 women. The Austrians are, I hear, behaving very ill, and at Tivoli have cut down the olive trees for fuel. A thing never heard of before in Italian war.

---

149 A long cape or elaborate mask worn at a carnival to conceal the wearer's identity.

150 Lady Charlotte Lindsay, née North (1770-1849), a daughter of the 2nd earl of Guilford. She married Lieutenant-Colonel John Lindsay in 1800 and was a lady of the bedchamber to Caroline of Brunswick from 1808 to 1817. She had been required to give evidence in 1820 to the House of Lords regarding the queen's relationship with her servant Pergami.

151 General Guglielmo Pépé took command of the Neapolitan army upon King Ferdinand's failure to keep his promises to introduce liberal constitutional reforms in Naples. The general sought to defend the defiles of the Abruzzi against the Austrians.

English, I think, are getting *en mauvais odeur* [in bad odour] with the government, which I am glad of. Appony[152] cannot digest Lord Castlereagh's declaration in the H. of Commons.[153] In bed tonight at 5. George came home half an hour after and I got up to eat cold turkey.

Monday 5th. Up at <u>one</u>. Strolled about with Corbett. Dined with the Aylmers, Vyvyan and Graham. Lady Drummond's a very good Ball in the evening. George as Lady Wronghead[154]—a good mask, but quite found out. Just come home with a conscience load of his upon me.

Tuesday 6th. Been down to the Ponte Molle to see a fresh attachment of Austrians and managed to bungle a little German with one of the men. Only one Regiment, Frimont's Hussars.[155] Report of Pepe's turns out to be a forgery and the man is in prison for it. This evening the Moccoletti begun and the Carnival ends.[156] The streets are full of people with lights and blowing out and kissing is the great fun, singing all the time in the way of the old Priests *Muore, Muore, Muore, Muore il Carnivale*. At a given signal all the lights are put out and then comes one loud shout of *È morto* from thousands of voices, and all is over. Ball at Mrs Starke's and a masked party at Lady Ellenborough's. In bed very late.

Wednesday 7th. Out of bed very late, 2 o'clock. Walked with Edsell to the Villa Pamphilj Doria—very curious excavations going on of Columbaria—beautiful mosaic pavement. One in this pattern, alternate black and white squares with white squares in the black ones. In the evening dined at home, called on the Duchess of Hamilton, and went by invitation to Lady Westmoreland. We have hid George out of Lady W. and it rather lies on my conscience.

Thursday 8th. Went out shooting with Edsell. Moderate sport, but a good walk of 25 miles. Dined with Mycielski and staid till 2 in the morning. Of course did not go to Sir G. Talbot's. Account from Frimont of his having with three thousand men beat the Neapolitans with nine.[157]

---

152 Count Antal (Anton) Apponyi (1782-1852), the Austrian ambassador to Rome.
153 While opposing calls for support of the revolution in Naples, Lord Castlereagh (1769-1822), the British foreign secretary, criticised the military intervention in Naples.
154 A leading character in John Vanbrugh's comic 1697 play *The Provok'd Wife*.
155 General Johann Frimont (1759-1831) was commander of the Austrian army marching towards Naples.
156 The carnival-like Festival of Moccoletti, occurring on Shrove Tuesday, involved crowds celebrating in the streets in masquerade, with each person carrying a candle called a 'moccoletti'.
157 General Johann Frimont defeated General Pépé's Neapolitan army at the battle of Rieti

Appony very cock-a-hoop, but nobody believes the account, or at least everybody thinks it exaggerated.

Friday 9th. Looking at this journal this morning I see Consalvi's alarm on the 12th of last month. I have since heard it accounted for. Cardinal Pacca[158] had been to the Pope in the morning: had denounced Cardinal Consalvi and his measures, and returned to his Bishopric of Frascati. Consalvi, receiving this intelligence in the evening, imagined that Pacca had bribed the Governors on the other side of Albano, and that he was betrayed, and the Neapolitans really at Albano without his having heard of their approach. This story shows the *friendly* terms on which the Cardinals are living together.

Horrible accounts of the state of Madrid. It is reported that the King has been assassinated. Been down with Vyvyan, Malcolm and George to see the Austrian infantry of whom there are 9,000 just arrived. They are almost all Hungarians and seem fine men, but rather slight made. They have got but a moderate bivouac, some of them being nearly midleg deep in water. Dined at Mr Clive's. Went to Princess Borghese's, which I thought agreeable. Returned to Mr Clive's. Asked to dine with Borghese on Tuesday, and having refused her on Sunday obliged to accept, though we are already engaged. Met James Brougham there and like what I saw of him very much.[159]

on 7 March 1821. Frimont had a total force of 14,500 soldiers while General Pépé commanded 10,000 troops.

158   Cardinal Bartolomea Pacca (1756-1844).

159   James Brougham (1780-1833) was the younger brother of Henry Brougham, 1st Baron Brougham, who was lord chancellor from 1830 to 1834.

VOLUME 2

Rome—Naples

10 March to 27 May 1821

Saturday March 10th. Austrians still passing through, but no news. Dined with the Aylmers, Lord and Lady Ruthven,[1] Lady Westmoreland, Hutchinsons, Brougham, Hornby and I. Long argument with Lady W. about General Church, whom she steadily defends. Lady Drummond in the evening—no Ball and I thought it dullish.

Sunday 11th. Went to the Vatican and passed all the morning there. Dined with the Duke of Hamilton, old Princess Czarterinka,[2] Count and Countess Ludorf, Baron Cassia,[3] Duke and Duchess, H. and I. Mrs Canning's in the evening. The war is over and the Neapolitans deserve all that happen to them. They have abandoned the defiles of Borghetto and Antrodollo, almost without question, and have allowed the Austrians to advance to Aquila.[4] One regiment of the line has already gone over to the Austrians and General Church went from here last night for the honourable purpose of taking command of the deserters.

Monday 12th. I have today taken my first lecture with Nibby. Parts of it are very interesting, but parts dry and tedious. This, however, being only an Introductory Lecture and chiefly upon the Topography of Rome, I

---

1   James, 6th Lord Ruthven (1777-1853) and his wife Mary, née Campbell, whom he married in 1813.
2   The Polish Princess Izabela Czartoryska, née Flemming (1746-1835).
3   The Maltese Baron Cassia (1778-1867).
4   After the Neapolitan defeat at the battle of Rieti, a provincial capital of the Papal States, on 7 March 1821, the Austrians marched into Naples. General Pépé went into exile, travelling to England via Portugal. See *The Memoirs of General Pépé Written by Himself*, 3 vols (London, 1846).

expect much from the others. Dined today at Ld. Colchester's—pleasant dinner—sat next to Miss Talbot, who is a very nice unaffected girl, though not pretty. Our party Sir G. and Miss Talbot, Ld. and Lady Ruthven, Gen. Ramsay, Miss Fanshawe, Cartwright, G. and myself. Went nowhere in the evening.

Tuesday 13th. A number of baggage and store waggons gone past this morning. One of the soldiers tells me no troops are coming this way, but I suspect this is not correct as I hear there will be some on the 16th. Reading Nibby's *Le Mura di Romano* all morning, very ingenious and I think tolerably satisfactory with some exceptions. Dined with Pauline, Falconieris, Mariscottis, Marinetti, Hautmesnils, a Spaniard I think Salines, several other Italians, Duke of Hamilton, Crescentini, George and I. In the evening Canova came in—nice, etc. as usual. Got into a scrape at dinner by mentioning the intended marriage of Lucia, daughter of Mr Wyse. Pauline, however, very gracious and particularly amusing. Gave Comte Falconieri and me a long account of Bonaparte's escape from Elba and the part she played on the occasion.[5] Promised to present me to Madame Mère and begged us to be at the D. of Hamilton's tonight. Called on Madame Massini[6] to enquire; Lady Ellenborough in the evening, an Improvisatore. I am glad I heard him and he was certainly ingenious, but I do not wish to hear him again. My Italian master tells me that this man, whose name is Feretti,[7] is better in the *buffa* line, and I can conceive it. The hopes of the war do not seem quite given up. Last night, where all are hot politicians, they seemed to be yet tolerably confident, and if once there is a republic all Italy will be up in arms.

Wednesday 14th. Letters arrived yesterday from Charlotte and Edmund[8]— wrote Charles on Monday. Nibby's second lecture very interesting, but most of it in his book on the Forum. Dined at home. Lady Westmoreland's in the evening—too full, but good. Lies on both sides, Austrian and Neapolitan. The latter that the Austrians have been beaten near Tivoli, and the former that their flag is flying on Gaeta.[9] I believe neither.

---

5   Princess Pauline was the only member of the Bonaparte family to visit Napoleon during his exile on Elba.

6   A much-admired soprano singer.

7   Jacopo Feretti (1784-1852), an opera librettist who worked with Donizetti.

8   Presumably Edmund Hornby (1773-1857), who married Stanley's aunt Lady Charlotte Stanley in 1796.

9   Gaeta is a coastal city 60 miles north of Naples.

Thursday 15th. Wet day. Was to have shot with Edsell—no going out. Dined with him—dullish—sat a long time after dinner, Lord W. Russell, Mr Power, Clayton and I. Torlonia's in the evening—very bad—crowded and bad company. Horrible news from Naples, proposals or rather submissions come to the King and Austrian colours really flying in Gaeta.[10]

Friday 16th. Went to see the Palazzo Colonna—finest room in Europe, 200 feet by 34, but about 20 feet on each side taken off by a separation by two pillars of *giallo antico* [ancient yellow marble]—very rich in marbles, some good pictures, but lamentably going to decay from the late Prince having no sons and his property being divided between a nephew and two daughters. Very interesting lecture with Nibby—see end of Book. Dined at Suli, went nowhere.

Saturday [17th]. Out shooting with Edsell—not much sport. Went to Lady Drummond's in the evening—dull.

Sunday 18th. Nothing particular.

Monday 19th. Bad day. Nibby's lecture Coliseum good, but all in his Book. Dined with the Selwyns, did not admire our party. All sorts of reports, no one knows what to believe. Revolution of Piedmont, however, is certain.[11]

Tuesday 20th. Went with George to the Corsini palace, the Guercino after all is <u>the</u> picture, though there are many very fine ones. Portico of Octavia, but little to see now as it is so blocked up and the stench quite intolerable. Dined with Corbett, Otway, Edsell, Edwardes and ourselves. In the evening went to Lady Westmoreland's—pleasant party as there is always. Lady Ellenborough's afterwards, where Corbett and I came in after everybody was gone away, except the <u>elect</u>.

Wednesday 21st. Went with Corbett to the Borghese. I like this collection better every time I see it, the Albanos, several Titians, 2 Domenichinos, a small Annibal Caracci, the Pietro da Cortona,[12] etc. are superb. Nibby did not come. Waited till four and then went away. He came afterwards and was disappointed. Dined at Lady Ellenborough's and staid late. Clive hooked for the eldest. It is said L. has broken the hook and got away.

---

10   On 24 March Frimont and his Austrian army marched into Naples.
11   In the face of the Carbonari and the threat of military insurrection, Victor Emanuel, king of Piedmont-Sardinia, abdicated on 13 March 1821 in favour of his brother Charles Felix. He had refused to grant a liberal constitution.
12   Pietro da Cortona (1596-1669).

Thursday 22nd. In our morning walk today out of the Porta Portese Corbett and I were overtaken by a thunderstorm and escaped into a fisherman's hut. His mode of fishing is one common enough here, but such as I never saw elsewhere. It consists merely of a large square net, which is let down and drawn up from time to time by a rope secured through a block on an upright pole. Our friend had ten of these, but said it was not very profitable. A labourer whom we saw said that he gained by his labour 22 *bagocchi*, about 1s a day, and if this be true is very well paid, as 1s here will go as far as 2s in England. Dined with the Aylmers, Burys, Lady C. Lindsay, Sir W. Gell, Brougham. Did not go to the Vatican at night.

Friday 23rd. Wet day. Nibby in the Capitol. Dined at home, Mr Parke, Brougham, Edwardes, Aylmer, Graham and ourselves. Duchess Borghese, she looked very ill, rejoicing over the Catholic question. Duchess of Devonshire, good party, a little formal in the music room, but plenty of other rooms.

Saturday 24th. Fine day, but sharp and cold *tramontana* [chilling north wind]. Drove to the Temple of Deus Rediculus. Has been a pretty temple and very well built, but the steps which I suppose to have been there have been removed and the vaults underneath united to the Temple, which gives it inside a preposterous elevation. Stopped on our way back at the Tomb of Scipios. Not a great deal to see, except for the name. Dined at home. Lady Drummond's in the evening. Dull, nothing but *rouge et noir* [a card game] and no conversation.

Sunday 25th. Walked a little while with Otway, but my foot obliged me to come home. Dined at home and alone.

Friday 30th. Lost the account of a week or near it, but I do not think there has been much in it worth mentioning. Shoals of English going off to Naples, some gone already. Just come home from dining with Sir W. Drummond—a dull dinner, Mycielski, Hutchinson, Hope,[13] Abbé Campbell[14] and a Mr Cholmondeley. Shall not go out. Nibby employs me morning, noon and night.

---

13   Thomas Hope (1769-1830), banker, author, art collector and a patron of Thorvaldsen.
14   Abbé Campbell (1753-1830), an Irish Catholic priest based in Naples and a friend of Sir William Drummond and Sir William Gell. He was employed as a spy by the British government.

April 1821

Sunday April 1st. Went with the Aylmers to see the Villa Mattei,[15] the property of the Prince of Peace.[16] It might be made into a nice house, there are some charming pictures by the Caraccis,[17] and the grounds are beautiful; but there is the malaria! What a scourge to the country this mysterious disorder is, which makes whole tracts of land uninhabitable! Went to the Gardens of the Villa Pamphilj Doria; more like English park ground than almost any, and the further part of them very beautiful; I had never been in that part of them before. A heavenly day and I hope the fine weather is setting in.

Monday 2nd. I forgot yesterday we visited the Temple of Claudius as it is called, which is nothing more than a Church [Santi Giovanni e Paolo al Celio] built in the 6th century by Simplicius[18] and mentioned as such I believe by Anastasius.[19] Nibby again today. Dined with Sir W. Drummond, Mycielski, Hutchinson, who go off tomorrow, two Austrians, Lady Lismore,[20] Lord and Lady Ruthven, Gen. and Mrs Canning and ourselves. Called on Madame Massimo and Duchess of H. where we were to have dined, and went to Madame Appony's in the evening—crowded and bad, all men. Report from France of very serious disturbances. Piedmont goes on they say.[21]

Wednesday [3rd]. Lady Westmoreland's gioci di Sacchia I thought rather *seccatura* [a nuisance], spite of the water. Was to have dined with D. of Hamilton, but he dined at five and I could not go.

Friday 6th. Set at four in the morning to Praneste[22] with Corbett and Sir G. Talbot. Doubtful morning, but turned out most fortunately a beautiful day. Four hours and a half in going, about five there, and ditto coming

---

15   The Villa Mattei, now known as the Villa Celimontana, is situated in the south-east of Rome on the Celian Hill.

16   Manuel Godoy de Faria (1767-1851), prince of the Peace and 1st duke of Alcudia, was formerly the first secretary of state of Spain, but by 1821 he was living in exile in Rome.

17   The brothers Agostino Carracci (1557-1602) and Annibale Carracci (1560-1609), and their cousin Ludovico Carracci (1555-1619).

18   Pope Simplicius, holder of the Holy See from 468 to 483.

19   Anastasius I Dicorus (*c.* 431-518), Byzantine Emperor from 491 to 518.

20   Lady Eleanor Lismore, who was married to the Irish Whig politician Viscount Lismore. She was travelling the Continent alone, and they divorced in 1826.

21   At the end of March 1821, King Charles Felix asked for Austrian military assistance in suppressing the insurrection in Piedmont.

22   A town 22 miles east of Rome, now known as Palestrina. It was known as Praeneste in the classical period.

home: home before 7. Sir G. Talbot a very good man to go on an excursion with. Temple of Fortuna at Praneste must have been superb. The
remains are inconsiderable and part hidden in the Barberini Palace.[23]
Muro Cyclopeo [the cyclopean walls] a stupendous work.[24] Not great
remains of antiquity at Palestrina, but a great deal of beautiful country,
and the view from the *cittadella* well repays the trouble of the ascent
[up Monte San Pietro]. Tried for antiques, terra cotta, etc., but found
nothing worth bringing away. I am very glad, however, to have seen this,
which few Englishmen go to.

Saturday 7th. Today an execution took place in the Piazza del Popolo,
the meaning of which offence I have not yet found out. Set off about
one-o'clock, a cloudy day but fair, to Tivoli.[25] Passed on our way the
sulphurous stream which comes from Lago di Fortano (the ancient
Avernus?) the day being calm, the smell of the water was very perceptible
at the distance of 200 yards and close by it was quite intolerable.[26] I was
not so much struck as I had expected with the first view of the city.
Drove to the Regina [the main inn at Tivoli], agreed for dinner at 5
Pauls, bed at 2 and breakfast 2. Walked out to the Cascade and still
disappointed, though there is some beautiful scenery. Returned to our
Inn, which we found tolerably comfortable and an excellent dinner.

Sunday 8th. Still a cloudy day, but took our Ciceroni and sallied forth.
Before we went out our Landlord said he could keep us no longer as
there were twenty people coming that day and he had let the rooms. As
we knew a large party were coming we thought this was possible, but
soon found our Innkeeper thought he had made a bad bargain with us
and could make a better, and unluckily the waiter offered us worse
rooms below. On which we said the party might take these and we
would not turn out, and in proof of this we locked the doors and put
the keys in our pockets. We heard nothing more about it. Quite satisfied
and more than satisfied with the Cascade and Cascatelle, which on the
whole I prefer.[27] The Villa is called Gregoriana must have been superb.
Its situation is quite enchanting. Returned to luncheon. Sallied out again,
hurried through the Villa d'Este [by the Porta Romana in Tivoli] and
to the Villa Adriana, but we had not time to see it as it should be seen.

---

23   A deserted fifteenth-century palazzo.
24   Cyclopean masonry was an ancient type of stonework using large boulders.
25   Situated on the slopes of Monte Ripoli, Tivoli is 18 miles north-east of Rome, following,
     for part of the route, the Via Tiburtina.
26   Lago di Fortano is also known as Lago di Tartaro.
27   The series of waterfalls formed by the waters of the Anio.

Hope, however, to see this country later on next season, for the leaves are hardly out yet.

Monday 9th. Bad raining morning and almost thought we should have been obliged to sit at home all day, but towards one it seemed to clear up, and we set out in hopes of reaching Vicovaro, Horace's Barria, or perhaps even Subiaco [28 miles from Tivoli] the end of our journey. The road, however, was atrocious and I should on first sight of it have given it up as quite impracticable for a carriage, being worse than that in which I remember Phipps[28] and I broke down on our way to Lady Mary Ross's in Rosshire. The country is, however, splendidly beautiful, being varied mountain scenery, and the situation of Castel Madama and Vicovaro itself above description.[29] George took two or three sketches and we arrived in very good time at an Osteria of so unpromising an appearance that our hearts sank within us. Sleeping there was out of the question as they had no rooms, and eating was nearly so to anyone who had smelt and seen the kitchen. I believe the only room. What was to be done? Our carriage was put under a rock, our horses in the stable, and a man in the crowd offered to share a *casa partricolare* where we could be received. Accordingly we found a decent looking house, the first floor of which was occupied by the family and served as a kitchen, the second by two Geometri [surveyors] sent by the Government to make plans of the properties hereabouts. The Geometri, however, were turned out or put to sleep together to accommodate people of such consequence, and we were put into rooms in a horrible a state of dilapidation, but looking like part of an old family house and with a Chapel belonging to them. Here we waited three hours for dinner and at last given Trout, an old Hen, as the man honestly called it, and the water it was boiled in full of rice for soup; besides this we had eggs and cheese. We had, however, good beds and were comfortable enough. While waiting for dinner walked to the charmingly situated Convent of S. Cosimato.[30]

[April 10th.] Tuesday morning. Woke by the rain pouring onto my bed through the ceiling and found it had been raining all night and was still pouring. Consequently our excursion to Horace's Villa for that day or the next was out of the question. After consultation we determined to

28 Phipps Hornby (1785-1867), George Hornby's uncle. He became a midshipman in the Royal Navy aged twelve, and had a very distinguished naval career. He was knighted, became an admiral, and eventually was made a lord of the Admiralty.
29 Vicovaro is a village perched on a hill above the road.
30 The convent of San Cosimato is located 2 miles from Vicovaro on a rock above the River Anio.

go on to Subiaco and see the country as we came back, and we set out with heavy rain and in answer to an enquiry whether the road was as bad as yesterday had from the Vetturino the comforting assurance '*Sempri lui peggio assai*' ['It was worse for him']. This, however, we found not the case, though the first eleven or twelve miles were horrible. But afterwards, for the last seven or eight, was as firm as can be imagined.[31] Day horrible and only consoled, in passing through a charming country which we could not see, by the recollection that we must repass it and probably in better weather. Arrived at Subiaco about four: a vile looking Inn and stank horribly. I never shall forget, however, the first impression of Subiaco, when we suddenly could catch a view of it rising on its own high eminence and backed by six distinct rows of mountains. We set out to look for a *casa partricolare,* but found none, though we routed out of bed a poor man with some chronic disease as he told us, who said it would be his pleasure and honour to receive us, if he had room. Returned to the Inn, found it cleaned and now decent, and managed to sup and sleep there.

Wednesday 11th. Set out to see the country. Fine morning at last after raining all night. Walked to the Bath of Nero[32] and the Cascade above. Scenery enchanting. San Bendetto [where Saint Benedict retired in about 450] and S. Scholastica [founded in the fifth century], the latter of which, consisting of 15 monks is possessed of a yearly income 18000 Pauli and give bread daily to 1000 poor, whom they thus help to maintain in idleness. Was obliged to hire an ass to carry me home as I have hurt my foot and think very likely I shall be obliged to lay myself up to get it well again. Having seen all at Subiaco worth observation, and not being able to go to the Lago Fucino, not having Neapolitan passports, we returned to Vicovaro, crossing the Teverone [now called the River Aniene], now Licenza, leaving Carsoli, now Arsoli, and Mandela, now Cantalusso Bardela, to our right and after many perils arrived safe at Baria. Found ourselves just as the first time and, while the *gallina* [chicken] is being *assaggate* [tasted] and the same dinner preparing, have found time to write this. I should add we have every prospect of a wet day for tomorrow.

Thursday 12th. Awoke by the customary shower on my bed. The day, however, cleared and became fine and warm, though not sunny. Set out for Horace's Villa. The country on the road not so beautiful as some we have seen, but immediately about it is romantic to the highest degree.

---

31   The road followed the bank of the River Anio.
32   One mile from the town on a hill above the river.

Horace's description of it holds good to this day, and the Fountain of Blandina, now Fonte Bello, corresponds with the account he gives. The fountain has perhaps suffered some alteration, but still the *loquaces lympha desiliunt cavis de saxe*[33] and their rocks on each side of the narrow gorge in which it springs, under Mt. Luesetites, are covered with the Ilex in profusion. It is still *rivo dare nomen idoneus, ut nec Frigi Thracam nec purior ambiat Hebrus*[34] and we enjoyed much a draught of it with our luncheon. The clods were very civil and communicative and I had an admirable scene today talking over Horace with them, which I had in my hand. They enjoyed catching at the names Licenza, Blandina, Mandela and Varia, and repeated over and over again *due mil 'anni fa*! By the way, our Cicerone asked us *en route* whether this Horace was an Englishman. I suppose because none but English come here. The Villa which is shown as Horace's has been lately bought by a man who possesses, it is said, 30,000 Pauli, and is always grasping at more. He first told me that with the <u>dissertation</u> written by Horace himself of his Villa, he had made out all the plan. On which I rather confounded him by pulling Horace himself out of my pocket. He next prepared to show us a small piece of mosaic said to belong to the Villa and always hitherto exposed to view; but being covered by him with a shovelful of earth, he asked us first *Quanto si spende per aprire*? ['How much do you spend to reveal?'] To which we answered *'Nienti'* ['Nothing'] and left the vineyard. This put him in a rage and he began to be very impudent, on which we recommended him to hold his tongue for fear of consequences. The whole business turned the laugh quite against my friend and all the clods kept laughing and repeating *Quanto si spende*? Our Cicerone told us afterwards he meant to demand 3 Piastres! We returned home, I mounted on a mule, George on a donkey, in good time for dinner, which though very abundant deserves to be particularised. In the morning we had seen a small lamb killed under our window and guessed the consequences. Accordingly there appeared first Rice Broth. Then the usual *gallina*, flanked by two shoulders of lamb, taken out of the soup; next fried liver and <u>entrails </u>of <u>lamb</u>, very good; next ribs of lamb boiled with garlic; then roast leg and loin of lamb and omelettes completed the dinner.

Friday 13th. Set out on our return, fair day with showers, to Tivoli, whence I write while the horses are baiting [being fed], after a dispute with the . . .

---

33 A reference to Horace's description of the fountain in *Odes* III.13: 'Fies nobilium tu quoque fontium, me dicente cavis impositam ilicem, saxis, unde loquaces, lymphae desiliunt tuae.'

34 A quote from Horace's *Epistles* I.16.

May 1821

Monday night May 7th. My poor Journal! What a gap in it! And how shall I ever get it up? Better not attempt it. There is no need of describing the ceremonies of the Holy Week, at least those that I saw. Though I hope I shall see them again. On Monday April 30th we left Rome for Albano[35]—a tolerable Inn, but the noisiest town at night that I was ever in. Took a cursory view of the Lake [Albano] that night, which is pretty but tame.

Next morning Tuesday 1st May set out for Frascati—beautiful day and fine drive. At Grotta Ferrata[36] a beautiful picture by Domenichino the Demonic Boy, the boy in strong convulsions and the Mother on her knees watching him are perfectly beautiful.[37] Bad day for Frascati, and did not go up to Tusculum. I think on the whole it disappointed me. Villa Marconi very pretty room and some good statues. Returning went to see Emissary of Claudius,[38] very wonderful and quite perfect, and the Lake appears to advantage from this side, but it is a tame production always.

Wednesday May 2nd. Took asses and a guide and ascended Monte Cavi[39]—beautiful ride: Via Triumphalis[40] very perfect from some little way above Rocca di Papa, and at the top a Convent of course as in every beautiful situation; probably on the spot of the Temple of Jupiter Latialis.[41] Immense stones yet remain forming the Convent garden and one can hardly imagine but that the road led to the Temple. Fine view all around, but particularly the Lakes of Albano and Nemi.[42] Rode back through the Nemus Diana, to Genzano.[43] Met our carriage after a six hour ride and went to Villetri. Bad Inn. Luckily arrived before diligences and got things more reasonable than we otherwise should have done.

---

35 A town 14 miles from Rome.
36 A small village 2 miles from Frascati, the location of the chapel of St Nilus and St Bartholomew, which is decorated with frescoes by Domenichino.
37 Domenichino's fresco had been restored in 1819.
38 Part of the aqueduct Aqua Claudia.
39 Monte Cavi or Monte Albano, the highest point of the chain of mountains that bound the Campagna on the east and south, nearly 3,000 feet above sea level.
40 The well-preserved Roman road ascending towards the summit from Rocca di Papa.
41 The convent of the Passionist, built in 1783 from the remains of the Temple of Latialis.
42 Lake Nemi was the centre of the cult of Diana, the ancient Roman goddess of the hunt, the moon and nature. The lake was called Diana's Mirror.
43 A small town built on the slopes of a steep hill above the Rivotanto.

Thursday 3rd. Crossed the Pontini Terracina, fine view of sea to Fondi a continued defile—shameful to have deserted it.[44] Country and climate change very suddenly. (Capua saw a specimen of Neapolitan bullying over-bullied by Austrian Authority, with the remark to us 'Signor, conosce Lei i Napoltani' ['Sir, you know the Neapolitans']) First view of Mole di Gaeta superb. Inn pretty good, but very dear. Mrs Arbuthnot arrived next day.

Friday 4th. In Naples. Before quitting the subject of the Roman territories I put down one or two hints for me next year as to prices. Lodgings in Rome very good for 2 people 50 Scudi a month.[45] Graham and Greaves had good ones Via Nuova No. 10 for 24 Scudi. Carriage for 60 to 75 Scudi. *Laquais-de-place* 6 Pauls a day. Posting 5 Pauli a horse. Postboys about 5 Pauls, quite enough, and just as well driven as if you pay 10. Dinner a Scudi.

Naples. May 5th. Austrians are of course all in all here, and it is even said that Sir W. à Court, our Minister here, finding himself a mere cypher, applied for leave to resign, which, however, has not been granted. On entering the Town General Frimont, having previously refused all terms, convened the Officers of the Neapolitan Army, told them that he did not intend to interfere with the internal government of the city, but that if any treason were attempted towards his army, he added, I will hang, hang, hang! On which the Officers gratefully bowed and retired. This fact, if it is a fact, I saw in a letter from Col. Evans. Soon after the entrance of the army some of the soldiers were privately stabbed, on which Frimont issued a proclamation that, the next time such a circumstance happened, he should take the ten first citizens he laid his hands on and hang them for each soldier that was stabbed. This had the desired effect. The people seem at present not all discontented and on very good terms with the soldiers. Nothing destroys their eternal gaiety. But they have not yet felt the weight of the load they have brought on themselves. Meantime, arrests are going on every day. Many persons, even of rank, have been publicly flogged through the streets. That is the account I have received from people who were here and I have seen a proclamation condemning the applause which the people bestowed on these just instances of rigour, however praiseworthy might be the sentiment which excited it. Above 100 are now in the Castel dell' Ovo.[46] Many have been sent to Alessandria [the location of the main fortress in Piedmont] and

---

44 Fondi was on the boundary of the Neapolitan territories. It was abandoned by Neapolitan troops in face of the Austrian advance.
45 The scudo was the currency in the Papal States until 1866.
46 The Castel dell'Ovo is situated on a small island connected to the mainland by a causeway.

there shot, and there is reason to believe that some have privately suffered here. All is done by the Neapolitan Police, under private orders from the Austrians. The Officers have all the best rooms in all the Hotels and pay for none of them. The Government promise to pay, but do not say when, and the Innkeepers seem to think never.

We have been in great luck to come in for the festival of the patron Saint S. Gennaro, whose blood miraculously liquefies three times a year.[47] Had I not seen it I would not have believed that there could still exist so much superstition and bigotry or that in any Christian worship there were exhibited such ridiculous scenes as I saw in this procession. In the morning, towards *mezzogiorno* [twelve o'clock], Mass is celebrated in the Cathedral Church of S. Januarius. After this, his head in a gilt case, with the mitre on, is carried in procession, though a very poor one, from his Church to that of Santa Chiara, where he holds his *levée*. I should not forget that during this ceremony I had my pocket picked and a rascal, who was caught with his hand in another man's pocket, went off lifting his eyes to Heaven, crossing himself and making all possible signs of devotion. About 2 o'clock, at this time of year about ½ past 3, the second procession begins to form. The silver statues of all the saints, to the number of sixty or more, are brought to the Church privately, and after Mass take their places. First, come some poor looking people. I should think from the Hospital in the town. Then a long train of mendicant friars, then priests and boys with torches, then the saints in order, beginning with the inferior ones, and lastly under a canopy the sacred blood of the Saint himself, which thus goes to visit his head. It is followed by the Bishop his successor, and all the people take off their hats, not to the Bishop, but to the blood. Besides this, each man takes off his hat to his patron Saint, or his relation—for almost all the lower orders claim relationship with some saint or another. In coming out of the Church St. Michael lost his balance and was near falling, and a cry of horror ran through the crowd, who seemed much consoled when he righted again without damage. The common people know all the statues perfectly and look up to them with the highest reverence. It has been twice proposed to melt them down as they are estimated at 400,000 Piastres. Once in the time of the French, when they were rescued by a contribution, and again in the heat of the late disturbances. But the Saints had the good fortune to escape. As they made the tour of half the city we had plenty of time to get to the Church of Santa Chiara, who by the way figures in the procession, and on whom it is rather hard to be received as a guest in her own Church; particularly as St. Gennaro

---

47   This was one of the three annual ceremonies of San Januarius, the Latin name for San Gennaro, held on the Saturday preceding the first Sunday in May.

has three of his own. The side aisles were full, but the middle one was reserved for the procession. I was stopped on going up by a Neapolitan soldier, but flung him off and said I should go where I saw others going, on which the Officer interfered and said *è forestiere, lasciatilo passare* ['a foreigner, let him through']. I am convinced he took me for an Austrian, as one of the sentinels did this morning in the place of the Cathedral. I went up to the steps of the grand altar, the steps of which were crowded with English and Austrians, and after a short time the procession came in, in the same order as we had seen it go out. Each person bowed to St. Januarius, and passed on, and the Saints bowed one by one, at least their bearers knelt and then passed by. On the right of the grand altar in a privileged place were the relations of the Saint, headed by the *principali parenti*, an old woman with a face I never shall forget, who stood on a chair and sometimes honoured a Saint by shortly relating his history as he passed, sometimes screaming the Credo and Paternoster, in which she was joined in full chorus by all the relations. The merit seemed to be in screaming as loud as possible, and the noise they made when they were well backed up is not to be described or imagined, except by those who have heard it. When the blood comes to pay its respects to the head a little bell was rung, and many a watch was out to observe the precise moment. All this time Hecate[48] and her crew were making such a deafening din that an Austrian officer fairly put his hands to his ears, and I was very near laughing aloud, though they say it is dangerous to laugh at these absurdities for fear of a stiletto. I was not near enough to see the miracle nor did I very much care about it. The observing the watches is because it is said that there is some blood on a stone at Pozzuoli where he was beheaded which liquefies at the same moment. I should not forget to say that Corbett strongly suspects the *principali parenti* of having picked his pocket, which somebody certainly did in the Church. The miracle was complete this year in nine minutes, which seemed to give satisfaction. If it is too long delayed the howls of the relations become dreadful, they tear their hair, fling themselves on the ground, and almost like the old priests of Baal gash themselves with knives. When Murat[49] was here he sent to say that he understood the miracle was likely to be delayed, he sent his complements and intended to be present with all his Officers, and should be much disappointed if it did not succeed. The hint was taken and the miracle performed to a miracle. This reminds me of another story of much the same kind which I heard the other day. Miracles were till lately pretty common in Austria and there was one saint whose statue's

---

48   The ancient Greek goddess of magic and witchcraft.
49   Joachim Murat (1767-1815), the French general who Napoleon crowned king of Naples
     in 1808.

hair grew every year, and for the cuttings of which immense sums were given. The Emperor, however, disapproved. He issued an edict against miracles. All the saints obliged and no more have been heard of. The favour of some of the Saints is but precarious here. Some time ago the *Lazarroni*[50] found out that S. Anthony was a gentleman, for which they called him a ... and flogged him all round the town. He is now, however, restored to favour. So much for Saints and miracles.

Sunday May 6th. Did nothing but walk about the Town—saw nothing. The Quays are beautiful and the people look so happy and contented one can hardly pity them. I think Naples will be quite *enchantment* [under a spell]. Tonight a procession by torchlight in honour of S. Gennaro.

Monday 7th. Walked with Corbett to the Grotto of Posilipo, which is very curious, but not the least pretty or fine, being a long passage through the mountain, broad enough in some places for three carriages, but quite dark, and the stench horrid.[51] Corbett and I stepped 800 paces exactly, including only the covered part, for the rock is cut into for some way on both sides. Walked on to the beach by the Island of Nisidia, a very fine view of Pozzuoli, Bacoli, etc. Tried to get round or over the cliffs but failed and were obliged to return the way we came. Wrote to my Grandfather.[52] Hope he will get it, as I was very cautious about politics.

Tuesday 8th. Today we hired a carriage at three Ducats to take us to Pozzuoli or anywhere we chose. We passed through the Grotto and came out on the beach not very far beyond where C. and I had been. A beautiful drive along the shore on a road made by Murat, and with magnificent views both ways. From Pozzuoli walked about a mile and a half to see the Solfatara [a dormant volcano]. This is quite evidently the extinguished crater of a volcano. On stamping with your foot the ground rings with a hollow sound, and in some places there rises a light smoke. It is a dead flat surrounded by a continued circle of hill, now planted with broom and other shrubs. From thence we went to the Amphitheatre [located behind the town] where S. Gennaro was put to death, and where, therefore, he has a chapel erected. Here is, I believe, the miraculous stone, but I did not see it. The Amphitheatre has been respectable in size, and the vaulted gallery around one half is yet in good preservation. It stands, however, in a vineyard so full of trees that at present it is impossible to see the rest of it, or to take one view of the whole extent. From the

---

50   The poorest class in Naples, including the fisherman and boatmen.
51   In 1819 J. M. W. Turner painted the view of the entrance to the grotto of Posillipo, a
      long tunnel linking Naples to Pozzuoli.
52   The 12th earl of Derby (1752-1834), who was a committed Whig.

Amphitheatre we returned to the carriage and drove on to Lucrino Lake. The bridge of Caligula, from Pozzuoli to Bacoli, or rather the ruins of it are worth observation. You pass by a house called that of Cicero (he certainly had one here) and soon after one stopped; the road made by Murat having been destroyed by the sea, as they say, but I suspect never having been finished. We walked there a mile or a little more along the sand, till we came to the Lucrino Lake. Horace is literally true when he says *undique latius extent visentur Lucrino stagna lacu*,[53] for it is now no larger than a moderate sized fishpond; having been shrunk to this insignificant size by the tremendous earthquake and eruption of the 29th September 1538, which destroyed the village of Tripergola, with all its inhabitants. Formed in 48 hours the mountain called the Monte Nuovo, occupying the site of the village, part of the lake and of the Portus Julius, and cut off the communication of the Avernus with the sea. This latter lake is small and not very beautiful; it bears, like most of those I have seen between here and Rome, the appearance of an extinguished crater of a volcano.[54] There are some ruins upon its banks which look well from a distance and bear the name of the Temple of Apollo. The Grotto of the Sybil we did not see, not having brought torches with us, but I suspect we had no loss. In returning we stopped at the Temple of Serapis,[55] which the Guide Books say was built in the sixth century of Rome, but I suspect that in the Republic Serapis was not introduced among the Roman Gods, and from the profusion of beautiful marbles, and from the style of the workmanship, I should place it full as late as Adrian's time.[56] I should say indeed later, had he not been so ardent a worshipper of the Egyptian deities. The Temple itself is circular, standing in the centre of a square court. The circle had 16 columns around it, of which three of Cipollino marble still remain, much eaten into by the salt water which lies more than a foot deep on the splendid marble pavements. Around the square are 42 little chambers, most of which, whatever purpose they anciently served, are now converted into Baths and supplied with mineral waters. In the town are a pedestal with an inscription and bas relief round it to Tiberius[57] and another surmounted by a statue of Flavius the Senator.[58] I could not read the inscription. The Church of S. Proculus is built on the site of the Temple of Augustus, but little remaining except

---

53 Horace, *Odes* II. 15.
54 Because of the poisonous fumes emitting from it, the ancient Romans believed Lake Avernus to be the entrance to Hades.
55 The Temple of Jupiter and Serapis. Serapis, a Graeco-Egyptian deity, was adopted by the Romans in the third century BC.
56 From 1806 to 1811 extensive excavation was carried out at the site.
57 The second Roman emperor who ruled from AD 14 to 37.
58 Possibly Flavius Optatus (d. AD 337).

an inscription and three pillars which are built into the wall. In returning to Naples we turned off to go to the Lake of Agnano, another crater, near which is the celebrated Grotto del Cane and close by this are the sulphurous baths. Here is also a royal Palace and Chase, but it is on the further side of the Lake.[59]

Wednesday 9th. This morning there is a proclamation announcing the report of a <u>Court Martial</u> held on a baker for furnishing arms. He was found guilty and it adds the sentence has been executed!! Very hot and Pharaoh's plague of flies beginning. Dined at three o'clock. After dinner drove up to the Royal Palace of Capo di Monte. The Palace itself is a miserable old building, quite in ruins, but the views from the whole of this hill are the most beautiful that can be conceived, the rich gardens interspersed with Villas going down the hill, the Plain scattered with houses, Portici, the Bay, and lastly Mount Vesuvius, with all the other mountains around in all the light and shade, made a complete picture. By the way, this is the first place where we have seen what one is accustomed to call Italian scenery. The buildings too are here quite Italia, flat roofs, verandas, balconies, awnings over terraces, etc. Returned on foot, a beautiful night. Remarked today a man cutting hay, his scythe formed thus . . . Bought some oranges coming home, 3 for 2 *grana*.[60] Saw the people buying their iced lemonade at a *grano* a glass. The town is well supplied with ice, boats coming over from the mountains with loads of it twice a week. They are heavily fined if they do not arrive at their right time.

Thursday 10th. This morning we have been to the Accademia Reale,[61] where we have seen the papyri, some fine paintings found at Nola, the Bronzes and Etruscan vases. The papyri are exceedingly curious. Their first appearance is that of lumps of stone calcified, and the beginning is much the most difficult part of the operation, being so more burnt than the rest. We saw the process of unrolling which is very singular; the manuscript having been begun (how I know not) is suspended in a machine of three or four cords with screws in the top, by which it is gently drawn up. The manuscript is then lightly brushed for the space of about an inch with gum water, upon which a piece of gold wafer skin is placed, and, with the additional consistency which this gives, they bear being drawn up and thus unroll themselves. They are then handed over to the decypherers, of whom there are six. The K. of Naples

---

59   Lake Agnano was drained in 1870.
60   One hundred and twenty grana made up one Neapolitan piaster.
61   The Accademia Reale was founded by King Charles VII of Naples in 1752.

at present bears the whole expense. The Nola pictures are almost all single figures, or at least not much grouped together. They are terribly spoilt, but there is some good drawing in several of them. There is a curious Murder of the Innocents said to be by Raphael on a china plate. One figure struck me as absurdly bad and the others good. From there we passed into the Library, a fine room 230 palmi[62] by 80 high, coved roof and floor of Dutch tiles. It has some other minor rooms adjoining. Manuscript room closed. Next came the Bronzes, mostly utensils of common domestic use, but curious from their antiquity, and many of them resembling our own. Among these were some surgical instruments, medicines, Ladies toilets, rouge bottles, children's playthings, etc. etc. Then succeeded the ancient armours, which no man will ever persuade me was really worn; I could hardly lift one of the helmets, and the rest in proportion, so that a man accoutred could not have moved, but must have been very like Sancho Panza armed in the midnight alarm. After these we saw the Etruscan vases, but I had not taste enough to admire them. Lastly we looked into the room ordinarily shut up on account of the extreme indecency of all the figures. There are, however, one or two of beautiful workmanship and curious as exhibiting a picture of the ideas of decency of the old Romans. The numbers of different *Custodi* who tax strangers and all of whom I saw put together what they got from us is very disgraceful, and for me a striking contrast with the liberality of the Vatican and Florence Galleries.

Dined at three as we shall do regularly. Drove to Virgil's tomb—a beautiful situation, but nothing in the tomb except the recollections attached to it.[63] A vile Inscription put up by I know not who which I cannot construe. This is it: *Qui cinares? Tumoli virtipa conditor diem. Ille hoc qui circunt pascua riora duces.* Saw the unfortunate lapdog's tomb hurled from its elevation. Passed along the Strada Nuova. Beautiful Villa of the old Margravine of Anspach,[64] drove along the top of the hill meaning to go to St Elmo, but were too late. A charming drive.

Going up Vesuvius tonight. About 11 o'clock we set out from Naples in Dr Fitton's carriage which he had sent over for us, having a villa at Resina.[65] Our party consisted of Otway, Corbett, Dr Fitton and myself.

---

62   The palmo was a Neapolitan unit of measurement: one palmo was equivalent to just over 10 inches.

63   Near the eastern entrance to the grotto of Posillipo.

64   The margravine of Anspach was born Elizabeth Berkeley (1750-1828), daughter of the 4th earl of Berkeley. She married the 6th Baron Craven in 1767, but they divorced in 1783, having both had affairs. In 1791 Elizabeth married the margrave of Anspach, who died in 1806. She lived in Villa Craven, Posillipo, and was a friend of Queen Caroline. While Caroline was princess of Wales, Elizabeth served as her chamberlain, and it was she, during their tour of Italy, who engaged Bartolomeo Pergami as courier for the princess.

65   William Henry Fitton (1780-1861), an Irshman, became president of the Geological Society

We left his house about one o'clock, a beautiful night, and the freshness of the air and the beauty of the moonlight soon made our ride delightful. We had, however, tried for two of the party and went, therefore, very slow, besides which we wanted, for no reason I could find out, a considerable time at the Hermitage.[66] Day was beginning to break before we left our mules by the crater of the late eruption. We made, therefore, as much haste as we could to gain the summit before sunrise and I had no conception of the labour of the ascent before I attempted it. On arriving at the summit of the first cone I was quite beat and great was my horror on finding a long plain of deep sand, succeeded by the second cone. The appearance, however, of this plain of lava, which I believe is of 1663, is very singular, sulphurous smoke issuing in not less than a hundred different places in all directions. Here we had a fine view, daylight having begun. But, tired as we were, we pushed on up the second cone and were delighted to find the Sun not risen. A light smoke rose from the crater and, the wind being easterly, we were near suffocated till we got round. We has not been up five minutes, indeed two of our party had not arrived, when the Sun suddenly rose like a ball of fire from behind the Apennines and the clear twilight suddenly flashed into day. The effect was very fine and our shadows upon the smoke had a most singular effect. As the day advanced we had a most splendid stare all round. To the west of us lay the Bay of Naples, with the town looking like a baby house, the promontory of Posilipo, the Islands of Ischia, Nisida and Procida, further to the right the promontories of Mola de Gaeta and Terracina, between which was a vast plain covered with villages and towns which had a very singular appearance, each being enveloped in a little cloud of vapour, the plain remaining clear. To the North lay Cassino, to the East the Apennines, ridge above ridge, to an immeasurable extent, finishing in the promontory on which stands Castella there between this and Vesuvius lay Pompeii, of which we could distinguish the amphitheatre like a garden well; and the whole panorama was closed by the very beautiful island of Capri, whose bold cliffs, from whatever point they are seen, make a superb break to the vast extent of the sea. Between us and the Bay lastly were Resina, Herculaneum and Torre del Greco, and we could plainly trace the dark grey torrent of lava which destroyed the latter in the tremendous eruption of 1794, the new town being built upon the ruins of the old. The shipping in the Bay dwindled to nothing but their white sails sparkling in the morning Sun, while the long conical shadow of the mountain itself extended over half of it, were wonderfully beautiful. Having satisfied ourselves with observing the view, we began to examine

---

in London in 1827 and was published extensively in the *Edinburgh Review*.

66   The Hermitage was a stopping point on the ascent up Vesuvius from Resina.

the crater and the appearance of the mountain itself.[67] Dr Fitton being a geologist was most interested in it. Indeed, it is for this purpose he [has] taken the villa and I think he intends to publish. It seems pretty evident that Monte Somma, Vesuvius, and the mountain behind have at some time been one hill; that the top has been blown off, probably by the great eruption of 79, and from the top of the present crater you trace the line of the old large crater in its whole extent, except in this side towards the Bay where repeated streams of lava have passed. You see, indeed, more, for you find nature performing the same operation again. Vesuvius itself has now divided into two tops, in the right hand of which is the present crater, the cone having been formed by the accumulation of ashes, and having formed for itself a crater, so that the left hand peak bears to the right hand one precisely the same relation, as Monte Somma to the whole of Vesuvius. Below is the present appearance of Vesuvius which will illustrate the above. The crater itself is horrible; the rocks which appear on one side are quite perpendicular and the rest is composed of loose earth and ashes, are constantly giving way. Indeed, as we lay on one side, leaning over to look down, I thrust my stick completely through the place where my body had been. The depth is perhaps equal to that of the core itself. The upper core and the bottom appear to be of shingly loose soil. From several parts sulphurous smoke is constantly ascending and as you walk round it repeatedly bursts up under your very feet. The side where it chiefly issues is perfectly yellow with sulphur. Altogether the appearance is awful and horrible to the last degree.

In descending we remarked on the right a hill completely covered with white crystallised sulphur, and with one yellow spot resembling a spring in a morass. At the bottom of the second cone, just by the spot where we left the mules, is the crater where the Frenchman threw himself in during the late slight eruption. It was still hot enough to light a stick, and we boiled our coffee and eggs here previous to descending. It was now 7 o'clock or near it and the Sun was already so powerful we were glad to find any shade. Arrived at Dr Fitton's about 10. Otway above three hours at breakfast. Got to home about ½ past 2. Excursion cost us 3 Ducats each. Went to bed for a couple of hours. Dined with O. and C. about six and took a short walk afterwards.

Saturday 12th. Went to the Museums into the Statue Gallery—much exceeds my expectations, Hercules, Flora, a little fragment of a Psyche or Leda, Antonius, Aristides, Hermaphrodite, 2 Venuses, but particularly Callipyge [buttocks] and many others are quite superb. I shall often be

---

67   The most recent volcanic activity on Vesuvius had been in April 1820, when large amounts
      of lava had poured from it.

there. Dined at three. In the afternoon drove to Portici, saw the pictures of Herculaneum and Pompeii, which surpassed my expectations. Though much damaged the colours are very fresh, and after seems that it is impossible to say the ancients did not understand foreshortening and perspective. The royal palace is horrible without, but has some good rooms within. The King, with characteristic good taste and feeling, keeps Madame Murat's books, family pictures presents made to her, and on the beds are the French Eagle, and on some of the chairs the cypher G.[68] I should not forget to say here that in the Palace of Naples I am told he has a screen worked by Madame Murat herself, on which he has taken out her cypher and substituted his own. We <u>should have</u> seen the theatre Herculaneum, but went with the Otways and when we were near the bottom Mrs O[69] took fright and would return, but we can go another day. Tonight San Carlo opens, but I shall not go for a first representation.[70]

Sunday May 13. Visited this morning the Palazzo Reale, fine palace and well furnished, but the pictures very second-rate—some good, but much trash. Very pretty Chapel, fitted up by Murat at great expense and good taste. A copy in the Palace of the three Graces altered into the three Virtues by Annibal Caracci, even worse than Giulio Romano at Knowsley. Dined with Sir William à Court, very civil. Like the Prince of Hesse,[71] Ficquelmont,[72] several Austrian officers, Weymouth, K. Craven,[73] a Mr Chaloner. I mean to go to Baiae tomorrow.

Monday 14th. Wild stormy day. Shall not go to Baiae. Greatly disappointed at receiving no letters today, of which I felt sure, particularly on Charlotte's account. I trust, however, no news is good news. Been to the Academy again. The pictures are very second rate, or even lower. One or two very good Raphaels, a beautiful Domenichino, and a superb Danae

---

68   Caroline Murat, née Bonaparte (1782-1839), was a younger sister of Napoleon. She married General Murat in 1800 and was queen consort of Naples from 1808 to 1815. In 1815 she went into exile in Austria.

69   Sarah Otway Cave (1768-1862), the mother of Robert Otway.

70   The Teatro San Carlo was built adjoining the Royal Palace in 1737, and the new Teatro San Carlo was inaugurated in 1817 following a devastating fire. Rossini, artistic director of the opera house from 1815 to 1822, premiered a number of his operas at San Carlo during this period.

71   Philip, landgrave of Hesse-Homburg (1779-1846). He was a field marshal in the imperial Austrian army and Austrian governor of Naples from 1821 to 1825.

72   Karl Ludwig, count of Ficquelmont (1777-1857), the Austrian ambassador to Naples.

73   Richard Keppel Craven (1779-1851) was the son of the margravine of Anspach and a friend of Sir William Gell. In October 1820 Craven appeared as a witness for Queen Caroline before the House of Lords, stating that he had never seen any act of impropriety between the queen and her servant Bartolomeo Pergami. In 1821 Craven published *A Tour Through the Southern Provinces of the Kingdom of Naples*, which included a detailed eyewitness account of the 1820 revolution in Naples.

by Titian, but a great many copies and an amazing quantity of trash. There is no catalogue yet published. Went again to the Statues. After all I prefer the Venus Callipyge to any, but the collection is a noble one. The Bronze room contains many very beautiful Statues, and several curious ones. There is one which, having been found at Pompeii wrapped in cloth, bears the impression of the grain of the burnt cloth deeply marked on the rest which covers it. The Drunken Faun, the Mercury, the Horse, the Antonius and a little Amazon in the act of darting her lance, struck me as particularly good.

There is a most absurd order come out today respecting the King's entrance. All marks of applause are strictly forbidden, as well as approaching the King's carriage under pretence of touching it. Plenty of Austrian troops in attendance. Among other triumphal Arches is one in the Toledo of wood and canvas Corinthian pillars etc. with an inscription *Ferdinand I Semper Augusti Clementia Ord populous Neap.*

Tuesday 15th. Today the old King of Naples made his triumphal entry among his *ornatissimi suolditi*. The streets were lined with Austrian troops two deep through the whole of the town. Corbett and I got a good place behind a complete way among them. His conversation to an old woman, who he would call nothing but *amorosa mia* was the very best I ever heard. He and another soldier insisted on talking German to me. They might as well have talked Hebrew in great part. The King, G. thinks, was well received. There was certainly some shouting, but it proceeded from a mob of the <u>very</u> lowest of the people who ran by the side of his carriage and were probably paid. The people at the windows took no notice of him whatever. When he shewed himself at the Palace the shouts were very feeble and were all begun by one man who stood close by me. He looked grim and sulky and hardly spoke to the P. Regent,[74] though he was very gracious to Ficquelmont. In the evening and for three nights illuminations by order of the police. An attempt was made last night to burn down the triumphal arch and 23 persons are in custody for it.

Went to S. Carlo which was illuminated, very brilliant, but I think the praise of the Theatre, though a splendid one, have been exaggerated. Very stupid opera and ballet La Donna Selvaggia,[75] and the Virgin of the Sun.[76] Decorations splendid, but no dancing.

---

74 Francis (1777-1830), son of King Ferdinand, who succeeded his father as King Francis I of the Two Sicilies in 1825.

75 A two-act opera composed by Carlo Caccio (1782-1873), first performed in 1813.

76 An opera by Henry Bishop (1786-1855), first performed in London in 1812. In 1853, Bishop was commissioned to write a piece of music to mark the occasion of Stanley's appointment as chancellor of Oxford University. Stanley was then the 14th earl of Derby.

Wednesday 16th. Called on K. Craven, Sir W. à Court, etc. dined at 3. Drove in the cool of the evening to Herculaneum.[77] The theatre must have been very magnificent and it is a great pity that it cannot be entirely excavated on account of the village of Resina which is from 60 to 70 feet above it. The parts of the theatre which are excavated are very interesting, the Orchestra, a sort of private box for the Consul, some rooms behind the stage, part of the seats, and a back corridor. In part of the lava there is a very curious and perfect impression of a bronze mask. Having no Ladies this time, we had plenty of time to examine the whole. Stopped in coming home and walked a little in the gardens of the Palazzo Reale at Portici. Beautiful night and glorious full moon. I forgot to say we saw the Favorita[78] today, a pretty little casino enough, but rather too near Vesuvius, which is, as the Custodi told us, *a cattivi vicinio*. He had been there 28 years. Pretty changes he has seen in that time! Illuminations tonight again, coming from Portici the effect of the Bay and hill up to the Castel S. Elmo very beautiful.[79]

Teatro Fondo, *Cenerentola* and a grotesque Ballet.[80] Very pretty little Theatre, and much better singing and acting than S. Carlo.

Thursday 17th. Set off this morning with Otway for Cumae and Baiae. Fine day and beautiful scenery, but in the way of *antichità* [antiquities] much less than I expected. In short, next to nothing to which one can attach any interest. All is lost in uncertainty, and Baiae presents but a mass of almost undistinguishable ruins, and a great name.[81] Returning home our Cicerone was discontented with our pay, and finding he could get no more, actually spit at us as we were in the carriage. I jumped out, but he was off like a shot, and after a long chase he beat me. When finding I could not take the law into my own hands I lodged a complaint at the Police, and shall go over to ensure him a trouncing. Detained some time by this, but it afforded us a laugh; and will perhaps give us some trouble. But I am determined to go through with it now. Another invite from Sir W. à Court for Saturday, but we are going to Paestum at half past three in the morning! Oh! Oh! Oh!

---

77   Herculaneum, along with Pompeii and Stabiae, was buried by Mt Vesuvius's eruption in AD 79.
78   The Real Villa della Favorita.
79   The Castel Sant'Elmo was built on the summit of a hill behind the city, originally in 1343.
80   *La Cenerentola* is an opera by Gioachino Rossini (1792-1868). The libretto was written by Jacopo Ferretti. It premiered at the Teatro Valle in Rome in 1817.
81   Baiae was a favourite resort for wealthy Romans in the first century AD, with a reputation for hedonism. The lower part of the town was later submerged by the sea due to volcanic activity.

Friday 18th. No letters again today. I am not surprised, because I am sure they have been written and not arrived, but it is very provoking.

Saturday 19th. Set out at 5 in the morning (having been ready at 3) with Wellesley and Arnstein for the Temples at Paestum. Fine morning, but the weather is getting too hot for travelling in the middle of the day. Stopped at the ruins of Pompeii, of which we visited the farthest part, viz. the two theatres, Temple of Hercules, Amphitheatre, etc. The Amphitheatre and the two theatres, but especially the former, are in a wonderful state of preservation, and there are very interesting ruins, giving you a perfect idea of what they must have been. Indeed, the Amphitheatre is as perfect almost as ever, and in a couple of days looks as if it would be ready for representations. In the theatres the Bronze letters even, announcing the names of the Duumvir for the Games still remain in the pavement. We had not, however, as much time as we wished, or at least as I did, for W. and A. were impatient to be off.

The road itself is here ugly, but the country very beautiful. The view of Vesuvius and the opposite hills are very fine. About three miles further there is a peak with a ruined building upon it, very picturesque and beautiful. Le Cava is well known for its splendid scenery, as well as the Gulf of Salerno, which however will not bear comparison with the Bay of Naples. We overtook, soon after we left Salerno, a man on a horse which he had for sale. We had some talk with him and after riding four or five miles he stopped at a house and brought out some wine, for which he refused anything or let us give the servant anything. He then went on a mile or so till we came to two roads, where pointing to a casino near he said, *anche quella casa é mia, e per conseguenza in occasione anche la vostra* ['that house is mine, and in consequence yours too']. and then wishing us good morning galloped off. We arrived by five o'clock at Eboli, a little town where we slept and was tolerably comfortable.[82]

Next morning Sunday 20th, we were off again at five for the Temples. The plain in which they stand has been much abused, but to my mind it is very beautiful. It is flat and without trees, but it is well cultivated, surrounded by beautiful mountains which slope down to the sea, of which from two of the Temples there is a fine view. I had been prepared by the accounts of other people to find the Temples very small and was therefore agreeably undeceived. That which they call the Temple of Neptune is magnificent indeed,[83] but I was well acquainted with all of them from

---

82   Eboli is elevated above the plains. The single inn, when Stanley visited, was the Locanda Nobile.

83   The Temple of Neptune is 195 feet in length and 78 feet in breadth, with columns 29 feet high.

models before I went. The quantity of birds of all sorts which build in the Temple of Neptune, and deafen you with their cries, is really astonishing. The last ruin [the basilica] I believe to have been a Temple also, though the line of pillars up the middle is singular. Might it have been one Temple dedicated to two Deities? The division lengthways is extraordinary, but I should not think this impossible. The walls of the city remain nearly perfect, and one of the gates, which W. and I went down to.[84]

We returned to Naples about ½ past 10, having had a hard day's work, but no adventures of any kind. We hear tonight that our friend the Cicerone at Pozzuoli is in the clutch of the Police, and they will do, I dare say, anything we please with him. We will go over there tomorrow, to save the Judge the trouble of coming here on Tuesday, which he left word he would do. I do not quite like what I have seen of Arnstein during this excursion. He gives me rather too much the idea of an adventurer living upon his wits. Wellesley is a sensible and I dare say an agreeable man, but he seems shy and reserved. Our horses cost us 24 ducats. The engagement being to take three, change at Salerno, and do the whole in two days.

Today, being Sunday, I was surprised at not seeing more variety in the costumes of the peasants. In England one talks of the dress of Italian peasants. At Rome people say, Oh it is not here, but at Naples that the dresses are so picturesque. At Naples they say, Oh it is not here, but in the country further south, and then again they talk of Sicily and Malta. The greatest variety of dress that I have remarked was at Florence. Here they are mostly very ill dressed and with nothing extraordinary except now and then a black veil, or a gold laced jacket. Roman buckles have disappeared. I saw a woman yesterday in an old Hussar's jacket, which nobody seemed to think extraordinary.

Monday 21st. Today we have been witnesses to a curious scene. Last night arrived a message from the Judge at Pozzuoli to say that the man had been arrested and he wished to see us; but as we were not come home, he would call on Tuesday morning. Today, however, we drove over to save him the trouble, thinking he wished to take our evidence. Not at all. On entering the village we were assailed by half the population, headed by the Brother with *Por l'amor di Dio. Quel povero chè è incarcerato, ma parole da loro lo farà liberare* ['For the love of God. That poor man is imprisoned, but one word from them will set him free']. We marched to the Judge's and found he was not in, but his Secretary was there, who wished to know if we were satisfied with what had been done,

---

84   The walls are 2.5 miles in length, and the eastern gate, which is nearly 50 feet tall, is still complete.

and what further punishment we wished awarded him. In vain did we try to explain that we had complained not for our own satisfaction, but for public justice. This was an idea that never entered into their heads, and we accordingly wrote to the Judge saying we were satisfied and requested his liberation on refunding the money we had paid him for the use of the poor, as he had already had four or five days imprisonment. Can anyone wonder at the middling ranks, much the best informed in Naples, wishing by any means to get rid of such administration of Justice? I forget to say we went to the Prison, saw the man through the grate, who was as cringing and mean as he had been insolent, touching my fingers and then kissing his own hand, the very deepest mark of respect. We came home about 6, dined at the Villa di Roma,[85] strawberries and cherries have long been in. Today we had apricots.

I forgot in my Paestum journal to give the curious instances, one of the fertility of volcanic soil, and the other of the way in which the fertility of the country is abused. At Pompeii we saw several crops of lupins, which had grown to the enormous height of at least 7 feet, as I could not reach the top of them, and in the plain near Paestum was a fine crop of oats, in full ear, and which would have been ripe in less than a month. Five men were employed in cutting it for fodder for cattle! The vines here, though many of them produce excellent wines, are spoilt by being trained up to the top of high poplars, which border the roadsides.

22nd. Drove this evening along the Strada Nuova, a beautiful road made by Murat for about four miles, but the last two miles, having been left unfinished, the present active government have done nothing to it and the road remaining useless except as a public drive. It is even going to ruin in one or two places from neglect.

We hear today that, in consequence of the Convent of Monks having been carried up to the mountains by the Brigands from Frascati, Appony is gone up there under a strong guard of Tyrolese tirailleurs.[86] Another note from the Margravine asking us for Thursday, Friday or Saturday! In coming home the other evening from Paestum we were stopped near Pompeii and looking out saw an Austrian soldier, who made the carriage go at a foots' pace that it might not make dust where he and his comrades were sitting! Military luxury!

23rd. Walking the streets this morning observed to my great surprise a public building for Vaccination. The first measure of public utility I have heard of being adopted here by the Government.

---

85   The Villa di Roma, located on the slope of Posillipo, was known for its gardens.
86   *Tirailleurs* were light infantry trained to skirmish ahead of main columns.

Thursday 24th. Dined today with the old Margravine of Anspach.[87] She was very civil and pressed us to come whenever we liked to her house or her Villa. She is a fine old woman, preserving still the appearance of having been a handsome woman, much rouged, false flaxen hair and eyebrows, and false teeth. At dinner she did not talk much. She does not speak good French or speak it with facility and I think talking to foreigners she feels *gèneé* [shy and self-conscious], but I have no doubt she can be amusing. She opened a little purse in going to her Villa and talked of her memoirs, as having a heap of notes which she would publish, if it was not for the trouble.[88] They would be very amusing. She affects royalty and is always called your Highness, calls the gentleman who is to lead her into Dinner, etc. Our party were the Duchess and Duke Bracciano with his son and daughter, Lady Herbert and her brothers, a Prussian who is here I believe as a *chargé d'affaires*, but I do not quite know who, K Craven, G. and I. She spoke of her son in very warm terms, and I believe he deserves it. His conduct to her is exemplary. Took to her Villa and amused us by her account of the way she got it. Observing the beauty of the situation and laughing with Prince Leopold,[89] she said she should like to have it. The P. said if you have any fancy for it I am sure the K. will give it you. She said, tell him I have a great fancy for it. He did and it was promised her, but nothing ensued till one day at the Drawing Room she presented him with the least possible piece of paper with nothing on it but Strada Nuova. She had the Villa next day. Her architect has been Sir William Gell, who has succeeded wonderfully. The situation is superb and she will make it a very pretty place. At present it wants shade.

Saturday 26th. Went over this morning, the hottest day we have had, to Pompeii. The remains are so perfect that this is a most interesting excursion, described over and over again, Sir W. Gell's *Pompeiana*.[90]

Sunday 27th. High wind, but very hot being a Sirocco. Called on old Gargallo, but he is not arrived. Yesterday on the road to Pompeii observed the harvest begun. There is not much cut, but a great deal ready.

---

87 In 1821 the margravine was seventy-one years old.
88 In 1826 the margravine published her colourful recollections, entitled *The Memoirs of the Margravine of Anspach Written by Herself*, 2 vols (London, 1826).
89 Leopold, prince of Salerno (1790-1851), was the sixth son of King Ferdinand I of the Two Sicilies.
90 Sir William Gell's *Pompeiana: The Topography of the Edifices and Ornaments of Pompeii*, 2 vols (London, 1817-18).

VOLUME 3

Naples—Venice—Tyrol—Switzerland

27 May to 18 September 1821

Sunday May 27th. Dined with Sir W. à Court, a very odd party and not a very good one. All English, but one unhappy Austrian. I did very well being between Sir W. à Court and General Church who was very civil, promising letters for the Abruzzi, etc. One delightfully vulgar man, but I could not find out his name.

Monday 28th. Very glad we did not go, as we intended, to Caserta, the Sirocco has ended in a determined drizzling rain. No letters again today and I have hunted the Post Office through. I begin to think there must have been some mistake about directing and that we shall find oceans at Venice. A good deal amused by a story of the P. of D.[1] and the Patrole.

Tuesday 29th. Today the Austrian troops, 15,000 in number, are gone over into Sicily, while we sit by and idly look at them. Just as the fleet of transports was gone out an English 20 gun brig came in. She is from Genoa and ordered to touch here and then proceed to Malta, whence she expects to be sent immediately to the Ionian Islands.

Called on the old Margravine who begged us to come and drink tea. Her exceeding vanity is admirable and the way she tells us what her dress was fifty years ago is too ludicrous.

---

1   Crown Prince Christian of Denmark (1786-1848) was a patron of the Norwegian Romantic artist Johan Christian Dahl (1788-1857) who in 1820-21 was a guest at Villa Quisisana where the crown prince resided. Dahl was there to paint dramatic scenes of Vesuvius. In 1839 the crown prince succeeded to the throne as King Christian VIII of Denmark.

Wednesday 30th. What we did I know not, but I know we did <u>not</u> go to Caserta and did go to Sir W. à Court's box at the San Carlo, which was brilliantly illuminated.

Thursday 31st. Set out on our adventure to Beneventum,[2] *olim* Maleventum as it proved to us. Breakfasted at Arienzo where we ordered dinner, meaning to return and there sleep. Arrived at Benevento about 2 o'clock. Trajan's Arch very fine, but cruelly blocked up with buildings.[3] About three sent for to the Commandant. Thought the message was a trick, the same having been played on Edsell and Corbett three days before, and returned a light answer, till it was enforced by two Gendarmes, whom we followed to the Commandant. He immediately began a gross abuse of us, high words passed. I put on my hat. Another man not in uniform, but whom I since learn to be a Lieutenant, attempted to strike it off, on which I knocked him down. I was immediately arrested, as well kicked as these Gendarmes could do it, but being Papal soldiers it was not very awful. Hornby arrested soon after. We were both confined for 7 hours in the most filthy holes in the world. At night allowed a less disgusting room. But for 24 hours not allowed to write to our Ambassador or see the Governor. Meanwhile, the Commandant, who has lied through thick and thin, sends off his own false statement about us to Rome and Naples.

June 1821

Friday 1st June. Allowed to see the Governor, after being told there was none. He is a Roman Monsignore and a sneaking fellow, though civil enough to us. His Secretary has found us apartments in the Marquis Mosti's house, and we remove there on Saturday morning. Our passports returned from Giustiniani[4] who says they are *en règle* [in good standing].

Saturday 2nd. Moved to M. Mosti's house, quartered on the younger brother, who has separate rooms, and the most curious medley of splendour or at least comfort and filth that can be imagined. As for instance, *item* silk beds, *item* bugs in them, *item* five servants, *item* an excellent dinner, *item*, but two books in the house, one of which, a preparation

---

2   'Beneventum' is Latin for 'good wind', and Stanley is referring to the town of Benevento, at the confluence of the Calore and Sabato rivers. The ancient name for Benevento was Beneventum.

3   Trajan's Arch or the Porta Aurea once spanned the Via Appia. It was erected in AD 112, and is one of the best-preserved Roman triumphal arches in existence.

4   Cardinal Alessandro Giustiniani (1778-1843), the papal *chargé d'affaires* in Naples.

for death, he insisted on our taking with us, as well as a picture of his patron Saint, and a paper of sausages. He is a good vulgarish Bachelor of 50, very kind and civil, and says the only return we can make for his hospitality is come for as long and as often as we like, and send any of our dear friends there. Benevento, he says, is in a horrible state, anybody at night without a lantern arrested. Murders going on between the political parties and all, in short, in the greatest confusion. I saw a couple of fellows whipped this morning—very pretty operation, and served me as an excuse for bilking a Churchwarden. Received tonight a <u>very</u> kind note from Sir W, à Court, who is exerting himself.

[June 3rd] Sunday morning. Monsignore frightened. A disgusting note from Giustiniani talking of *Comte de Derby, un des premier pair Angleterre , etc. etc.* Liberated and returned to Naples in a Noah's Ark. Admirable woman at Arienzo—*Caro figlio*! I was as much grieved as if it had been my son—*Ommaggai un pollastro la sera—Aspettai fin' alle quattro—oh qaunto mi piace di rivedervi*—charming mixture, which a piaster converted into pure gratitude, and she was so tender on George that I hurried him away, but not before she devoutly kissed his hand. He promised to marry her and we parted.

Monday 4th. Letter from Henry & Tom's Book. Very pretty <u>poetry</u>, but not a good <u>poem</u> I should say. <u>Some beautiful</u> lines, but very unequal. Employed in justifying ourselves to Sir W. à Court, who is <u>quite</u> satisfied, & Giustiniani. Rode with Otway & Corbett in the evening.

Tuesday 5th. Employed the whole day in memorialising Consalvi, through Giustiniani and Sir W. à Court. Dined with the Margravine, met Madame Zupari, Sir W. Gell, K. Craven, and a Mr Lynch—an agreeable dinner.

Wednesday 6th. Rode with Corbett, looked in at the Chartruse,[5] magnificent in marbles, a fine picture by Spagnoletto[6] of a descent from the Cross. Lord Bristol said to have offered 80,000 Piastres for it. Some good frescoes by Cav. Arpino and by an artist who died very early, Finoglia.[7] Prophets by Spagnoletto some very good.

Dined at the Villa di Roma. Austrian frigates returned from conveying the transports. Went to the Fondo—*Barbiere di Siviglia*.[8]

---

5   La Certosa di San Martino.
6   Spagnoletto was the Italian nickname of the Spanish painter Jusepe de Ribera (1591-1652).
7   Giuseppe Cesari (1568-1640), known as Cavaliere d'Arpino, and Paolo Domenico Finoglia (*c.* 1590-1645).
8   *The Barber of Seville*, a two-act opera buffa by Rossini, was premiered in Rome in 1816.

Friday 8th. After dinner today with Otway, rode out with him and Corbett on <u>my</u> white mare, which I find was the favourite Charger of Joachim Murat!! Such are the changes from men down to horses!

Saturday 9th. Dined with Sir W. à Court, Prince of Hesse, Prince Butera [a Sicilian title], Sir W. Gell, General Hauwitz and three or four other foreigners, one Englishman whom I did not know or admire. Sir William promises to send a letter for me to the Duchess of Hamilton containing some verses which, not to lose such a valuable performance, I enter in my Journal, though written long ago.[9]

> When the tale of affliction from Susan[10] I heard,
> Of death, which though hopelessly feebly deferr'd
> Still hangs o'er the fair and the young:
> What magic enchantment my senses professed?
> Whence the deep admiration that swell'd in my breast,
> And trembled to burst from my tongue.
>
> 2
>
> Was it Beauty's fond spell that around me was thrown?
> Oh no—nor that voice's soft musical tone;
> 'Twas the heart, 'twas the warm feeling heart,
> Whose generous sentiments, spurning disguise
> Now throbbed in her bosom, now swam in her eyes,
> And mocked at the language of art.
>
> 3
>
> Of the parent she told, who in silent despair,
> And, sleepless and speechless and helpless sits there,
> To gaze on the gradual decay:
> As she hangs o'er her Child, not a tear dims her sight,
> But in agony wakes she the long gloomy night,
> And the cheerless unvarying day.
>
> 4
>
> Lone, widow'd and childless, no husband to throw
> The mantle of love o'er the desolate woe

---

9   The poem was written following a moving account given by the duchess of Hamilton of 'old Princess C' and her fifteen-year-old daughter, whom the duchess described as 'charming'. When in Rome the daughter became dangerously ill and her father very reluctantly agreed to his wife and daughter going: 'Eh bien,' he said, 'allez donc, mais ramenez moi mon enfant.' The distraught mother was in despair as she devotedly nursed her daughter, comforted by the child's grandmother. At the same time 'Madame L', the daughter's aunt, attended the parties in Rome affecting to deplore the necessity of her going out in such circumstances. See *Early Poems (1809-25), Edward Geoffrey Smith Stanley 14th Earl of Derby* (Stevenage, 2013), p. 77.

10   Susan-Euphemia, duchess of Hamilton.

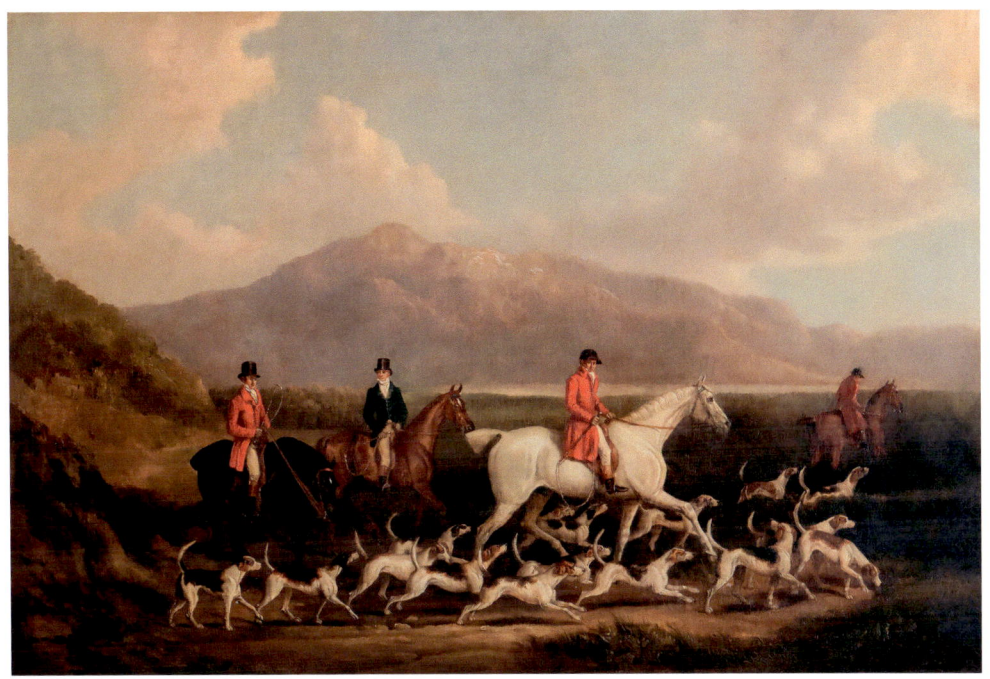

James Barenger, *The Earl of Derby's Staghounds with Lord Stanley, his Son the Hon. Edward Geoffrey Stanley, and the Huntsman Jonathan Griffin on Spanker and the first Whipper-in on Noodle, c.* 1822-23, oil on canvas. *The Derby Collection*

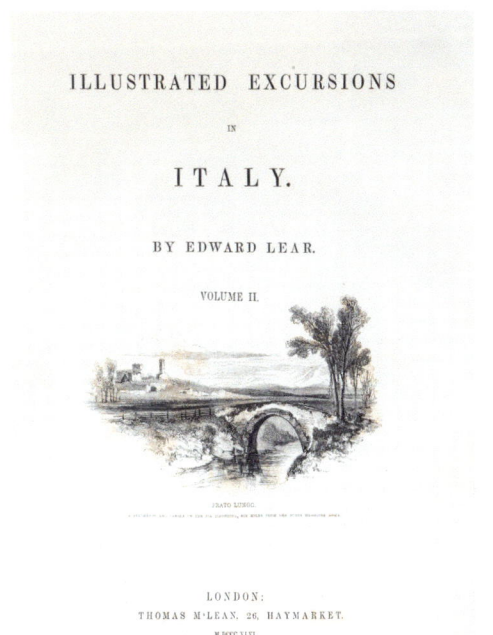

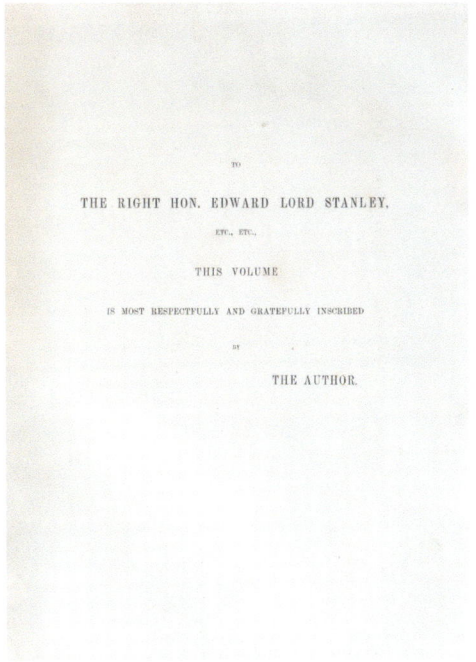

The titlepage and dedication to the Right Hon. Edward, Lord Stanley from Edward Lear, *Illustrated Excursions in Italy*, vol. II, London, 1846. *The Derby Collection*

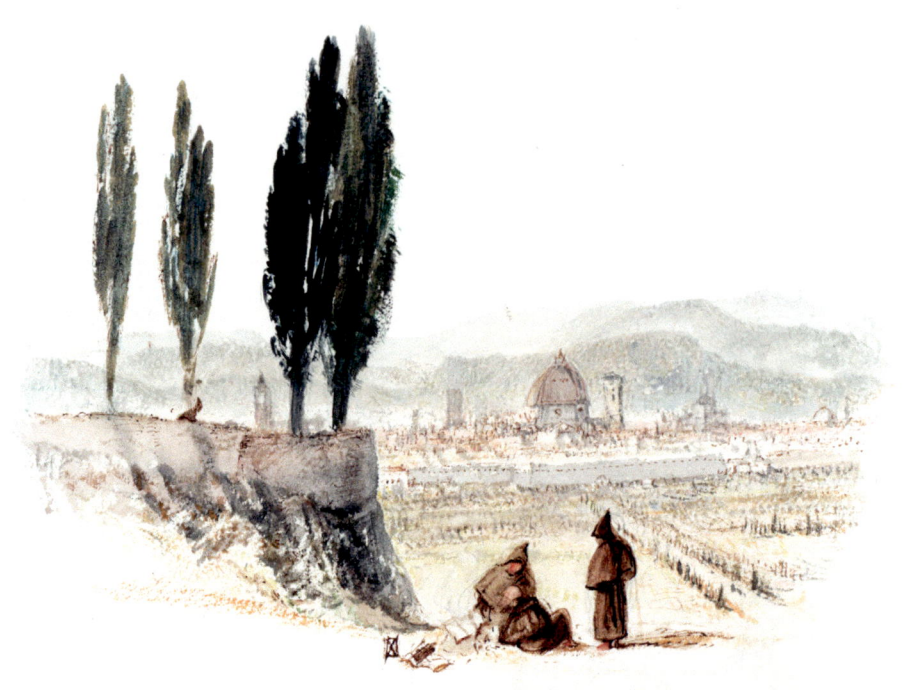

J. M. W. Turner, *View of Florence from Fiesole*, *c*. 1826-27, watercolour. *Tate*

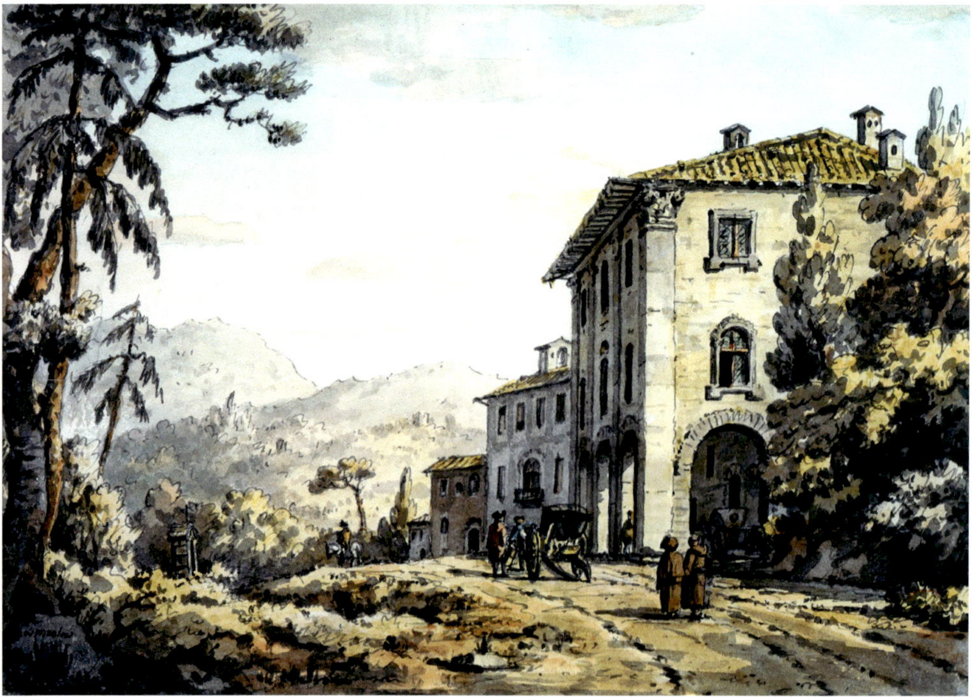

William Marlow, *A Post-House near Florence*, *c*. 1770, watercolour over pencil. *Tate*

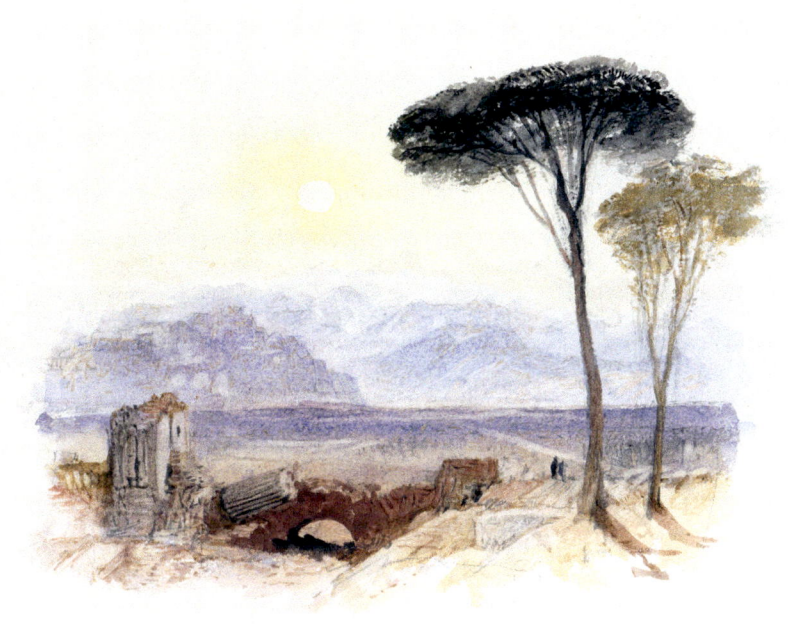

J. M. W. Turner, *View of Perugia*, *c*. 1826-27, watercolour. *Tate*

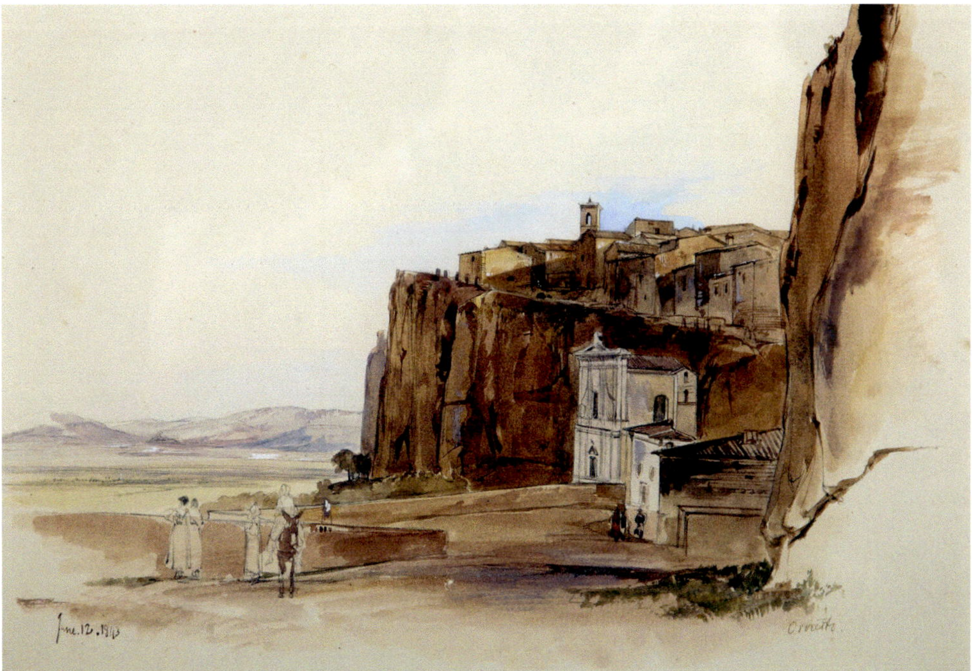

Edward Lear, *View of Orvieto*, 1843, watercolour. *The Derby Collection*

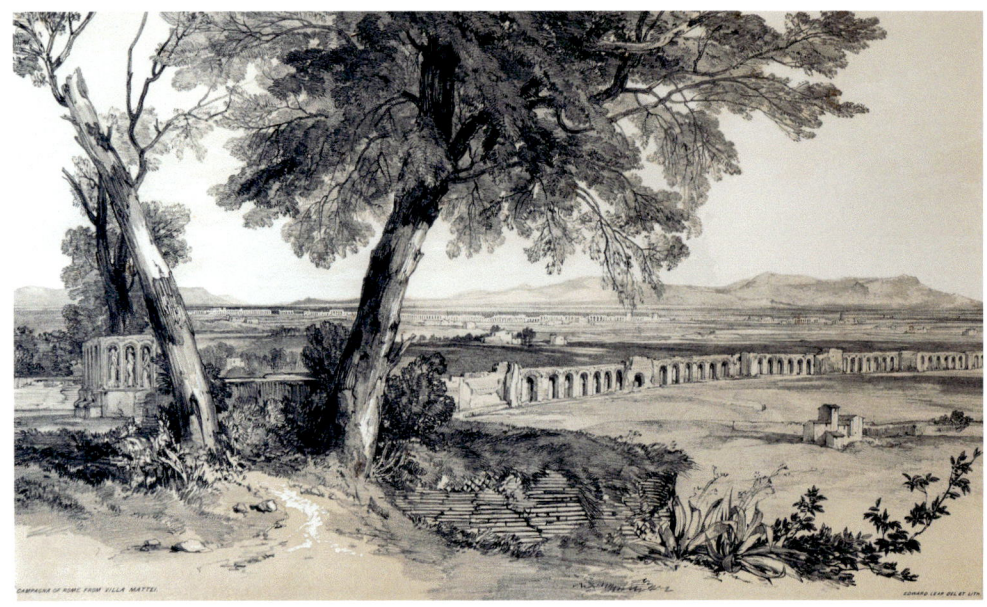

Edward Lear, *Campagna, and the Walls of Rome, looking to the Alban Mount from Villa Mattei*, lithograph. Plate 3 from Edward Lear, *Views in Rome and its Environs: Drawn from Nature and on Stone*, London, 1841. *The Derby Collection*

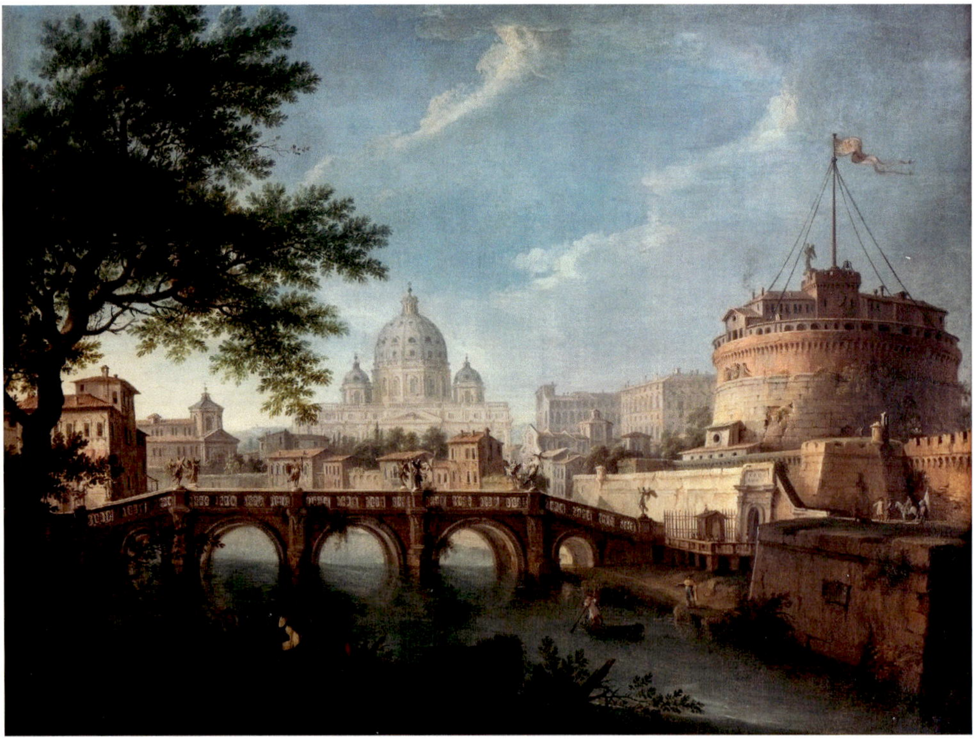

Attributed to Filippo Falciatore, *View of the River Tiber, Rome, with the Castel and Ponte Sant' Angelo, with St Peter's Basilica, c.* 1750, oil on canvas. *The Derby Collection*

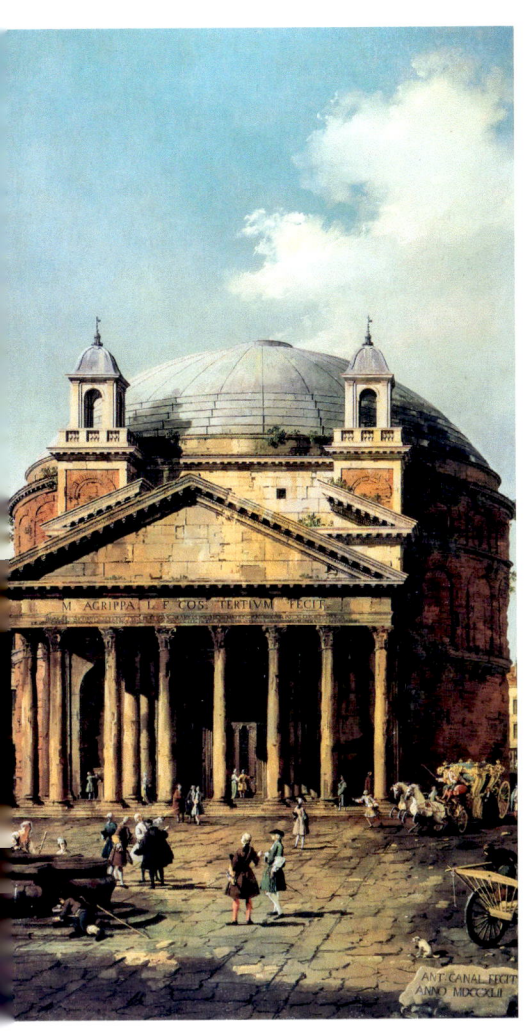 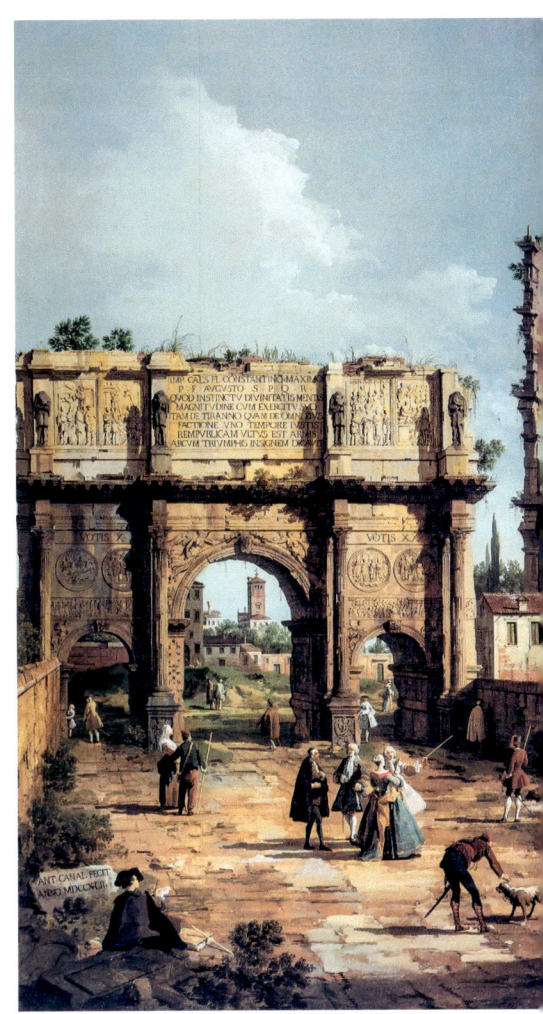

Above left: Antonio Canal, known as Canaletto, *The Pantheon, Rome*, 1742, oil on canvas. *The Royal Collection*

Above right: Antonio Canal, known as Canaletto, *The Arch of Constantine, Rome*, 1742, oil on canvas. *The Royal Collection*

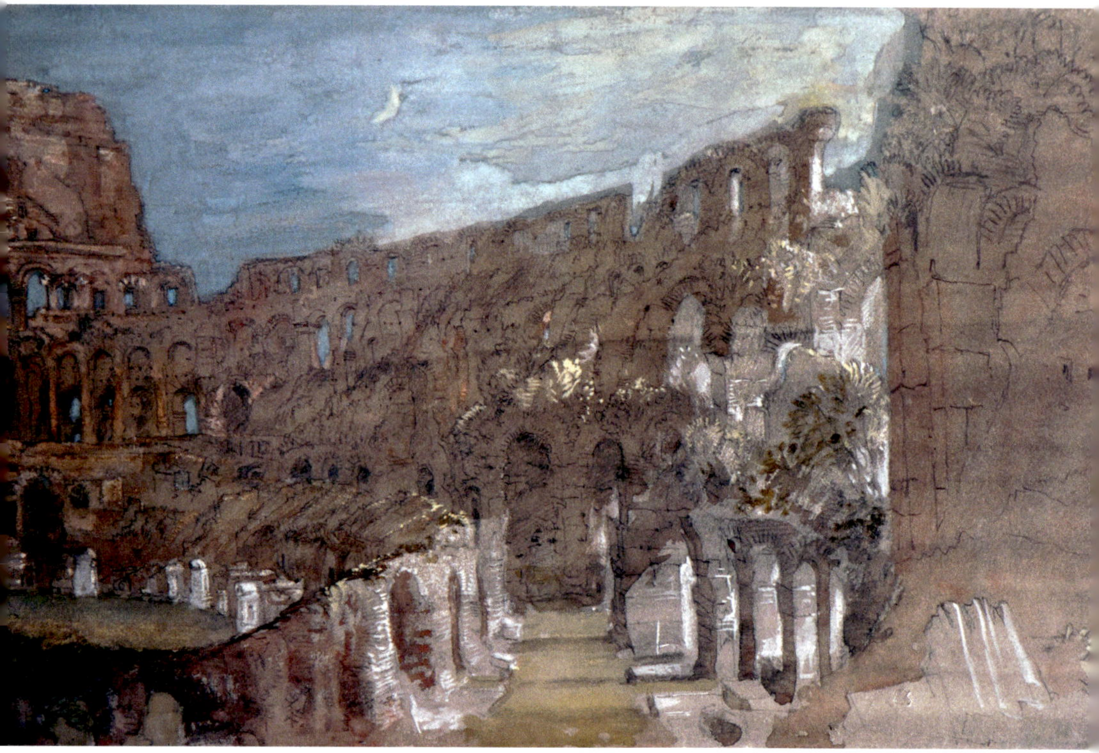

J. M. W. Turner, *The Colosseum, Rome, by moonlight*, 1819, watercolour. *Tate*

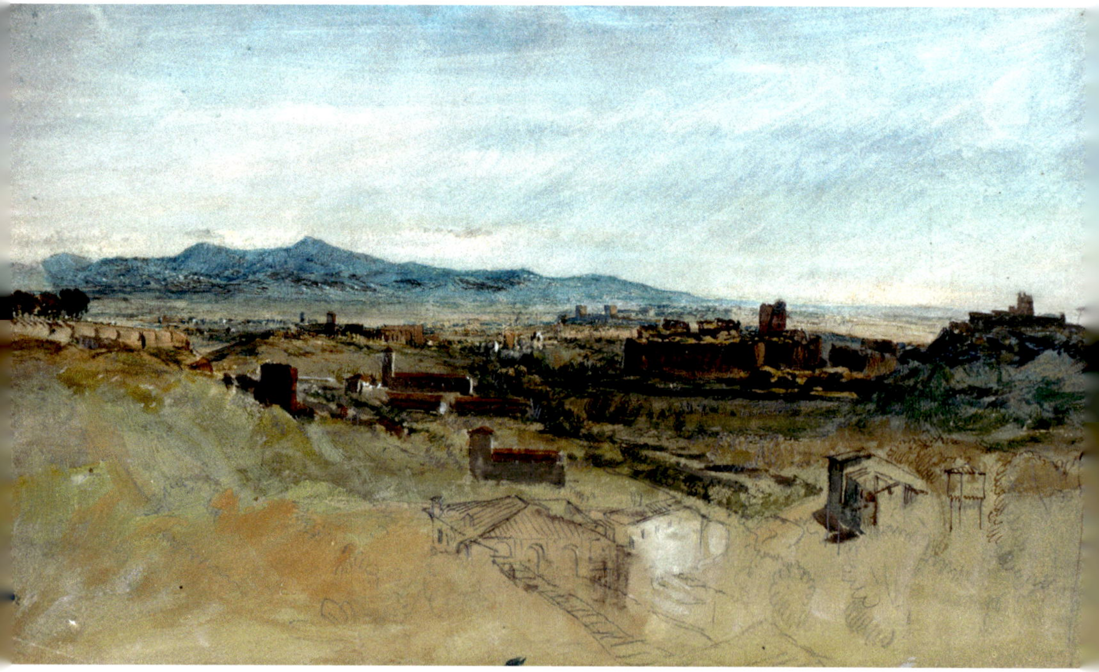

J. M. W. Turner, *View of the Baths of Caracalla, from the Palatine Hill, Rome*, 1819, watercolour. *Tate*

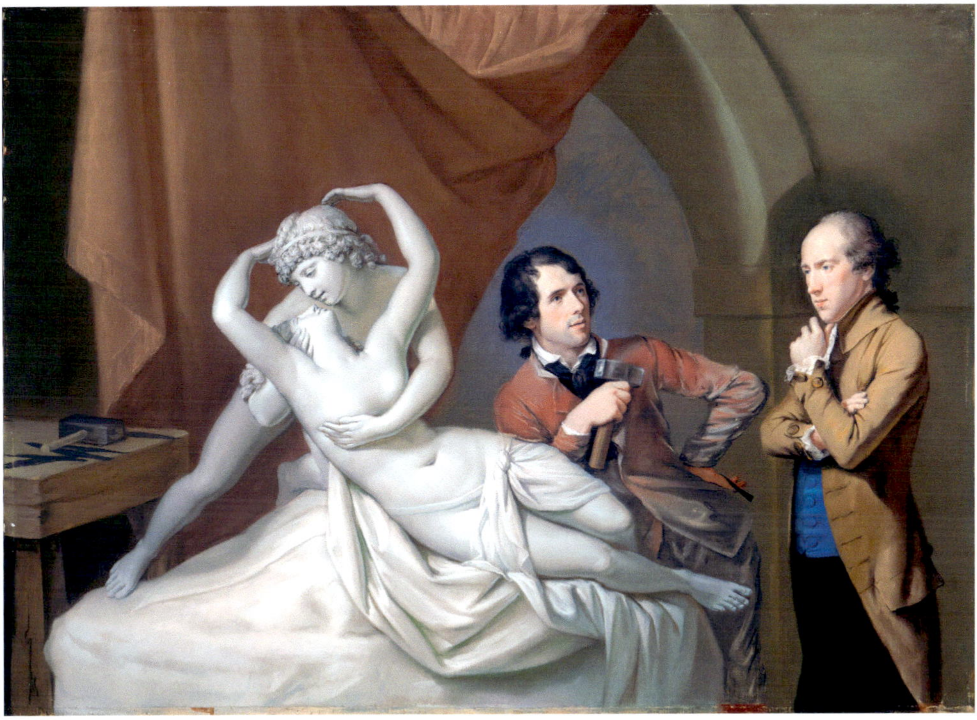

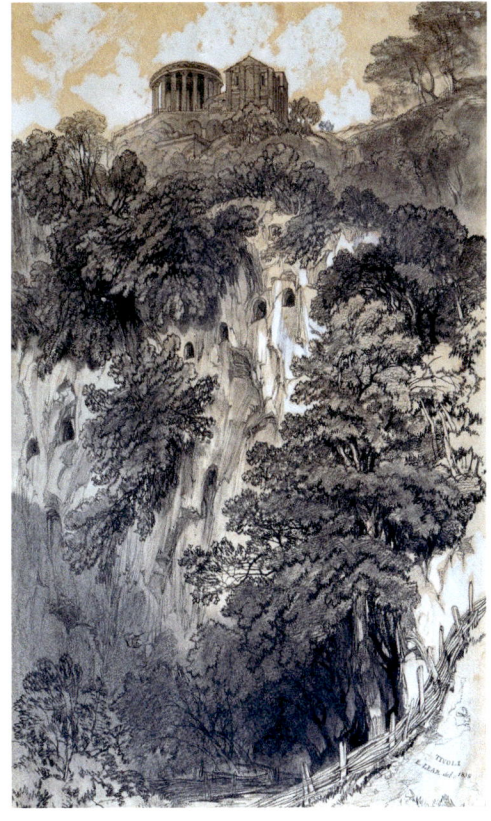

Above: Hugh Douglas Hamilton, *Antonio Canova in his studio in Rome with Henry Tresham and a plaster cast of Cupid and Pysche*, 1788-91, pastel on paper. *Victoria & Albert Museum*

Right: Edward Lear, *Tivoli*, 1838, pencil with wash and white heightening. *The Derby Collection*

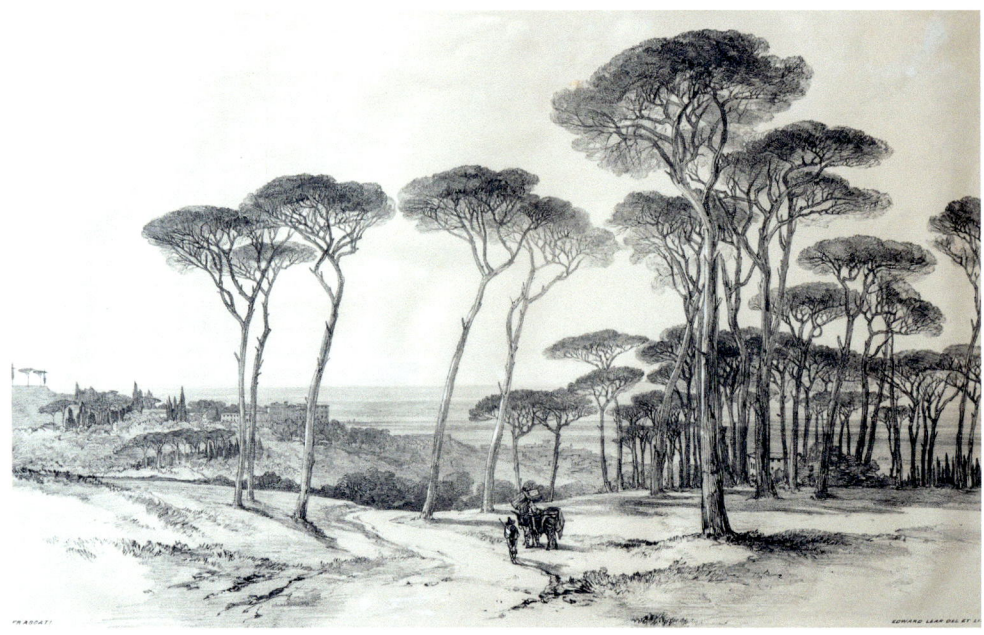

Edward Lear, *Frascati from the Villa Mondragone belonging to the Borghesi*, lithograph. Plate 7 from Edward Lear, *Views in Rome and its Environs: Drawn from Nature and on Stone*, London, 1841. *The Derby Collection*

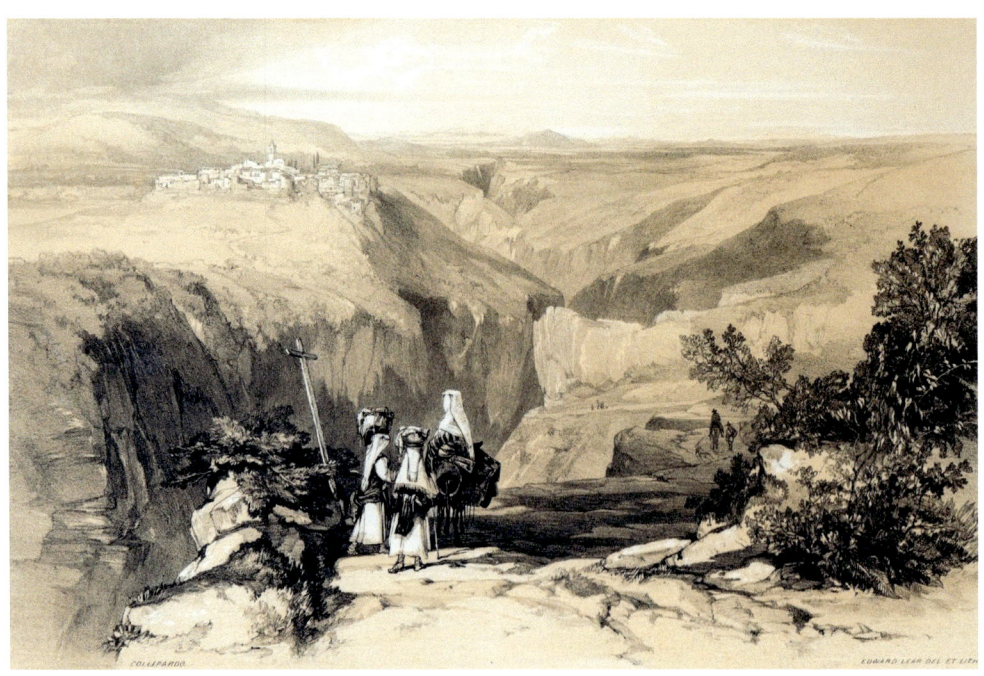

Edward Lear, *Collepardo: a small Town near Alatri, district of Frosinone*, lithograph. Plate 6 from Edward Lear, *Views in Rome and its Environs: Drawn from Nature and on Stone*, London, 1841. *The Derby Collection*

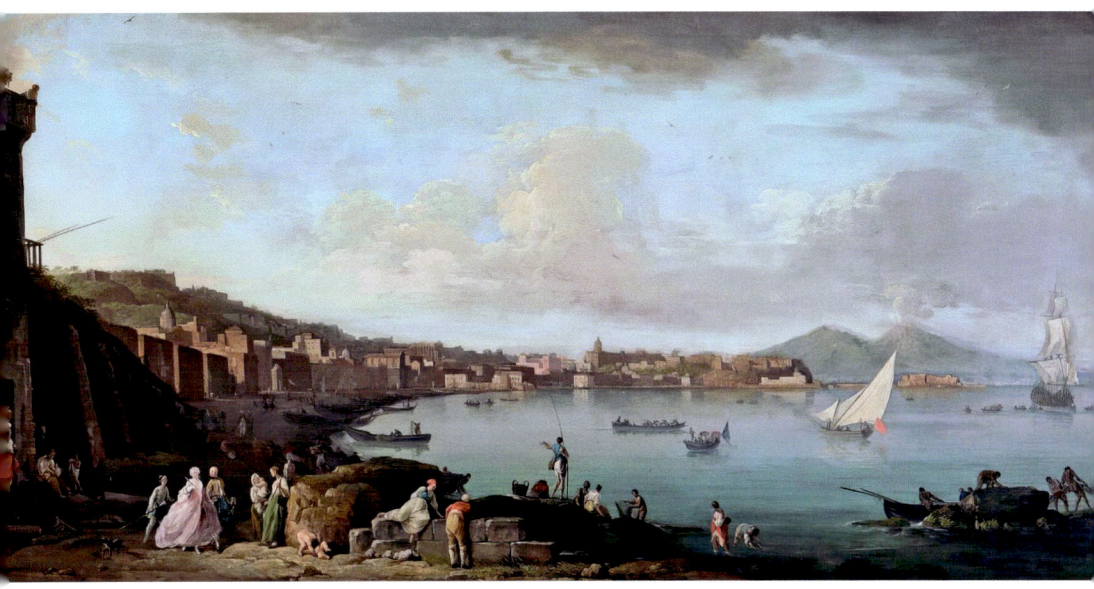

Claude-Joseph Vernet, *View of the Bay of Naples from Mergellina, c.* 1740, oil on canvas. *Collection of the Duke of Northumberland*

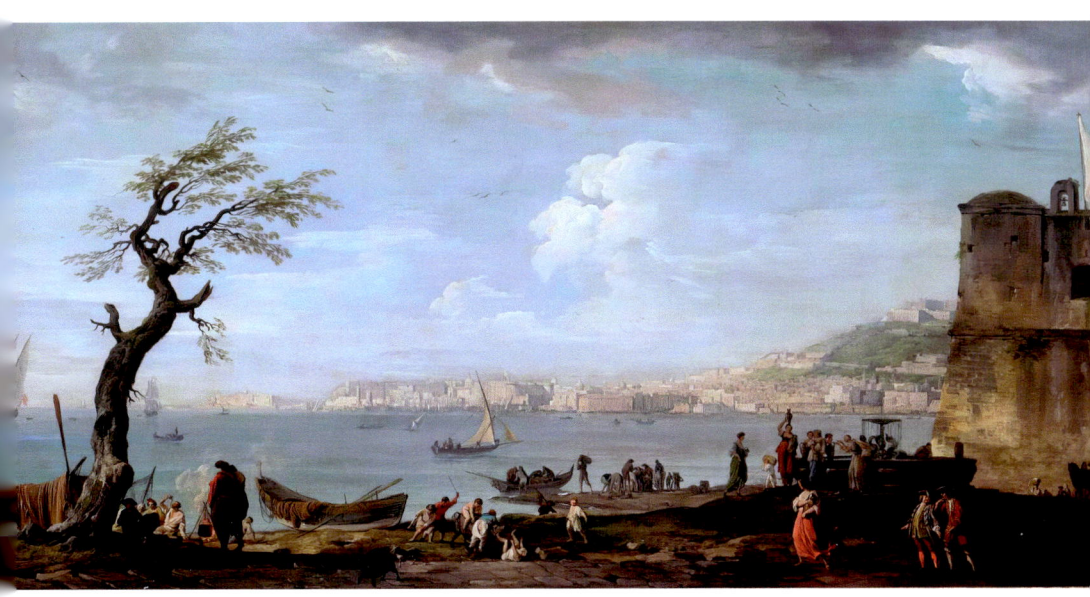

Claude-Joseph Vernet, *View of the Bay of Naples from the Marinella, c.* 1740, oil on canvas. *Collection of the Duke of Northumberland*

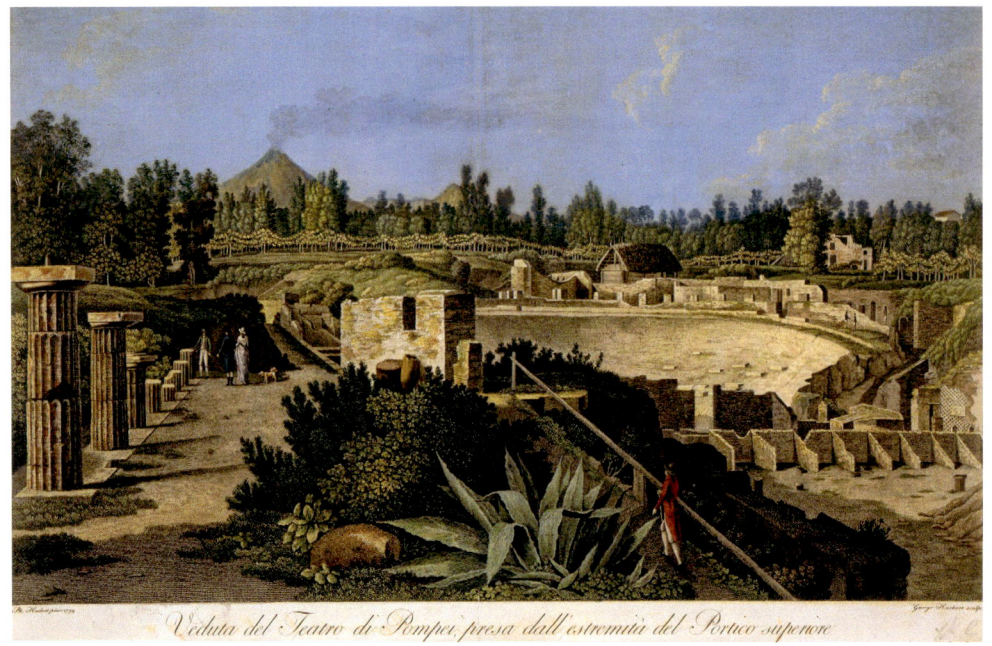

Georg Abraham Hackert after Jakob Philipp Hackert, *View of the Theatre, Pompeii*, 1793, hand-coloured etching. *The British Museum*

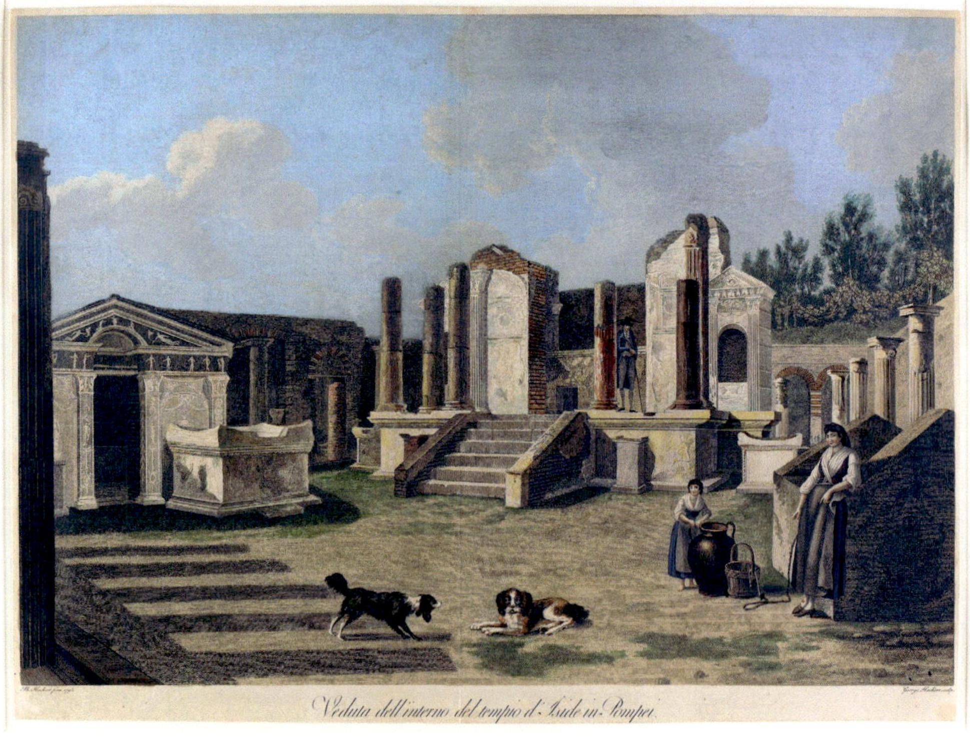

Georg Abraham Hackert after Jakob Philipp Hackert, *View of the Interior of the Temple of Isis, Pompeii*, 1793, hand-coloured etching. *The British Museum*

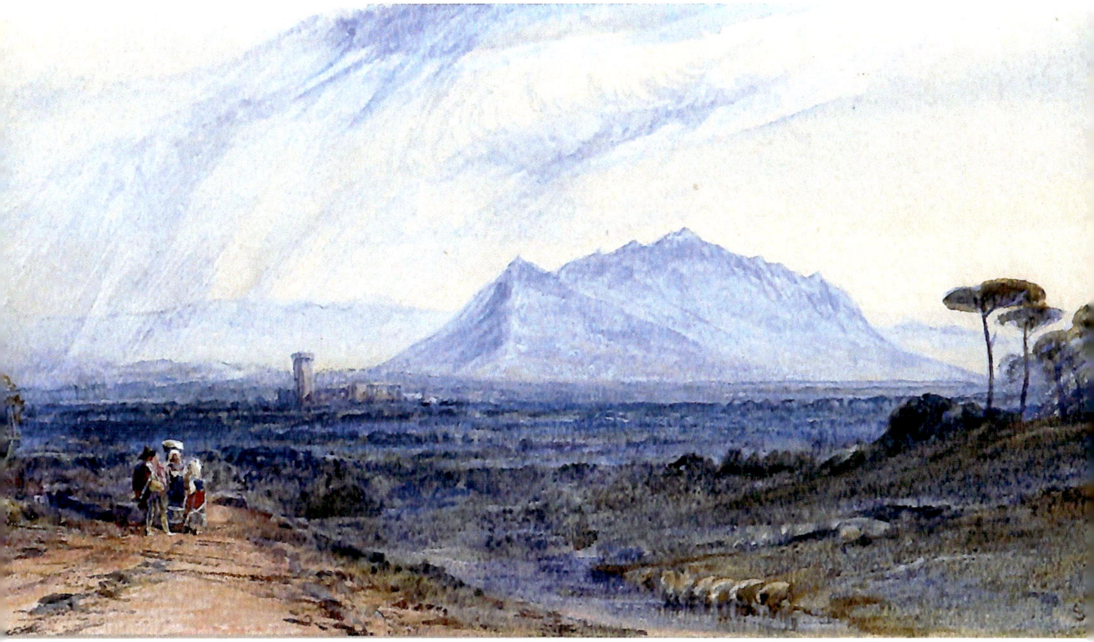

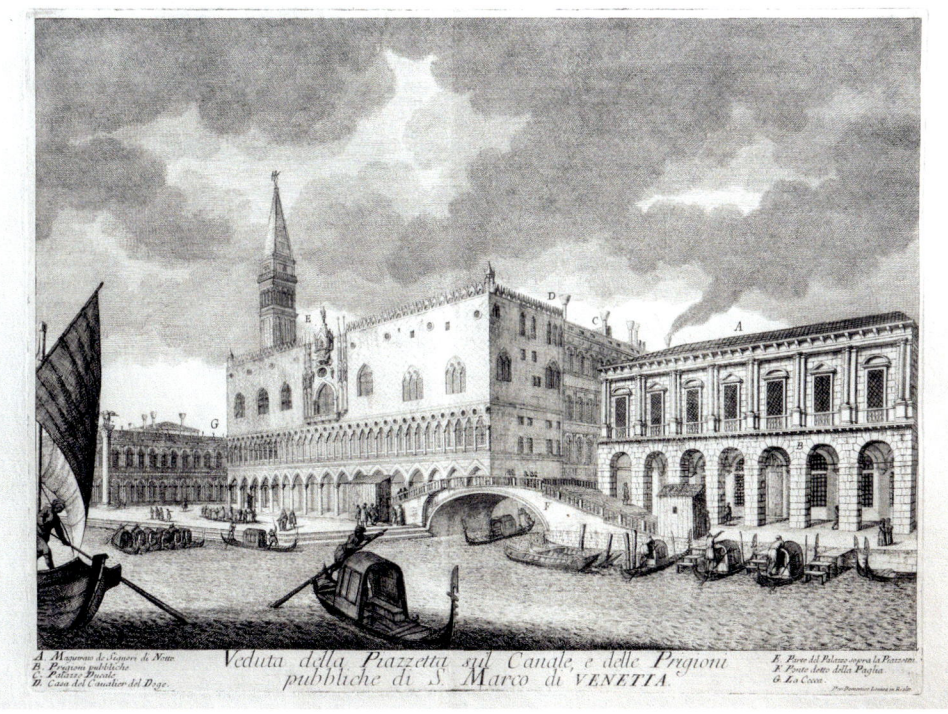

Edward Lear, *Monte Soratte*, 1880, watercolour. *The Derby Collection*

Unknown printmaker, *View of the Piazzetta from the Grand Canal, the Doges Palace and the public Prisons of S. Marco, Venice*, 1720, etching, published by Domenico Lovisa, Venice. *Private Collection*

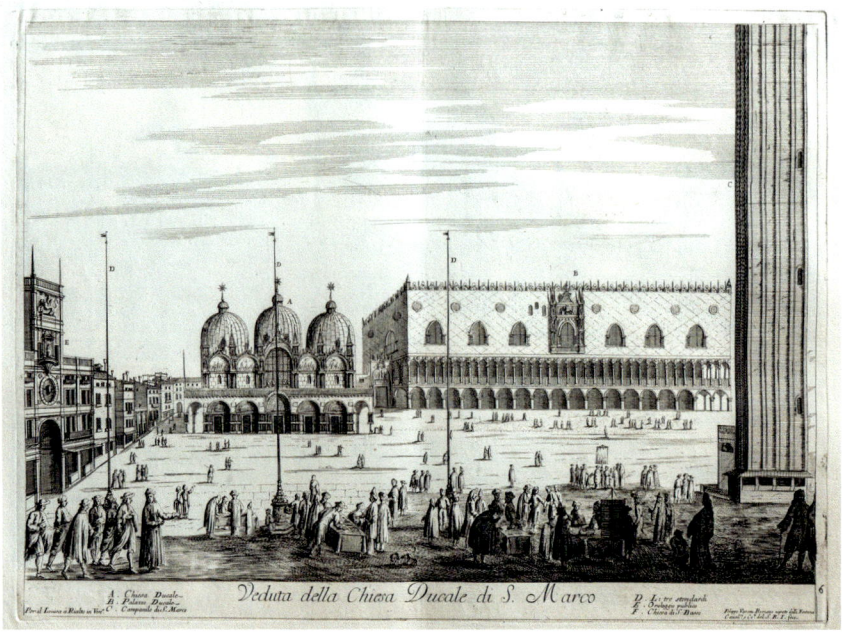

Filippo Vasconi, *View of the Basilica of St. Mark's, the Doges Palace and the Campanile, Venice*, 1720, etching, published by Domenico Lovisa, Venice. *Private Collection*

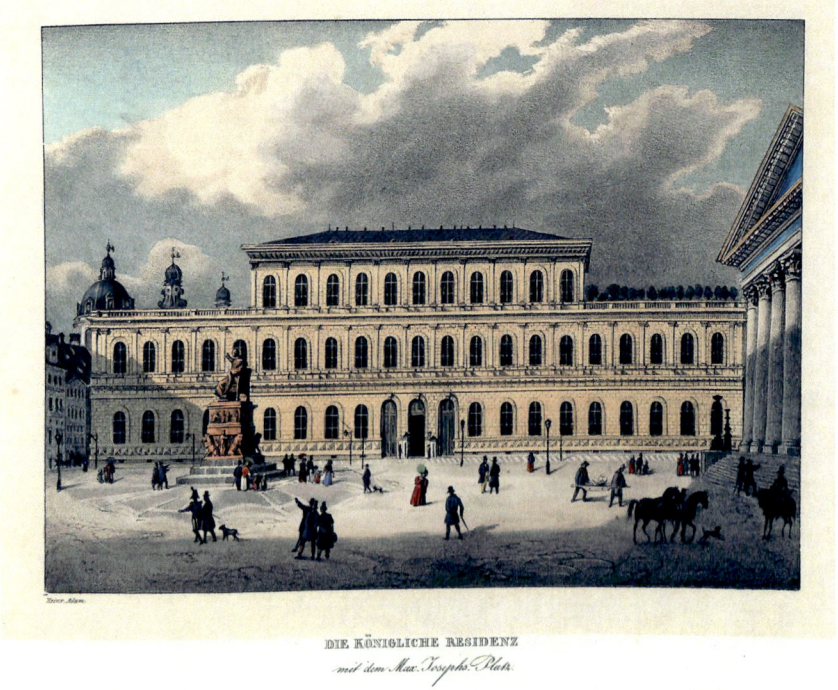

Heinrich Adam, *The Royal Residenz and Max-Joseph Platz, Munich*, *c.* 1830s, hand-coloured etching. *Private Collection*

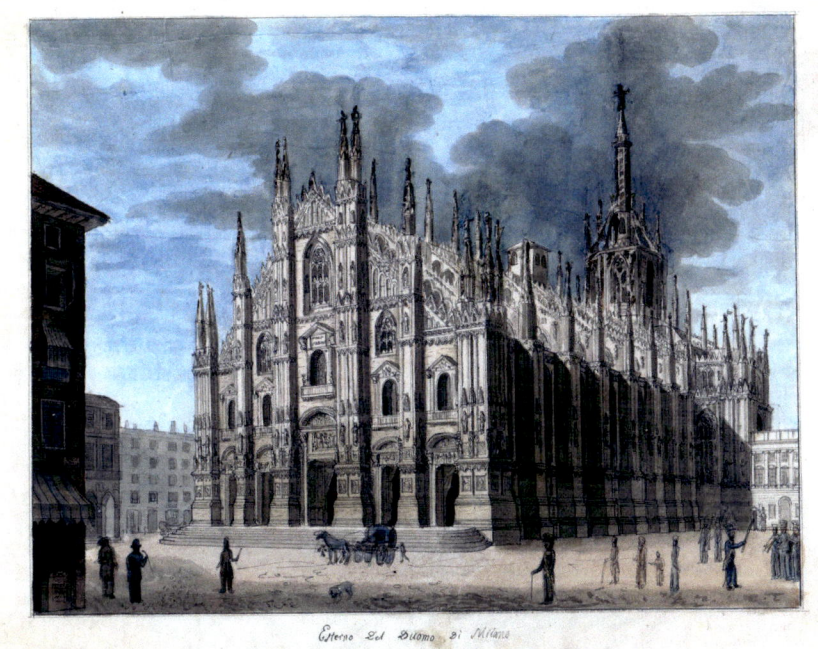

Unknown artist, *View of the Duomo, Milan*, *c*. 1820s, pen and ink with watercolour.
The British Museum

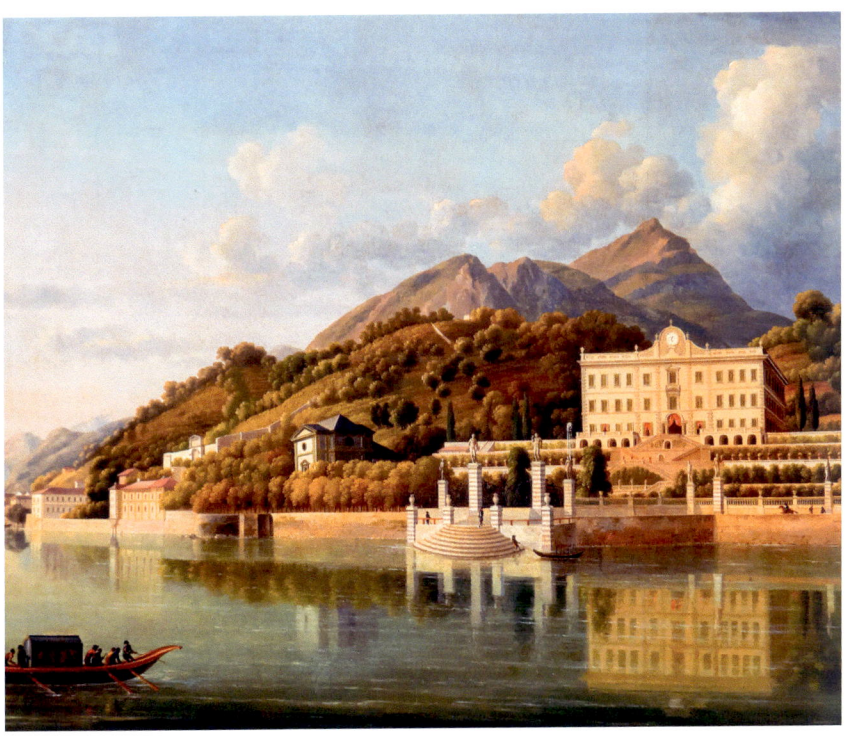

Giuseppe Bisi, *Villa Sommariva, Cadenabbia, on Lake Como*, 1823, oil on canvas.
Villa Carlotta

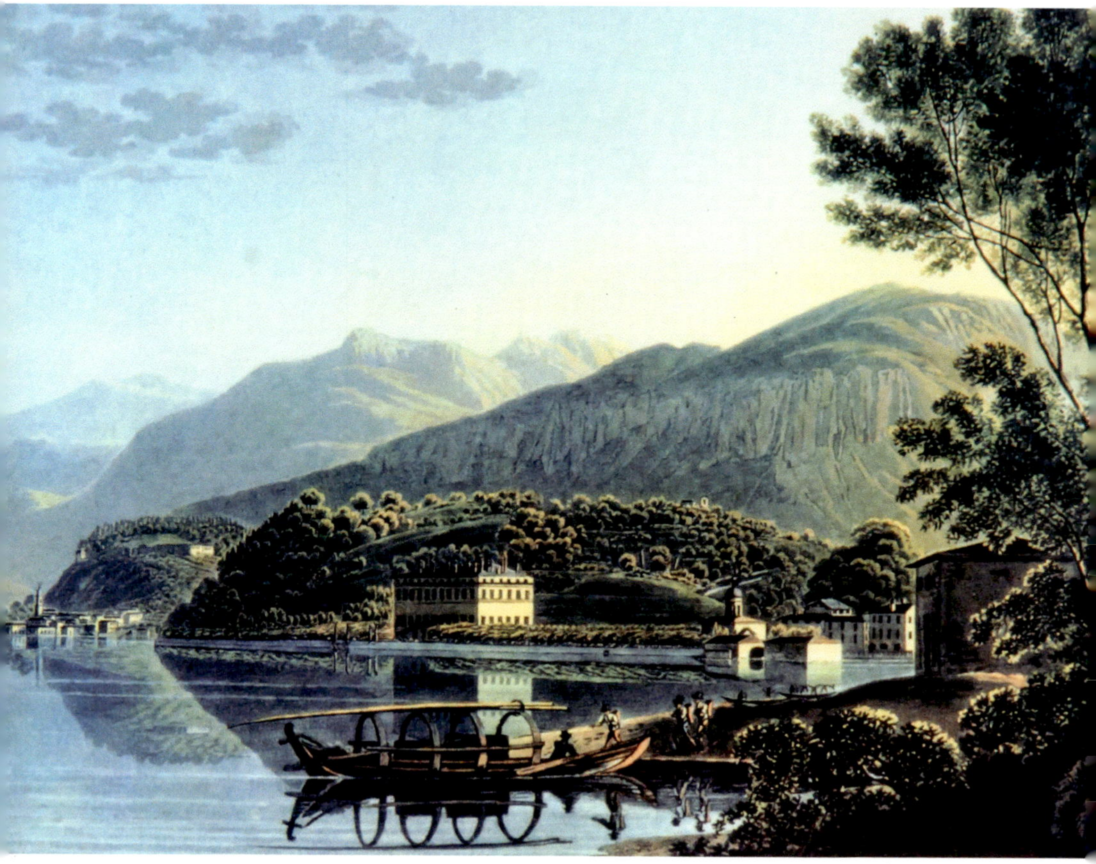

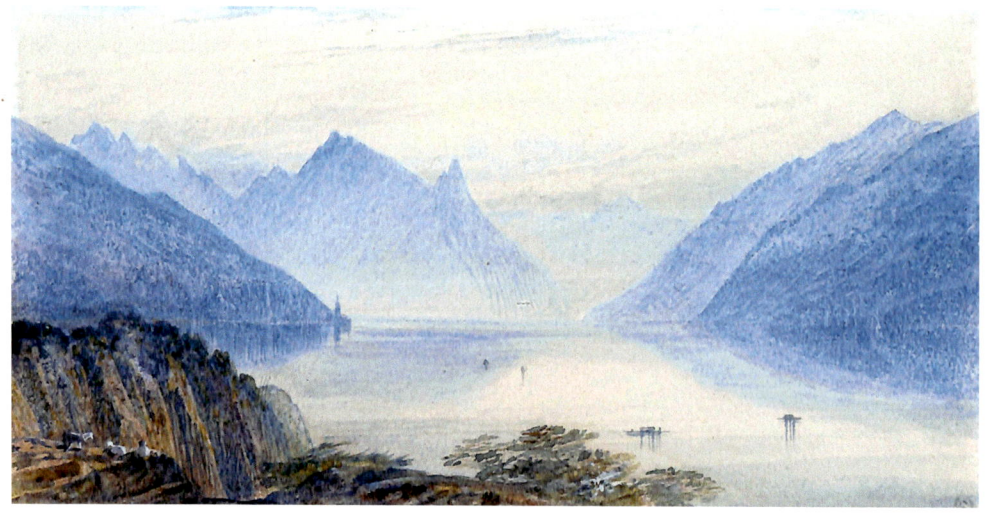

Johann Jakob Wetzel, *Villa Melzi d'Eril, Bellagio, on Lake Como*, 1822, hand-coloured aquatint. *Villa Melzi d'Eril*

Edward Lear, *View of Lake Lugano*, 1880, watercolour. *The Derby Collection*

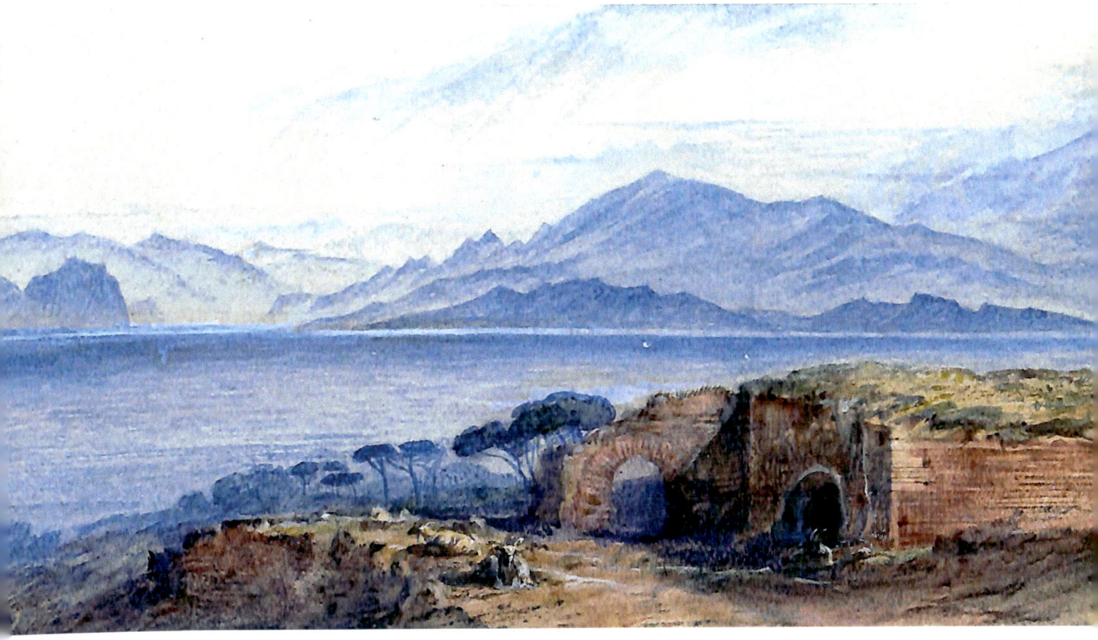

Edward Lear, *View of Lake Garda*, 1880, watercolour. *The Derby Collection*

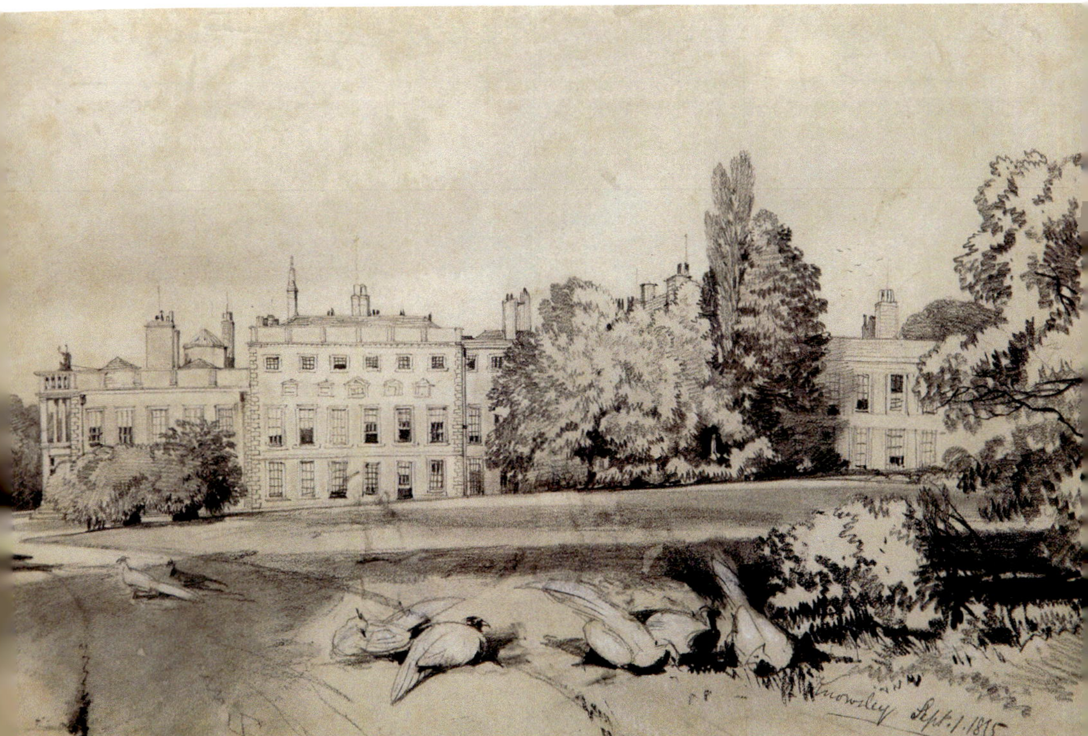

Edward Lear, *View of Knowsley Hall, Lancashire, from the East*, 1835, pencil. *The Derby Collection*

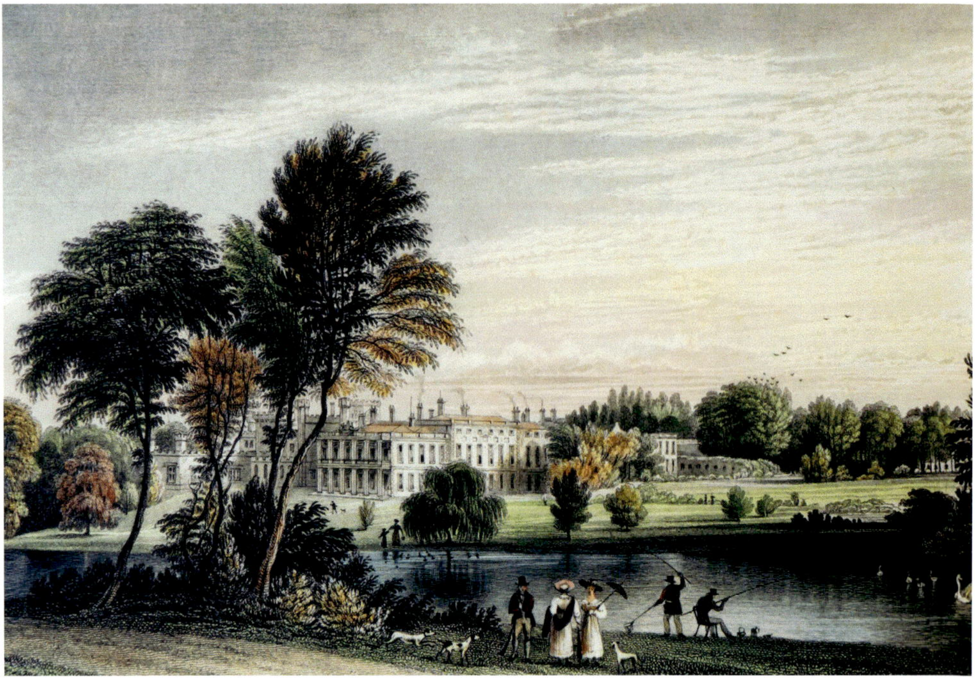

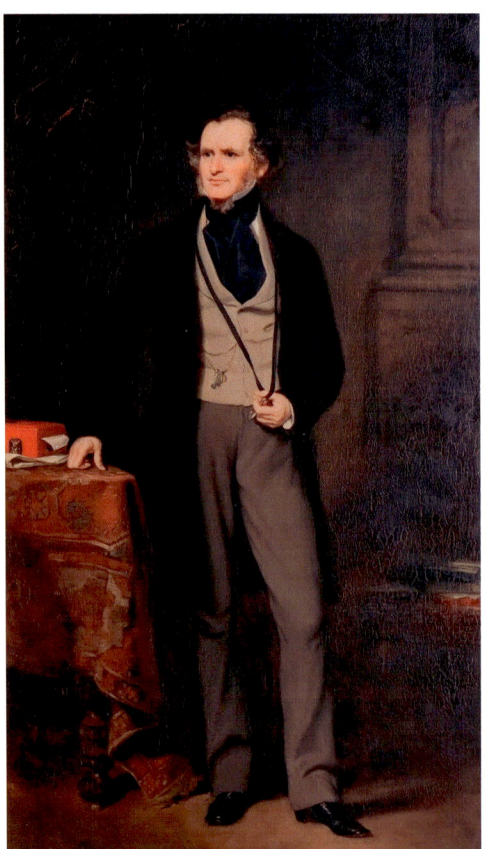

Above: W. Taylor after G. Pickering, *View of Knowsley Hall, Lancashire, from the South*, *c*. 1832, hand-coloured etching. *The Derby Collection*

Left: Sir Francis Grant, *Edward Geoffrey Stanley, 14th Earl of Derby*, 1858, oil on canvas. *The Derby Collection*

His tenderness might have beguil'd:
Yet oft, in her anguish his form shall appear,
His words of foreboding shall ring in her ear,
'Then go—but Ah! Lose not my Child!'

5

And thus as she pitied a Mother's despair,
Be sacred the unbidden, the natural tear
From the eyes of a Mother that stole:
Or if haply a word by emotion were broke,
With how tenfold a livelier interest spoke
That half broken word to the Soul!

6

Of age too she spoke, which, nor selfish nor chill,
But with youth's warm affections, for misery still
Could in generous sympathy glow:
Yet could with heroic exertion suppress,
To lighten the load of another's distress,
Its own stifling emotions of woe:

7

Of deep resignation which looked to its God,
Which shrank from the blow, but which bowed to the rod,
By fervent devotion uprais'd:
And more firm grew her tone, as she warmed to the theme,
And the soul kindled fire of her glance made her seem
The heroine, the Christian she prais'd.

8

But of one when she spoke, who all heartless and light,
On the eddy of pleasure delusively bright
From the chamber of sorrow was borne:
How mantled the eloquent blood in her cheek!
And how did her clasped hands and flashing eye speak
Indignation, and pity, and scorn!

9

Oh thou, who so warmly for others canst feel,
Still temper'd with Mercy, may Providence deal
Thy allotted proportion of care!
May it ne'er be thy fate thus to hang o'er thy Child,
Nor to know by experience how fearfully wild
Are the pangs of a Mother's despair!

10

Yet since all have their suffering, if friendship have power
By partaking, to lighten one desolate hour,
Thou never canst sorrow alone:

For many a warm heart which thy kindness has felt
Should with thee in reciprocal sympathy melt,
And make thine afflictions their own!
Rome May 1st 1821.[11]

Sunday 10th. This morning Corbett and Otway sailed hence for Genoa. I fear they have got hold of a rascally Captain. Sir W. à Court expects Consalvi's answer today. I wish we could get it. I want to be off.

11 o'clock at night. Just arrived. He will not do anything and writes a very cautious letter, but we can get nothing else and must be satisfied. At any rate this enables us to leave Naples, which we shall do immediately.

Monday 11th. Today we consulted with Sir W. à Court and it was determined that we should send another note to Consalvi, though without much hope of success.

We dined with the Margravine *en famille*. That is with Mr Lynch and Sir William Gell and Keppel Craven, but I did not think she was particularly amusing. We were obliged to walk to dinner after waiting an hour for a carriage, but it was a great festive day today, that of *la Madonna dell' Arco*.[12] The Strada Nuova had a curious appearance, full of carriage loads of country people. Rode till late and a beautiful night.

[June 13th] Wednesday. We dined with Sir W. à Court, where there was nobody but Borel,[13] the Prince of Hesse, and Mons. de Fontenay, French *chargé d'affaires*.[14] Went to the opera. Saw Madame de Ficquelmont looking very well and Catherine [von Tiesenhausen] quite brilliant. Took a farewell supper (how sentimental!) at the Villa di Roma.

Thursday 14th. After waiting some time for Ficquelmont's letters of introduction to Austrian Commandants, which after all were only to Chieti and Aquila, we set out about two o'clock for Venice. General Church had sent us a number of letters the day before with a very civil

---

11   Stanley was familiar with close family bereavement. In 1809 his eldest aunt Lady Lucy Stanley died aged ten. Then in April 1817, while both were at Eton, his uncle the Hon. James Stanley died aged seventeen. Ten weeks later, on 16 June 1817, Stanley's mother, Lady Stanley, died aged forty-one.
12   The festival of Madonna dell'Arco was a popular procession with dancing, particularly the Tarantella, from Naples to the sanctuary of Madonna dell'Arco at the foot of Vesuvius. It drew large crowds from across the region.
13   Possibly Colonel Charles Fabvier (1782-1855), a distinguished French military officer. Having left France in 1820 accused of inciting a military conspiracy, he travelled to Greece under the assumed name of Borel to participate in the Greek War of Independence. At this time he would have been *en route* to Greece.
14   Monsieur le Chevalier de Fontenay.

note, recommending us to go to Caserta and deliver one to Marshal O'Farris, General of division for the district. We called on him, but he would not speak out. Said he was sorry he could not give us an escort, having sent out all his Gendarmes, but gave us a letter to the Commandant at Capua, whither we went. The Commandant said he believed the roads were safe and that they had *nessumissina informazione* [no information] to the contrary. On which encouragement we resolved to set out. I forgot to say General O'Farris was preparing a memorial of a robbery which took place 40 miles off six weeks before. The day we were in Gaeta— vigorous Police!

Friday 15th. Set out, delightful morning. Half a post before Formicola, at ten o'clock in the day met a *Vetturino* in full gallop, who stopped, after screaming to us *non andate* [don't go]. Told us there were four armed men a few hundred yards on, who had robbed a carriage, and from whose pursuit they had just escaped. This happening the first post and at such an hour, with General O'Farris's declaration, determined us reluctantly to give up our route through the Abruzzi, and by a cross road we reached the road to Rome, and arrived that night in good time at Terracina. Inn [La Posta] bad, dear, and full of vermin. Waiter drunk, but we got a good dinner. Plenty of Austrian troops.

Saturday 16th. Passed the Pontine Marshes and observed but little signs of ill-health.[15] Detained three hours at Albano by a breakdown, but reached Rome by 7 o'clock. Albergo di Porizi, nobody in the house and only one waiter. Rome quite empty, now that the strangers are gone, and George going to buy some English pencils was told they had none as their stock for the season was exhausted.

Sunday 17th. Nothing material, reached [the Speranza Inn at] Spoleto in the evening and were as before comfortable there.

Monday 18th. At Foligno left our former road, turning to the right among the mountains. The line of country we traversed today is extremely beautiful, and in every respect this road is far preferable to the one from Florence to Bologna, which crosses the same chain of Apennines. It becomes mountainous immediately on leaving Foligno and is particularly beautiful from Serravalle[16] to Macerata.[17] At Tolentino there was a great fair the day we passed and the country people were all dressed and

---

15   The Pontine Marshes were notorious for malaria.
16   A village located in a steep narrow defile dominated by the ruins of an old castle.
17   A town situated on a lofty eminence, mid-way between the Apennines and the sea, above the River Potenza.

looked contented and cheerful. They are a remarkably fine race of people. We slept at Macerata at the Post which is a good Inn and not dear.

Tuesday 19th. Here the valley begins to widen and from being mountainous the country becomes a constant succession of swells, well wooded and very pretty. The reapers whom we passed this morning exhibited more costume than I have seen in Italy before. Orange coloured tight breeches, very neatly tied, white stockings and straw hats gave them a very dressy appearance. Stopped at Loreto[18] and bought some beads and necklaces, which are the chief trade of the place. Went to see the Casa Santa with the Church built over it.[19] The place in which it stands is adorned with a beautiful bronze statue of Gregory 13th and the doors of bronze remarkably fine.[20] Two of these, however, are very far superior to the third, and I should say even to those at Florence. The Baptistry is by the same artist as the best of the doors, of beautiful design and execution, and the figure of St John baptising our Saviour struck me as peculiarly good. The Church is very fine and the grand altar built over the Holy house is ornamented with twelve beautiful statues of the Prophets and as many Sybils. One of which, by the way, is very like our friend at S. Gennaro's. The Treasury disappointed me. It was plundered by the French and since by the Pope, and contains now comparatively nothing. There is one beautiful picture of Guido in the Sacristy. The Palace contains nothing in my opinion worth the trouble of a visit.[21] The Q. of England was received here when at Loreto.[22]

On arriving at Ancona we leave the fine country: we did not stop in the town, and contented ourselves with a distant view of the Mole. The women here and at Loreto are very handsome, and at Loreto I should think not rigidly virtuous. The road now is flat and ugly along the coast to Fano—a wretchedly decaying town, and which gives me more the idea of wretchedness than any I ever saw.[23] The Postmasters say there is no travelling and they are ruined. That one of them keeps nine posts and had not had one carriage for 2 months, and this is confirmed at Pesaro. At Fano there is a figure of Fortune reckoned fine, but the attitude struck me as stiff and ungraceful.[24] There is also a very curious arch said to be

---

18   A significant place of pilgrimage situated on a hill about 3 miles from the sea with extensive views over the countryside.
19   The Chiesa della Santa Casa.
20   The bronze statue is in fact of Pope Sixtus V by Calcagni. The doors are the work of the sculptor Girolamo Lombardo (1506-1590) and his pupils.
21   The Palazzo Apostolica, designed by Bramante for Pope Julius II in 1510.
22   Caroline of Brunswick, who visited Loreto in 1814.
23   The Roman town of Fanum Fortunae.
24   The statue crowns a public fountain in Fano.

to Constantine.[25] I could not make out the inscription, but it has been made at two different times and the middle letters are considerably larger than the others. There is a model of the arch in the perfect state in bas relief by the side of it, by Michelangelo, giving an upper row of columns with a second pediment. Part of two columns still remain.

From Fano the road seems prettier following the sea coast, to Pesaro: where we slept at the Post, a good clean Inn.

Wednesday 20th. Soon after leaving Pesaro the country alters for the worse, and it is flat and uninteresting, presenting no object worthy of attention, except the remains of a fine Roman brick bridge, on the Emilian Way. Pesaro carries on a large commerce in silks, and we saw all the country people loaded with baskets full of silk worms going to market.

Slept at Bologna at the S. Marco[26] and determined to stay on a day and pay Crescentini a visit.[27]

Thursday 21st. In going to his house we met him. He seemed very glad to see us and pressed us to come and dine at his *campagna*, which we promised to do. Went to the Gallery[28] and admired again our old friends the great picture of Guido, his Samson, Crucifixion, and Murder of the Innocents. There is likewise a splendid Conversion of St. Paul and descent from the Cross by Ludovico Caracci,[29] and a splendid head of Guido by Annibal Caracci. I do not so like Elisabetta Sirani on second acquaintance.[30]

Crescentini gave us a good dinner and excellent wine of his own making, and talked with great warmth of the Duchess of Hamilton who staid here ten days ago and whom we were very near meeting. Went to the Opera in the evening. *La Feroni* (a Miss Feroni) quite infernal, but much in fashion here.

Friday 22nd. Passed through a horrible country full of marshes and ugly rivers, among which, however, are the Po and the Adige, to Padua.[31] Ferrara the boundary town [between Lombardy and Venetia] very wretched. The Austrian Police troublesome about passports and the money

---

25   The triumphal arch is made of white marble and was originally built to honour the Emperor Augustus, but was later extended by Constantine.
26   The Hotel San Marco, the oldest and best-appointed hotel in Bologna.
27   The celebrated castrati singer Stanley had dined with in Rome.
28   The Accademia di Belle Arti.
29   Ludovico Caracci (1555-1619).
30   The Bologna painter Elisabetta Sirani (1638-1665).
31   The plain of Polesine.

terribly confusing. Reached Padua in the evening and came to the Aquila d'Oro. A tolerable Inn, but with too much pretension.

Saturday 23rd. Took a Cicerone to make a tour of the town. The Grand Sala[32] is one of the finest, if not the finest room I ever saw, 125 passi by (I think) 53, and 100 feet high. The Church of Santa Giustina is I think the handsomest I have seen:[33] rich in marbles and some good pictures, though I do not admire the great Veronese.[34] S. Antonio has seen better days.[35] He was as rich as our Lady of Loreto, but is now reduced so low as to have wooden lamps silvered over. His private Chapel, however, over his tomb is still rich and handsome. The inscription to Livy in the grand Sala is long and bad, as all modern inscriptions in Italy are. The town of Padua contains many handsome buildings and fine Piazzi, but give the idea of going to decay. The great commerce was in silk, but that was ruined in the time of the French and has never recovered. The French also robbed here 70 Convents which were within the walls, and many of which had large incomes, turned the Monks adrift and allowed them 50 sous a day—an allowance still continued. We were taken to see a colossal statue in the Palazzo di Venezia, which I did not admire.[36] All our Cicerone knew about it was that it was antique and made where it stands. The Fall of the Angels cut out of one block of marble in the Palazzo Papafava is very curious and I think very bad—a pyramid of legs and arms.[37] There are there and have been for four years in their cases four statues by Canova, unopened. I forgot to mention at Ferrara yesterday the Cathedral, a handsome outside Gothic building and with the inscription:

> *Anno milleno Centeno ter quoque deno*
> *Quinque super latis structur domus hac Pietatis.*

The inside is Italian architecture and poor.

I must not forget to put down a collection of oaths from one of our postilions to a carter who ran against him. After swearing for some time very fluently *per Christo, sanque di Dio, corpo di Christo, anima della misericord à di Dio vengar accidente* ['for Christ, blood of God,

---

32   Presumably the Great Hall in the Palazzo della Ragione, built by Pietro Cozzo between 1172 and 1219. The hall is 240 feet long and 80 feet wide.

33   A thirteenth-century church supposedly built on the site of the Roman Temple of Concord.

34   Paolo Veronese (1528-1588). The painting to which Stanley is referring is *The Martyrdom of Santa Giustina*.

35   The Church of San Antonio, noted for the richness of its internal decoration.

36   A statue of Hercules by Bartolomeo Ammannati (1511-1592).

37   A sculpture by Agostino Fasolata (1714-1787) of Satan and his disciples being cast out of Heaven, made up of sixty figures carved out of one solid piece of marble.

body of Christ, soul of God's mercy come to an accident'], and wishing he could give him a *pistolata*, he finished by calling him *Buggerneccio futuro infame*—which amused me much. Another postilion to his horse said! *Che sii scoglionato maledetta bestia* ['May you be a cursed beast']! So much for Italian oaths, which in general are highly political—as *Folonina di Dio*, etc. A sort of Ladies oath is *per Bacco* ['for Bacchus'], and *corpo di Bacco* ['body of Bacchus'], and a very common one is *Cazzo di Papa* ['Papa's cock']! Tomorrow we reach Venice and hope to get letters.

Sunday 24th. Passed still through a very ugly country, though better inhabited than the last part of our route, to Mestre. Our road almost entirely along the banks of the Brenta, which exhibits now a very decaying commerce. We took a Gondolier from Mestre and arrived in good time at the Leone Bianco—a comfortable Inn [by the Rialto bridge] and very civil people. Walked out after dinner to the Piazza S. Marco. A splendid and very much improved by the new buildings of beautiful architecture added by the French. The side by Palladio is particularly striking.[38] The famous horses are placed so ill it is impossible to see them. We met Cox Hunter and M. Conte and took a turn in the garden, full of people, and exhibiting a very curious simple dance. Went into a Café on the Place S. Marco where we had our Limonata and returned to a 12 hour sleep.

Monday 25th. Sallied forth with our Gondola and Servitor di piazza, first of all to the collection of pictures called the Galleria Manfrin—very large and some very good, with many very bad. Giorgione shines very superior here, and I never saw any of his so good. One or two good Titians, a very fine Rembrandt, a beautiful Gerard Dow, and a good Carlo Dolci in the Café d'Opera here.[39] There is a good statue by a Neapolitan sculptor exhibiting the face through a veil with beautiful effect.[40] The Church of Scalzi is very rich in marbles and so loaded with ornament and wealth as to make it very ugly.[41] We took a general view

---

38   This reference to the work of architect Andrea Palladio (1508-1580) in Piazza San Marco is unclear. Presumably it refers to the Procuratie Nuove on the south side of the piazza, which was designed by Palladio's pupil Vincenzo Scamozzi (1548-1616). Scamozzi adapted one of Palladio's designs for re-facing the Doge's Palace, which the architect had rejected.

39   Stanley is referring to the following artists and paintings: *Woman with a Guitar* by Giorgione (*c.* 1477/78-1510); *The Descent from the Cross* and a portrait of Ariosto by Titian (*c.* 1488/90-1576); a portrait by Rembrandt (1606-1669); *The Physician* by Gerrit Dou (1613-1675); and the Italian painter Carlo Dolci (1616-1686).

40   A bust by Antonio Corradini (1688-1752). Corradini was born in Venice and died in Naples.

41   The Church of Gui Scalzi, built from 1680 to 1715, is noted for the richness of its interior decoration, which was almost completely destroyed in an aerial attack in the First World War.

of the whole city from the top of the belfry of St. Mark's, which gives a fine panoramic of this extraordinary town.[42]

Its commerce is lamentably going to decay, the population diminished from 160 to 120,000 souls, the Palaces all shut up, the inhabitants in wretchedness, and the nobles gone to Vienna and Milan. Such are the consequences of Austrian dominion. These, our generous allies, impose upon all sorts of English and French manufacture a duty of 60 per cent, amounting to a prohibition. The new Patriarch[43] who arrived six weeks ago is, from all accounts, a meddling injudicious man, a Hungarian, who seems disposed to treat the Greeks and Jews with great severity, wishing to shut up the latter in one quarter of the city, and forcing the former to have their worship with closed doors and without ringing of bells. In severity to whores and pimps he beats Alderman Wood,[44] and the other day confined and indeed banished 23 of the latter, because his Secretary had been importuned. His precautions here, however, will be of no use for all the women seem whores.

Tuesday 26th. Set out again sightseeing, which we intend to do rapidly for the eternal Gondola tires us to death. Went to the Salute, a handsome church outside though too much loaded with ornament.[45] Within it disappointed me. It is by Baldassare Longhena.[46] There is one good picture by Luca Giordano and two by Cerva, a painter of whom I never heard before.[47] S. Giorgio Maggiore is a beautiful church by Palladio, simple and noble. So is the Redentore by the same architect, but inferior.[48] In the former are two beautiful Tintoretto's quite spoilt.[49] The Accademia is the only institution here which seems well kept up, and it is a noble collection indeed.[50] There seemed a good room of *gessi* [plaster casts], but as we had seen all the originals statues we did not go in. The pictures are mostly in excellent preservation and among them are two superb Titians,

---

42   The Campanile, completed in 1155, reaches a height of 323 feet.
43   Ladislaus Pyrker (1772-1847) was patriarch of Venice from 1820 to 1827.
44   A reference to the vociferous radical Matthew Wood (1768-1848), lord mayor of London 1815-17 and MP for London 1817-43. He was considered a vain foolish man; Lord Brougham called him 'Jackass Wood'.
45   The Church of Santa Maria della Salute was built in 1632 as a monument of thanksgiving for the end of a plague which had killed 60,000 Venetians.
46   The Venetian architect Baldassare Longhena (1598-1682).
47   Luca Giordano (1634-1705) and Pier Antonio Cerva (1600-1670).
48   The Chiesa del Santissimo Redentore. While Stanley admired San Giorgio and the Redentore, Ruskin later wrote of his hatred of both, declaring them gross, barbarous and childish in conception.
49   The *Virgin Crowned* and the *Martyrdom of Saints* by Jacopo Tintoretto (1518-1594).
50   Gallerie dell'Accademia.

2 Tintoretto's, one the Miracoli di S. Marco, the finest I ever saw,[51] several of Bonifacio very good, one or two of Leandro Bassano and some others.[52] One very good Giorgione,[53] but this I think not equal to the one in the Manfrini. The great Titian was a good deal concealed by a scaffolding for two artists who are to make an engraving for Marie Louise.[54] But in a few days it will be removed and this Gallery deserves a second visit. The Church of S. Giovanni and Paolo is a very handsome one and not too rich, full of fine pictures, sculpture and architecture. A good Paolo Veronese, a very fine Titian,[55] the Martyrdom of S. Marco, same subject as Domenichino at Bologna, and some good Palma Vecchio's, who with Palma Giovane is buried here.[56] Here too we must go again. There are many fine monuments[57] and several beautiful pictures in a chapel which is so dark they cannot be seen. The roof beautiful by Tintoretto.[58] Some very beautiful *basso relievos* in the same chapel by different authors in Carrara marble, representing the History of the New Testament, rather, however, too much the effect of porcelain.

Wednesday 27th. Went early to the Palazzo Pisano to see two pictures. One of them is a moderate production, of the death of Darius, the other a magnificent Paolo Veronese, the reception of his family by Alexander.[59] Then to the Scuola di S. Rocco, where there is a fine Tintoretto of the Crucifixion and another good one on the ceiling of Moses making the water gush from the rock, but room after room with nothing but Tintorettos, and there several of them not in the best state.[60] In the neighbouring Church of S. Rocco[61] Titian is buried, without a monument because he died in the great plague, when they had not time to raise one,

---

51 Presumably Tintoretto's *Miracle of the Slave* (1548), one of the artist's most highly finished and virtuoso works.
52 Bonifacio Veronese (1487-1553) and Leandro Bassano (1557-1622).
53 Neither Giorgione's *La Tempesta* nor *La Vecchia*.
54 Marie Louise, the duchess of Parma.
55 *The Death of Peter the Martyr*, which was later destroyed by fire in 1867.
56 Paolo Veronese (1528-1588), Palma Vecchio (1480-1528) and Palma Giovane (1548-1628).
57 Monuments dedicated to the twenty-five doges buried in the church.
58 At this time work by Tintoretto was hung in the Rosary Chapel, but the reference to the roof is unclear. The painting on the ceiling of the Rosary Chapel is the *Annunciation* (1558) by Veronese.
59 The Veronese was acquired from the Palazzo Pisani by the National Gallery, London, in 1857.
60 The Scuola Grande di San Rocco was the meeting place of a confraternity, rather than an art gallery. It was decorated exclusively with the paintings of Tintoretto. Stanley clearly admired the work of Tintoretto, although it is Ruskin who is usually credited with reviving interest in the painter at a later date.
61 Stanley is referring to the Church of Santa Maria Gloriosa dei Frari, a neighbour of the Scuola Grande di San Rocco.

and posterity has never taken the trouble to supply the deficiency.[62] In this Church, where <u>was</u> the famous Titian the Assumption, now in the Accademia, there is still another of his which is said to be as good, but is, as the other was, covered with filth and spoiling with damp.[63]

The pictures in the Palazzo Barbarigo are much in the same way. For this house Titian worked for a number of years almost exclusively, and there is shown the last of his works, a San Sebastiano, unfinished and dirty, but struck me as very good. There is also a fine Magdalen, but too fat and blousy. In the Casa Grimani are several antiques, some very good busts, but mostly unknown and there is no catalogue. There is also a statue of Agrippa, which I own I had not taste enough to admire.

In the evening I took a drive in the Gondola and was much amused by the *Laquais-de-place* and my Gondolier, both of whom gave me a great deal of their histories. The latter had been four years prisoner in Plymouth, and four years more on board an English man-of-war, where he said he wished himself again. No letter arrived from Sir W. à Court.

Thursday 28th. Visited the Church of S. Mark, venerable for its antiquity, and beautiful for the richness of its mosaics and marbles. The four bronze horses are placed on the front of this Church and so high that they cannot be seen without going up, but when they are so they are well worth the trouble of going up to them.

We went afterwards to the Arsenal, a very fine locale and plentifully supplied with wood, with building yards, etc. They have one frigate nearly finished and 2 others, and two 74s on the stocks, where they have been without making any progress since 1811. The French employed 4,000 men in the Arsenal, the Austrians 800. There are confined there now 300 Galley slaves whom we saw pass by chained 2 and 2, and a sad rascally looking crew they were. The Armoury contains nothing very remarkable, except the armour of Henry 4th, a small gun made in honour of a Turkish Ambassador's arrival, by a Doge's son, a Banner taken from the Turks, and other memorials of the Republic which they ought to be ashamed to show in their present degraded state.

My Servitor has opened a good deal tonight. He tells me he is 71, which I do not believe—lived three years as Maestro di Casa to Lady Hamilton at Naples, when she was in the high tide of her beauty.[64] He

---

62   In 1790 Canova was commissioned to create a monument to Titian in the church, but
     the overthrow of the Venetian Republic by the French in 1796 prevented its completion.
     Much later, the emperor of Austria, Ferdinand I, ordered the erection of a suitable monu-
     ment to Titian, which was undertaken between 1843 and 1851.
63   Presumably the Pesaro altarpiece.
64   Emma, Lady Hamilton (1765-1815) was an English actress and famous beauty, and the

was sent by Sir W. as Courier to England, had been in the siege of Gibraltar under Eliott,[65] and narrowly escaped, had travelled with a Sicilian nobleman into Russia, and had been soon after the Battle of the Nile, Maestro di Casa to the Sardinian Minister at Vienna, where he again saw Lord Nelson, and where the D. of Hamilton, according to his account, then Mr Hamilton, related a most extraordinary story as having happened to himself, and which I told him I should certainly ask the Duke. That he was travelling in Italy with a very handsome English carriage, during a short armistice between France and England. That at some town, I forget which, he stopped to get some refreshment and sent his servant on some errand. That in the meantime Marshal Masséna drove up with a very shabby carriage and four horses.[66] That he ordered four more, put them to the Duke's carriage and drove off, leaving the Duke with nothing but the clothes he had on! This he swears to be sacro. As a proof of my friend's accuracy in history, beyond that of his own times, he talked of a fact (I believe the foundation of some Church) when Hannibal drove the Goths out of Italy *is prima tempi di qui revoluzionari l'Italia I terribili Goth id Astrogoti.*

Friday 29th. The last day of our stay in Venice, which I believe neither of us regret. George protests he shall be in raptures when we get out of this prison. His impatience is too invidious. We went this morning to see the old Palace of the Doges. A fine old pile of building and adorned with some very curious as well as beautiful paintings, historical and allegorical, by the first masters of the Venetian School, chiefly Tintoretto and Paul Veronese. The Library is a magnificent room, but the ceilings of all the rooms are rather heavy, from their exceeding richness not being sufficiently relieved by their height. A great part of the Palazzo is now occupied by officers, and some certainly destroyed, but the Council Room, the Hall of Audience etc. still remain to show what Venice was. The modern Palace is a wretched specimen of French taste, fitted up with tinsel and finery on the smallest meanest scale. The old Library, as if in shame of it, is a noble room and the roof beautifully ornamented with pictures and gilding, and coved, which takes off the effect of heaviness.

Saturday 30th. Left Venice without the least regret, passed through an uninteresting country for the most part, and reached Bassano in good

---

muse of the painter George Romney. In 1791 she married Sir William Hamilton, British envoy to Naples. She became the lover of Lord Nelson in 1798.

65   George Eliott (1717-1790), a British army officer famous for his command of the Gibraltar garrison during the Great Siege of Gibraltar, which lasted from 1779 to 1783. He was created 1st Baron Heathfield in 1787.

66   André Masséna (1758-1817), one of Napoleon's marshals of the empire.

time. This is a nice little town prettily situated upon the Brenta, with a curious covered wooden bridge.[67] Its chief trade is in iron and I believe in silk.

July 1821

Sunday July 1st. From hence to Primolano, the first post, and from thence part of the way to Valsugana the wood is very beautiful, but it afterwards worsens as the valley widens, and though there are some picturesque bits, the country falls very far short of my idea of the Tyrol. The chain of mountains about Trent [Trento] has the appearance of being very splendid, but we arrived so late at night that we could hardly see the town under our feet as we descended to it. On this road the posts are wretchedly served and the slowness of the travelling is dreadful. The wooden bridges I spoke of yesterday we find common enough.

Monday 2nd. Soon after Trent we enter upon the German Tyrol and begin to hear the German language the only one spoken. Before leaving it in the morning we went to see first the Cathedral, a Gothic building, handsome inside and partly so without, and the little Church of Sta. Maria Maggiore, where the great Council was held, but which has no other claim to attention.[68] Leaving Trent the road is itself nearly flat, but winds along a valley between stupendous mountains rising more abruptly and precipitously than anything I ever saw. The valley itself, however, is flat and mostly still. I continued disappointed with the Tyrol till I reached Bolzano. This is a very nice looking little town situated on the river (I believe) Eisack. Here the scene suddenly changes and instead of bleakness and desolation we find a beautifully cultivated valley, narrow, well-peopled and smiling, between noble hills, and the ground well variegated, as far as Brixen where we slept, or rather passed the night in a comfortable looking Inn, but in which between us we caught <u>seven bugs</u>. We should, however, have staid a day had not the morning proved bad, so that we determined it was better to proceed, even though the country was very beautiful, but would lose much by the unfavourable weather.

Tuesday 3rd. This day's journey was indeed highly beautiful, though in quite a different style—more wild, more romantic, and less inhabited; but so beautiful that it had not the least air of desolation even though

---

67   The thirteenth-century Ponte Vecchio.
68   The Council of Trent, held from 1545 to 1563, was an ecumenical council of the Catholic Church, which defined the heresies of Protestantism and codified the Tridentine Mass.

seen in the rain. The distant snowy mountains, wherever we could see them, were magnificent, and the first view of Innsbruck, situated in a plain at the confluence of the Sill and the Inn, is very striking. In this part of our journey we have seen more costumes than in any part of the continent in which we have been. In the men the broad belt with brass ornaments, the various coloured clothes, the large and singular shaped hat, the immense ring of silver, serving for ornament and as a weapon, and lastly the immense knives in the pocket, give them a very striking appearance: and the women are not less remarkable, with their green and yellow bonnets, their red stockings, immensely padded hips, and their bunch of keys dangling by a long chain behind them. They seem as far as one can judge (alas! not knowing the language) remarkably civil nice people. It is said, however, they are a little violent with each other at times: to strangers they are remarkably civil and hardly one passes without taking off his hat, and even many of the women nod or curtsey as they pass.

Wednesday 4th. Innsbruck is a remarkably nice town, well built, full of good houses, though with no splendid buildings situated upon the Inn, in a fine valley and abounding in beautiful scenery. Manufactures it has none and not much trade, but the people seem easy and cheerful. We have been all day about the environs, there being nothing curious in the town, except the fine old Gothic Cathedral, with the monuments of Maximilian in the middle, and fine bronze statues, many of them of good workmanship, representing old Kings and Emperors of Austria and other great personages, 14 on each side.[69] Among them appears Arthur, König von England! An authentic likeness no doubt! We hear that the Tyrolean peasants are a good deal discontented, the Emperor[70] having refused to confirm their old privileges according to his promise, and having as they say ruined their trade. This is a little hard after the noble and spirited proofs they gave of attachment to him in 1809 under Hofer, whose whole history we have had today.[71] They even showed a little of this feeling, it is said, when their army was raised to go into Italy. Well for them they did not show much of it.

---

69   The monument to the Holy Roman Emperor Maximilian I (1459-1519) was decorated with marble reliefs which were highly praised by Thorvaldsen. The surrounding statues were made between 1513 and 1583 by the brothers Stephen and Melchior Godl.

70   Francis I, emperor of Austria. He ruled from 1804 to 1835, having previously been styled the Holy Roman Emperor from 1792 to 1806.

71   Andreas Hofer (1767-1810), a Tyrolean innkeeper who led the rebellion against the Napoleonic invasion. He was captured and shot by the French, and his body was subsequently buried in Innsbruck. A marble statue was placed on his tomb and he came to be venerated as a folk hero and patriot.

Friday 6th. Left Innsbruck with regret and passed through a very pretty country, chiefly along the banks of the Inn, to S. Johann, where found a small comfortable Inn, with a roguish Landlord, and not a soul in the house who could speak either French or Italian. We got, however, a good dinner, though as it was Friday there was no meat. NB. The population in this country are remarkably strict Catholics.

Saturday 7th. From S. Johann the country becomes almost immediately mountainous and highly beautiful. We have seen, indeed, no scenery equal to it in Italy or the Tyrol and I cannot conceive anything finer in its way. The only *disagrément* is the slowness of the Postilions and the frequent recurrence of barriers, of which in consequence of crossing the confines of Austria and Bavaria, we had to pay no less than 9 in the last two posts; and we were altogether ten hours and a half in going 4 posts and a half, or about 35 English miles! Job himself would have sworn if he could have spoke German, but nothing will move the phlegm of a German postilion. Salzburg is well situated at the foot of some steep rocks on the river Sal [Salzach] forming in its general shape a fine semicircle. The Fortress stands very finely above. Inn, the Barca d'Oro, tolerably good, but people roguish and insolent.

Sunday 8th. This morning went out with *Laquais-de-place* and a liar of the first quality, who out-Munchausened Munchausen.[72] He was, according to his own account, obliged to leave France in 1804 for being concerned in the *Machine Infernale* plot.[73] Had been before taken prisoner four times by Austrians, once by the English and once by the Turks, and the campaigns he had served and the exploits he had performed were unheard of. He took us up to the Fortress, amazingly strong and extensive, commanding on every side splendid and varied prospects, and underneath, through the solid rock, is cut the old passage called the Porte Neuve, with the bust of the person who made it over the arch and the very neat motto *Te saxa loquuntur* ['The stones will speak of you'].[74] The Royal Stables are close to this, a fine building, with stabling for 700 horses, in three rows. Near there is the winter and summer *manège* [horse training area], with galleries cut in the solid rock for spectators. The Mirabell [Palace] has been a beautiful building, originally designed in the 16th century for the Bishop's mistress, with a covered passage to the

---

72   This is in reference to Rudolf Erich Raspe's 1785 novel, *Baron von Munchausen's Narrative of his Marvellous Travels and Campaigns in Russia*, in which the protagonist is known for his fanciful storytelling.
73   A planned assassination of Napoleon in 1800.
74   This person was the prince-archbishop of Salzburg, Sigismund von Schrattenbach.

Fort.[75] It afterwards belonged to the government and three years ago was totally, or almost, destroyed by fire, in which several lives were lost.[76]

The churches are nothing very extraordinary. The Cathedral is a fine handsome building and they say very old. This place is oddly held by a government I do not quite understand, between the Pope and the Emperor; and they send, if I did not mistake, a Resident here alternately. Yet the Emperor lays out immense sums for this place. I suppose for the sake of the Fortress. In the evening we walked to a beautiful place of Prince Schwarzenberg's,[77] laid out in the English style and with very good taste, and open to the public, whom he was always delighted to see here on Sunday and holidays. He seems to have been a very amiable man and was well spoken of here, and is much regretted. The two brothers, the Bishop[78] and the Marshal, died within a few months of each other, and the succession goes to another brother who lives at Vienna, and whose son is at Rome, so that it will probably be sold. A threatening day and turned to heavy rain at night.

Monday 9th. Heavy rain, in spite of which we set out to see the Salt mines. On arriving at Hallein[79] we found to our consternation that we had an hours walk before we entered the mine, but as we were there, we determined to set out, though cursing the man for leading us there. On the top of the mountain, which is I dare say very beautiful, we put on the miner's dress, or rather a pair of white trousers, a white jacket, a leather bum protector and a cap and gloves. George looked very much like a Cook and I like a Butcher. On entering the mine, we passed for some way along a covered passage, supported in places by timbers, but in most supporting itself. The earth, which is mixed with the Salt and Gypsum, is so clammy and elastic that it is used as cement and hardens on exposure. The whole mine is composed of these covered shafts all having their separate names, and interrupted only by occasional descents like the *Montagne Russe*.[80] Your guide goes 'first' and you seat yourself upon two polished fir poles which reach from the top to the bottom. On the right hand side is a rope which you hold to steady yourself and then slide down. The longest descent is 48 *toises*,[81] and the shortest twelve.

---

75 Prince-Archbishop Wolf Dietrich Raitenau built Mirabell Palace in 1606 for his mistress Salome Alt.

76 The devastating fire occurred in 1818.

77 Prince Karl Philippe Schwarzenberg (1771-1820), a field marshal in the Austrian army.

78 Bishop Ernst Scharwzenberg (1773-1821).

79 The Hallein salt mines are 18 miles south of Salzburg.

80 *Les Montagne Russe* were originally ice slides. In 1817, the concept was developed into the world's first roller coaster, the *Promenades Aeriennes* in Paris, with wheeled cars locked on to tracks.

81 A unit of measurement in pre-revolutionary France. One toise equalled roughly six feet.

There are also as many as 33 lakes in this mountain. The one which we saw gave me more the idea of Acheron than anything else.[82] Between the lake and ceiling was about 7 feet: the whole length of the lake was of ninety *toises*, and the circumference partly lighted with torches made darkness visible. There was too a boat with its Charon[83] in this subterranean abode, but we preferred walking around the along the edge. The bottoms and sides of these lakes are stopped with the elastic earth and their use is this. A certain number of them are constantly filled up to the ceiling; the passages are stopped with earth and the lake is left thus for three weeks: at the end of which time it has melted down about a foot deep of the ceiling. The water is then drawn off and purified to obtain the salt and the rubbish is cleared away. A certain number are always open for the purposes of passage. Soon after leaving the lake we were told we performed the rest of the journey by the post. This I did not understand: but presently arrived a long plank, upon four wheels, drawn by a man before and one behind. On this we all placed ourselves astride, one behind another and placing our feet on a plank below, were drawn off at a rapid trot. In doing this one must sit upright and steady, for the passage is so narrow as to have but a few inches on each side. It gives a giddy sensation at first, but that goes off. The whole length is 800 *toises* and for the last half you see daylight gradually breaking, and you are at length wheeled out at a cottage door, where you find your clothes and the town within ten minutes' walk. There are occasionally accidents here from inflammable air and the safety lamp is unknown.

On coming out we found the day had mended a little and we drove on to the Häffle, a tremendous gorge where the Sual passes below among rocks and woods, at a tremendous depth, and the most Salvatorish and magnificent scenery I ever beheld.[84] From thence we returned to Colline, where we left our carriage and went to the waterfall, which is singular and beautiful: the river rushes at once, at its source, from a large opening in the rocks near the top of the mountain and already a considerable stream falls suddenly down a deep chasm, over which there is an arched rock, with a tree upon it, above a vacant space, and above again a flying bridge. The second fall is below and not inferior in beauty; the hills around are clothed chiefly with larch and in fine weather must be charming, but here again came on the rain and lasted all night.

---

82   In the Homeric poems, the Acheron is a river in Hades.
83   Charon is the ferryman of Hades, who carries the souls of the recently deceased across the River Styx.
84   'Salvatorish' is a reference to the Italian painter Salvator Rosa (1615-1673), known for his haunting and dramatic landscapes.

Tuesday 10th. Gave up with reluctance our excursion to the lakes and set out in wretched weather across an uninteresting country at two hours a post of 8 miles, and 20 minutes changing horses. This is average. Rain all day, as it has been for six weeks. Slept at Wasserburg at a decent Inn.

Wednesday 11th. Yesterday repeated. The first view of Munich is fine, but it loses as you approach. Went to the Aquila Nera, a moderate looking house, in a good situation.

Thursday 12th. Visited first the Palace.[85] Detained a long time in an uninteresting set of bad rooms. The *trésor* of Bavaria which they have been fortunate enough to preserve entire, in spite of the war, is wonderfully rich and amongst it some very curious pieces of old plate: but I own my taste is so bad that the sight of it gave me little or no pleasure. The Chapel of the Palace is very richly ornamented with gilding and carving, and yet does not look gaudy. There is also a crucifix belonging to Mary Queen of Scots, with an inscription which I could not understand, till it was explained and after all it is very far-fetched. It is: *Maria etc. Exilii comes et carceria imaga, fuit, frisset cadis si vixisect*, which is said to mean, that she would have kept it till her death, if she had not been beheaded. It came here by her granddaughter the Q. of Bohemia. Visited the Gallery in the afternoon. A splendid collection.

Friday 13th. In the Gallery all day. The pictures are nobly fine, but in a wretched state from dirt and loads of varnish. Some splendid Van der Werff's, Gerard Dow, Teniers, Rubens, Rembrandt, Van Dyke, Snyders, etc.[86] A good lithographic press here, but prints very dear. Visited today the new Theatre, in company with a Swiss Officer, a Mr Boissin with whom we have been, indeed, all over the town. We first saw him at Salzburg and he amuses me and is very civil: he talks of going into England. The English Garden here is a fine extent of plain, well planted and laid out really in the English style.[87] Forgot to mention the Library, a noble collection, well worth seeing and well kept.[88] Some very curious old manuscripts, the bindings splendidly ornamented with gold and jewels. In another room surprised to meet with English books and even with some of our dullest and commonest novels.

---

85   The Residenz, the royal palace of the kings of Bavaria.
86   The Dutch painter Adriaen van der Werff (1659-1722); the Flemish artist David Teniers (1610-1690); and the Flemish painter Frans Snyders (1579-1657).
87   The English Garden was 4 miles long.
88   The library, the second most extensive in Europe, contained 400,000 books and 22,000 manuscripts.

Saturday 14th. Gallery in the morning and in the English Garden after-wards. Bad day: the town seems thriving, and there are a vast number of new buildings, but it has all the air of being unfinished. Today being the Queen's birthday it was a fête and the military band played in the grand palace in the evening.[89]

Sunday 15th. Set out for Augsburg. Stormy day with intervals fine. The country flat, tiresome and uninteresting, interspersed with vast fir forests and very monotonous. Augsburg a fine town, with large hand-some well-built streets. <u>Very</u> good Inn at the Drei Mohren. That at Munich was also a good one, the Schwarz Adler, but I believe the Hirsch is better.

Monday 16th. The Gallery at Augsburg [called the Golden Hall] is a beautiful room in the Town Hall, with a remarkably fine carved ceiling, but the pictures are most of them very second rate. The churches are many of them handsome in the second order. The Cathedral and Sankt Ulrich are the two best. The walk along the ramparts is well enough, and the whole town wears an air of cheerfulness and comfort. There is a spirit of universal toleration, and Catholics and Protestants fill alternately the offices in the town. No execution has taken place here for two years. The Inn is excellent and not at all dear. The owner has a large gallery of pictures, but many of them are copies from those at Munich which he calls originals. I had almost forgotten the small house here, neatly fitted up, belonging to Madame St Leu the ex-Queen of Holland.[90] Here are all the books in English, French and German that ever were written about Bonaparte and pictures innumerable of all the family. The pictures of Malmaison are here all selling off at fixed prices.[91]

Tuesday 17th. Across a plain ugly country, like all Bavaria, to Memmingen, a neatish little town, whose fortifications have been destroyed. Inn the White Ox moderate.

---

89   Queen Caroline of Baden (1776-1841), who had married King Maximilian I of Bavaria in 1797.

90   Madame St Leu was Hortense Bonaparte, née Beauharnais (1783-1837), Napoleon's step-daughter. She married Napoleon's brother Louis Bonaparte, who was king of Holland from 1806 to his abdication in 1810. After being banished from France in 1815, Hortense was given the title of duchess of Saint-Leu. She was the mother of Napoleon III of France.

91   The Château Malmaison in Paris was acquired by Empress Joséphine in 1799 as a resi-dence for her and her husband Napoleon. Her daughter Hortense fondly remembered it as a delightful place.

Wednesday 18th. To Lindau: the road was not much in beauty; the town is well situated and the mountains immediately about it are fine, but those further down the Lake want boldness.[92]

Thursday 19th. The country along the Lake is pretty enough, but nothing very extraordinary, even under the influence of a brilliant day. In Meersburg we took a boat to Constance across the Lake, which disappointed me much; indeed, it has not much beauty, except that of extent. Constance itself belongs to the Grand Duke of Baden,[93] who being Protestant has encouraged the Protestants, but mildly and sensibly. The convents have all been suppressed, but gradually and by letting the Monks die off. There are four still living in the Palace itself. Nothing but the town belongs to Baden, the country all around is Switzerland. Yet Swiss merchandise pays no duty, while all intercourse with Baden is under restrictions. The country round the Lake is portioned between Austria, Bavaria, Wittemburg, Baden and Switzerland.

Friday 20th. Hired a V*oiturier* for Schaffhausen. A pretty liveable country, very rich and well cultivated. This Canton, Thurgau, sends two Deputies. The property is all divided among small proprietors, there being no such thing as renting land. Labourers are well paid, receiving as much as a Florin a day (about 1s 10p). There is an institution for the poor, who are prevented from working by infirmity, which is administered by the *Gemeinde*, and the surplus of population go abroad to serve in foreign armies. This at least is the information I got from a wine merchant who was travelling to Schaffhausen and with whom I walked nearly half the way, talking German, and finished by drinking a bottle of wine with him. Before I joined him we went up to Madame St. Leu's little country house [at Arnenberg], well situated above the Lake, opposite Reichenhau, and in sight of one of P. Eugene's, and another of Mad. Gougelin her Dame d'honeur. In the evening ate a little honey and was immediately made violently ill and obliged to go to bed.

Saturday 21st. Much better, went to see the fall, with which we were both cruelly disappointed.[94] It is not to be named in the same year with Terni or many others, and in point of beauty it is not nearly equal to the falls of the Clyde in Scotland. Returned home and not being well put myself in physic.

---

92   The old town of Lindau is situated on an island on the eastern shore of Lake Constance.
93   Ludwig von Baden (1763-1830) was grand duke of Baden from 1818 until his death. Constance became part of the duchy of Baden in 1805.
94   The celebrated waterfalls on the Rhine are about 3 miles from Schaffhausen.

Sunday 22nd. To Zurich, an easy day, the country just pretty and in many parts not even that. The town well situated, but very moderate and its beauty very much exaggerated in all prints and drawings. I am much disappointed with Swiss scenery as far as I have seen it, and Ebel's much talked of book seems to me really bad, being full of the grossest exaggerations.[95] Went to the Sword [Hotel Schwerdt], dear and not good, tried the Corbeau, full, the White Horse, full and bad, and at last settled in the Stork [Hotel Storck], a small very comfortable Inn, cheap, good and people very civil. The situation just as good as the Sword.

Monday 23rd. Lounged about the environs of Zurich, which are pretty, but tame. Called on Mr Disbrowe,[96] our Minister here, who gave us some instructions for our route. There seems little to see about Zurich, but we were tired of wandering and glad to have a rest day.

Tuesday 24th. Same as yesterday, dined with Disbrowe. His sisters are living with him, niceish unaffected girls and must be a great comfort to him. We had also M. Talleyrand French Minister, M. Laidkerch, Dutch, two Deputies and one or two more. Went on the Lake [Zurich] in the evening.

Wednesday 25th. Set out from the Stork, with which we are quite satisfied, to Zug. A fine scene going over Albis and a pretty country about Zug. A fine day and a shooting match for prizes which lasts four days. Hired a guide to make a short excursion.

Thursday 26th. Meant to have gone up the Rigi, but the day not fine enough. Passed the Lake in a boat to Arth, a pretty village well backed by fine mountains.[97] Thence past the Spitzbühl[98] to Schwyz. This fall of a mountain, which swallowed up two villages, is most tremendous. It presents an aspect of desolation too horrible and only to be compared to a stream of lava magnified.[99] The little Lake of Lauerz is pretty enough

---

95 *The Traveller's Guide Through Switzerland* (London, 1818) by Johann Gottfried Ebel (1764-1830) was the first comprehensive guidebook of Switzerland to be published in English.

96 Edward Cromwell Disbrowe (1790-1851), secretary to the British legation to Switzerland, 1820 to 1822. He was later MP for Windsor from 1823 to 1826, where his father was MP before him.

97 Arth is situated between the Rigi and Rossberg mountains.

98 The pasture on the slopes of Rossberg mountain.

99 In September 1806, amid heavy rainfall following large amounts of snow, there occurred a spectacular landslide off the Rossberg mountain. In the space of five minutes, an estimated 40 million cubic metres of rock enveloped the villages of Golau, Bussingen and Rothen, covering an area of approximately 20 square kilometres and killing 457 people.

and the environs of Schwyz must in fine weather be beautiful, but we had a wet evening for it and could not enjoy them.

Friday 27th. Left at five to go up the Muotta river, a fine gorge [the Muotta Thal], up which Suwarrow led his army, cavalry, infantry and all, retreating from the French and fighting all the way, along paths little more than sheep tracks.[100] Returned to breakfast and thence crossed the mountains, fine wild scenery, to Einsiedeln. This is a most extraordinary town, a frightful situation with bare hills and black turf valleys. A fine convent very like (as G. says) that at Stoneyhurst, but containing nothing worth seeing.[101] The rest of the town, with few exceptions, composed entirely of Inns, of which there are above <u>forty</u>. On the 14th of September there are here sometimes as many as 22,000 pilgrims from all parts of the world, to visit the shrine of Our Lady of the Hermits.[102] The best Inn is the Peacock which is tolerable.

Saturday 28th. Returned to Zug from Einsiedeln quite convinced there is nothing there to repay the trouble of going. Met numbers of pilgrims on their way and in the morning, before setting out, saw them drink each at the fourteen fountain spouts of the fountain, for fear of missing the one our Saviour is said to have drunk at. How or when is not explained.

Sunday 29th. Wet day, came from Zug to Lucerne in the carriage, instead of going by Immersee and Shüssnacht. The evening was clearer and we got a walk along the lake and river, which are highly beautiful. Our guide did not make his appearance.

Monday 30th. Went to see General Pfyffer's plan of the great part of Switzerland.[103] It seems very exact, beautifully executed on a scale of 13 pouces to a league in relief.[104] Of course, it occupies a largish room. It is very curious and was an ingenious idea of which he had the merit. It was begun at the age of 50 and occupied him 25 years.

The next object we visited was the Lion which is cut from a model of Thorvaldsen's, in the solid substance of a perfectly precipitous rock.

---

100   Alexander Suwarrow, also transliterated as Suvorov (1729-1800), a Russian general, fought a valiant retreat over the Alps in 1799 with 23,000 troops against a French army numbering 80,000 commanded by General Massena.

101   The Einsiedeln Benedictine abbey. Stonyhurst College is a Jesuit school near Clitheroe, Lancashire.

102   The Black Madonna in the Graces Chapel was the object of pilgrimage.

103   Franz Pfyffer (1716-1802), military officer and pioneering topographer, made a relief map of Switzerland.

104   A pounce is an historic Swiss unit of measurement.

It is intended to commemorate the fate of the Swiss Guards, and is to be opened to the public on the 9th of August, with a great fête.[105] The execution is fine, but the design is a little obscure. It is a Lion, pierced with a spear, and expiring upon the shield of France. The Lion is 30 feet long.

The environs of Lucerne are charming. It is the first place that gives us an idea of Swiss scenery. The Jesuit Church has a fine altarpiece, but otherwise there seems nothing remarkable in that or the Cathedral.[106] Our Inn the Balances very comfortable and remarkably civil people.

Tuesday 31st. Wet morning and afterwards a dark gloomy day—mended towards evening, and we have hopes of getting off tomorrow.

August 1821

Wednesday August 1st. Splendidly fine day, but intensely hot. Set out, I on foot George on horseback, with our sack behind him and a guide. Crossed the corner of the Lake from Winkel to Stansstadt, Pilatus[107] magnificent upon our right, then through a pretty rich valley as far as Grafenort, whence we begin rapidly to ascend, through a particularly fine gorge, the finest valley I have yet seen in Switzerland and from which I begin to have better hopes for the future. The valley is well wooded, with gigantic cliffs towering boldly far above them. The convent itself is not striking in its appearance, nor perhaps so well situated as it might have been; it stands, however, in a fine semi-circular plain, backed by fine snow mountains, so that it requires the preceding scenery to make one quarrel with it. The Cascade some way further on is a great height, but the scenery is not remarkable. The Inn, the Engel, is very dirty and bad.

Thursday 2nd. Returned to Grafenort by the same road, then turned to the right to Buochs. All this valley well wooded and beautiful. Took a boat down the Lake, 5 Leagues to Altdorf. All this part of the Vierwaldstätter See is very fine, but more especially the part between

---

105 Designed by Thorvaldsen, the *Lion Monument* was executed by Lukas Ahorn in 1820-21 to commemorate the Swiss Guards killed in 1792 when revolutionaries stormed the Tuileries Palace in Paris.

106 The construction of the Jesuit church began in 1667, and it was the first sizeable baroque church to be built in Switzerland north of the Alps. What Stanley calls 'the Cathedral' is the Church of Saint Leodegar, named after the patron saint of the city.

107 Mount Pilatus, which rises to 7,315 feet above sea level.

Schwyz and Flüelen, by Tellesplatte, ½ a league from Flüelen to Altdorf, not remarkable in any way.

Friday 3rd. The whole of this day's journey has been highly beautiful, the first part to Amsteg is very pretty. From thence, it becomes immensely fine, wild steep mountains, covered with fir woods, and not gloomy looking. The new road, which is being made at the expense of the four Cantons, is a very fine work, but there are great doubts whether it will ever be finished. From Wassen it becomes more wild and trees almost disappear, but the hills are so fine, one cannot quarrel even with desolation. The Pont du Diable disappointed me on the whole, though it [is] certainly a striking thing, but not equal to its reputation.[108] The passage through the rock and the sudden view of Andermatt, situated in a plain and with some fir trees about it, is curious and pleasing.[109] The Inn at the Hospital is tolerably good and comfortable.[110] It is said to be a corruption from a family who lived there called the Hospenthaler, many of whom still live at Altdorf. Met two Englishmen who are coming our way and with whom we must have a race for our beds tomorrow. 8 leagues today.

Saturday 4th. Set out at 7 along an uglyish valley, bare and bleak to the Realp, a round grass mountain where there are three hills and a gorge very like the division between Brown Moor, Ashgill and Long Canny.[111] The next mountain we cross has a very fine view. It is the Furca, 6,700 feet above the sea, covered with snow, and finely desolate.[112] Below it appears the Glacier of the Rhone, said to be the finest in Switzerland. If so, it disappoints me, being neither in shape nor colours so magnificent as I had anticipated. When, however, one considers it, it is a noble thing, but it loses from the prodigious scale of everything around. In this part, we first see the beautiful flower the Rose des Alpes [*Rhododendrom ferrugineu*], which is so hardy as to grow close by the Glacier and so delicate as to die at Berne. On the top of the last mountain is a stupendous view of desolation, not a tree, not a shrub, hardly a blade of grass to be seen, but inconceivably fine rock and for wild scenery the most magnificent I ever saw.[113] The House, the Grimsel, is wretched: but the poor people only live there half the year, from March to <u>November</u>! and

---

108 A twelfth-century bridge constructed over the rocky gorge of the River Reuss.

109 This is the Hole of Uri, a 180-foot tunnel which leads to the valley of Ursereu.

110 The Hospental. The main inn was the Meyerhof.

111 Possibly a reference to the Ashgill Force, a waterfall which runs down a gorge in Cumbria.

112 The Furca Pass, which rises to 7,969 feet above sea level at its highest point.

113 The Grimsel Pass, which rises 7,100 feet above sea level at its highest point, connects the upper valley of the Rhône with the upper valley of the River Aare.

it is not to be expected the Inn should be very good. In fact, it is worse than anything I have seen, except King House in Scotland!

Dined with our two Englishmen and three Swiss, and slept well, in spite of fleas.

Sunday 5th. Today has been all downhill, but tolerably fatiguing. The first two leagues gigantic and bleak; then appears the Rose des Alpes, and a few stunted pines; soon after in our favoured spot a pine or two, which increased to a wood near the chalets of Handegg; here is one of the finest cascades in the world. At least it is very little if at all inferior to Tivoli or Terni, formed by two rivers [the Aare and the Aerlenbach] which meet at a rock on which you stand, and in the moment of meeting fall down into an almost immeasurable abyss between perfectly precip-itous rocks, whose tops are covered with wood. The double rainbow on this fall had a beautiful effect, and the fall itself is highly picturesque, whether seen from above or below—it ought to be from both. The next three leagues are rather uninteresting, but the two last to Meiringen are quite charming. Savage enough, but the valley cultivated and smiling. Find out I knew both my Englishmen at Oxford. They are not first rate, but one of them, Hill, is very well. Stopped at a cabin about a league from Meiringen where we found the people <u>waltzing</u>—very good fun.

Monday 6th. Cloudy day, but walked over to Brienz from whence we took a boat to see the Falls of the Giessbach; beautiful scenery and a fine fall, or rather continuation of falls from the top of the hills to the bottom.[114]

Tuesday 7th. Detained by rain. An admirable set of people at the *table d'hôte* and two women and a man quite delicious.

Wednesday 8th. Dull cloudy morning, but decided on crossing the Scheidegg instead of going again by Brienz, which is dull to a degree, though the tops of the mountains here covered. The Reichenbach [Falls] which we went to see is not worth the trouble. The road up the moun-tain is pretty enough, the view at the top of the Wetterhorn is very fine and fortunately for us cleared so as to enable us to see it. We saw several avalanches, but none of them very good ones. The higher Glacier at Grindelwald is very <u>very</u> superior to that of the Rhone; it advances every year about 14 feet, and must in a few years overwhelm a Chalet, the owner of which <u>now</u> begs of every traveller as an anticipated *dédom-*

---

114 A succession of fourteen waterfalls descend from the hills of the Faulhorn through the
fir forest.

magement [compensation]. The situation of Grindelwald is good and I am glad we took this passage instead of going to Interlaken.[115]

Thursday 9th. Today has been a hard, but very beautiful, day's work. Crossed the lesser Scheidegg, which by the way is much the highest of the two, and which commands a splendid view, being just under the peak of the Jungfrau, and descended into the valley of Lauterbrunn, the most beautiful and romantic valley we have yet seen.[116] The Staubbach is not, indeed, worth seeing, but the whole valley is charming, and the view on coming into it magnificent.[117] It continues, well wooded, bold and beautiful, all the way to Interlaken, where we arrived at 4, after a ten leagues walk. G. in ecstasy at meeting Mrs and Miss Siddons and Kemble and Mrs K. the most vulgar woman I ever saw.[118]

Friday 10th. Wet day, just found an interval to go the bridge of Interlaken. A very pretty little town in very pretty scenery.[119] Met here Vernon, who has been staying to shoot Chamois with Lord Anson,[120] but they have never seen me.

Saturday 11th. Wet day again, determined not to wait, crossed the Lake [Thunnersee] to Thun, which is pretty I dare say, got immensely charged for a bad luncheon, resisted and succeeded. Came with Kynaston and Hill to Berne in a *Voiturier's* carriage. The latter is a very gentlemanlike man, the former middling. Stopped at the Couronne[121] and found a bundle of letters.

Sunday 12th. Thoroughly wet day again.

---

115 Situated at 3,250 feet above sea level, the village of Grindelwald has long been known for the grandeur of the mountains that surround it.

116 The valley of Lauterbrunn is deep and narrow and contained by precipitous, nearly vertical faces of limestone.

117 The Staubbach, a waterfall between 800 and 900 feet high, is also called the Dust Fall because its small stream of water disperses into spray. It was celebrated by Byron in his dramatic poem *Manfred,* which he set in the Bernese Alps.

118 The actress Sarah Siddons (1755-1831), known for her tragic roles such as Lady Macbeth, and her daughter Cecilia Siddons (1794-1868). Kemble is presumably the actor John Kemble (1757-1823), younger brother of Sarah Siddons, who married the actress Priscilla Hopkins (1756-1845).

119 There is a full view of the Jungfrau from Interlaken.

120 Thomas Anson, Viscount Anson (1795-1854) was a Whig politician who became known for his extravagant entertaining and gambling, and prodigious debts.

121 The Hotel Couronne in Thun.

Monday 13th. Cloudy day, with showers of rain. Berne a beautiful town, charmingly situated and well built.[122] There are no <u>very</u> remarkable buildings, however, except the old Cathedral, which presents the curious and interesting sight of a Catholic and Protestant place of worship under the same roof. The door is beautiful and very curious workmanship.[123] Met here the Talbots, and Wellesley and Mr Bain, a friend of George's who dined with us.

Tuesday 14th. Staid at Berne, looked about the town and bought prints. Environs beautiful.[124] A Hospital with an admirable inscription: *Christo in pauperibus* ['Christ in His Poor'].[125] Turned to rain in the evening.

Wednesday 15th. Fortunately for our journey the weather began to clear, and we set out around the middle of the day for Bienne. After the first league or two there is nothing pretty or interesting in the country and Bienne itself is a poor little town, situated at the foot of the hills and near the Lake, and yet not pretty, though I do not know what it wants to be so.[126]

Thursday 16th. A heavenly day at last. Set out in very good time. The road over the hills to Sonceboz is a pretty miniature of parts of the Tyrol, but at the latter place the valley widens and becomes very ugly. From hence we went to see Pierre Pertuis, a natural area of rock, through which the road to Basel passes, but except the curiosity there is nothing worth seeing.[127] Over the arch is an old Roman inscription, but except to an Antiquarian, quite illegible. Here they began to speak the French patois, it quite gave me pleasure to hear it again. At Chaux-de-Fonds is the great *fabrique* of watches and musical snuff boxes, the mechanism of which is very curious, particularly that for the process called *guillocher* [ornamentation resembling braided or interlaced ribbons] to the case of the watch. Bought a silver watch for 36F (30 shillings) and am told I gave 5F too much for it. From Chaux-de-Fonds and in coming down the hill on Neuchâtel we had a splendid sunset view of the distant Glaciers.

---

122 Berne is situated on a rocky promontory formed by the River Aar.
123 The door, made in 1475-85, depicts in relief the Last Judgement, flanked by figures of the wise and foolish virgins.
124 Views of the Bernese Alps.
125 The Great Hospital in Berne was built in the 1730s. The Latin motto over its entrance is attributed to the prominent Bernese physician Albrecht von Haller (1708-1777).
126 Bienne is situated at the mouth of the valley of the Suze, at the foot of the Jura mountains, and on the Bielersee.
127 Pierre Pertuis is the name of a tunnel formed out of a natural opening in the rock. Pertusa means 'bored through'.

Friday 17th. Went from Neuchâtel in a *Char à banc* to Neuveville, and from thence to Rousseau's Isle.[128] The Island belongs to the Hospital at Berne, the *receveur* of which lives here. The top ridge covered with trees is pretty enough and has a good view. There is here every year a great fête at the vintage time, to which people come from all the neighbouring Cantons for 4 successive Sundays. The room Rousseau lived in is a miserable garret, much such a thing as they show for Shakespeare at Stratford on Avon. It is said he preferred it, on account of a trapdoor, still shown, by which he escaped troublesome visitors. Returned by the side of the Lake to Neuchâtel, which is a nice little town enough, and the Lake [Neuchâtel] is the best specimen of the tame genre I have seen, with a fine view of the distant Glaciers. Tho' it was a glorious day, the sunset was hazy and we lost our view, which we had been looking forward to all day. Set out for Lausanne tomorrow. There is no attempt at architecture in Neuchâtel except the Hotel de Ville, which sports a heavy colonnade exceedingly bad and clumsy.

Saturday 18th. A glorious day and the road from Neuchâtel to Yverdon pretty enough: when, however, we reach the farther end of the Lake it is very ugly; a plain bare shore, covered with reeds, flat, tame and ugly: the town of Yverdon stands near it, and in every direction from the latter branch alleys of poplars. Had not the curiosity to see Pestalozzi's Institute.[129] I was afterwards rather sorry for it, but if I had wished I could not have done it, as it is not open either Saturday or Sunday. The Inn here very moderate.

Sunday 19th. Weakly we allowed our *Voiturier* to take us today by a *chemin de traverse* [a cross-country road], which I believe he repented afterwards as much as we did, besides having the pleasure of being abused for it. It is a horrible road, particularly after wet, and nobody should attempt it except in very dry weather. It is, however, in parts prettyish, winding through some very fine natural woods, which reminded me strongly of the wood commons in Surrey. The view down upon Lausanne is very striking and would have been splendid if there had not been such a haze that we could not distinguish the distant mountains.

　　Established, after some difficulty, in some very bad rooms in the Lion d'Or. Before we had got out of our carriage we were accosted by a man, who said he must introduce himself as a friend of Mr Ashton's, begged we could dine with him that day, and added a necessary piece

---

128　Sankt Peterinsel or l'île Saint-Pierre on Lake Biel or Bienne.
129　Johann Pestalozzi (1746-1826) was a Swiss pedagogue and educational reformer who established the Pestalozzi Institute in Yverdon in 1805.

of information, his name, Mr Elliott. Lady L. here, first enquiry was after F.[130]

Monday 20th. There does not seem much or anything to see in the town, but the country about it is pretty. Rode over with Rice to see Virnaud, a country house of M. Pauline, very prettily situated on a hill between two wooded hills, which are like a very beautiful gentleman's seat in England. Returned at four to dine with Lady Alvanley. A party in the evening, Lord and Lady Quin, she seems a very nice person.[131] Most of the others I did not admire. Find Ramsay here *en pension* [a lodger in a private house] with Rice. Hill and Kynaston set out today. Lausanne seems a sad gossiping tittle tattle town. Like a second rate bathing place in England. I should not like to live here.

Tuesday 21st. Called on Mrs Siddons. She and old Kemble very civil, but the latter very infirm.[132] Mrs K quite detestable. Dined at 2. Went again to Virnaud with Rice and G., drank tea at his pension, and saw a great deal of lovemaking between Mademoiselle L. and a young Prussian.

Wednesday 22nd. Though we never have seen the mountains, owing to a sultry haze in the air, we set out for a nearer view of them. The country to Vevey is pretty and background quite beautiful. Arrived at Bex, we found there the young Archduchess of Tuscany, in consequence of which we were obliged to go on to St Maurice.[133] This, however, we did not repent as the country is extremely beautiful and the situation of the little town itself very striking. The bridge, called Roman, is very fine.[134]

Thursday 23rd. On returning to Aigle at ½ past 11 we found all the horses under <u>taboo</u> for the Archduchess and had, therefore, the pleasure of waiting there till ½ past 8, when we set out and arrived at Vevey, where we slept in a good Inn the 3 Couronnes.[135]

---

130   Presumably Lady Lismore, whom Stanley had dined with in Rome. 'F' was the sportsman and horse racer Frank Hall Standish (1799-1840). In October, when Stanley was in Milan, Lady Lismore and Standish arrived together. Stanley thought Standish a fool.

131   Possibly Windham Henry Quin (1782-1850). He married Caroline Wyndham (1789-1870) in 1810 and succeeded as the 2nd earl of Dunraven in 1824.

132   John Kemble died in Lausanne in February 1823.

133   Maria Luisa, archduchess of Tuscany (1798-1857) was the daughter of Ferdinand III, grand duke of Tuscany.

134   Though perhaps built on Roman foundations, the bridge at St Maurice was in fact constructed no earlier than the fifteenth century.

135   The Three Crowns or Trois Couronnes was described in later handbooks for travellers as one of the best inns in Switzerland: large, comfortable, clean, and with a reading room well supplied with newspapers.

Friday 24th. Returned early to Lausanne. Called on Lady Alvanley and set out for Geneva. The road is pretty enough at the beginning and at the latter end. In the middle it is tame enough. It passes by Morges, where we visited the Milliner, by a nice looking place of Joseph Bonaparte[136] and by the Château de Coppet the residence of Madame de Staël.[137] We got in to wretched little rooms at the Schawn. Found Sir G. Talbot was there and paid him a visit.

Saturday 25th. To my great disappointment received only one letter here. Others have been sent, I am sure, to Berne, but I hope still to get them.

September 1821

Sunday September 2nd. Here is another week's gap in my journal, occasioned by having nothing to say. Received about a week ago a packet of six letters which had lain here [in Geneva] some time. Established in the Balance [Hotel La Balance], a decent Inn in the town, which is itself well enough and in one part really handsome. There is, however, nothing to do, nobody here, and as far as I can see no inducement for people to make it a permanent residence. We have now been here a week and, though the weather has been tolerably fine, it has never been so clear as to see Mt. Blanc. I have kept myself alive by playing tennis. We have dined twice with Sir G. Talbot. Tomorrow I play tennis again and dine with the D. of Leeds[138], who is going on to Italy.

[September] Sunday 9th. Tomorrow we quit Geneva. The town itself is very dull and there is little society. I have been doing nothing but play tennis with the Duke of Leeds in the morning and drive with him in the evening. The Duchess is a very nice good-humoured woman[139], and Lady C. charming.[140] I have been there four times this week and it has helped me to pass the time much more agreeably than I should otherwise have done. They are going on in about a month to Naples, where I shall be delighted to meet them again.

---

136 Joseph Bonaparte (1768-1844), elder brother of Napoleon, was king of Naples and Sicily from 1806 to 1808, and king of Spain from 1808 to 1813. After 1817 he mainly lived in the United States.

137 The novelist and writer Anne Louise de Staël (1766-1817), who was much admired by Byron. She established a salon at the Château de Coppet.

138 George Osborne, 6th duke of Leeds (1775-1838), who succeeded his father to the title in 1799.

139 Charlotte, née Townshend (1776-1856). She married the duke in 1797.

140 Lady Charlotte Osborne (1801-1836), daughter of the duke and duchess of Leeds.

On Thursday I dined with Sir G. Talbot and we drove on to Ferney.[141] The house is nothing remarkable, but commands a fine view, and two rooms and the garden are left precisely in the state in which Voltaire occupied them. The inscription he put up upon the neighbouring Church has been removed by the Government—*Deo erexit VOLTAIRE* ['Erected to God by VOLTAIRE'] was certainly a little strong.

Our weather is, I fear, breaking up and in that we shall not go to Chamonix. I am rather ashamed of leaving Geneva without having seen it, though to say truth I have no great curiosity to see it. George quite raves of Italy. Received yesterday at Hentsch's[142] a brochure called *Reflections on the Conduct of the Allies*.[143] The greatest stuff I ever read and that, with the hit at me in the end, makes me almost sure it can be by nobody but old Gore.[144]

Wednesday 12th September. Having been detained by my arm, which I hurt by a fall in the Tennis Court, we did not set out till this morning and I believe George thought it a worthy celebration of the day that we are now leaving Switzerland. Met with an accident at Thonon, which detained us three hours, so that we did not arrive at St Maurice till half-past ten. The whole of this side of the Lake [Geneva], except the first post, particularly the latter end, is very beautiful and I have great expectations from the Vallois which we enter on tomorrow. At 11 o'clock drank Mr and Mrs James's health in some very bad wine, not forgetting our friends at Knowsley. Wished we could join them for a little while. We are quite sure my Grandfather [the 12th earl of Derby] has been wicked, and wish Louisa joy of the day she has past.

Thursday 13th. Much disappointed with the beauty of the Vallois. There are, however, some striking exceptions. The situation of Sion upon two high rocky knolls is singular and highly picturesque and as a cascade the Pissevache is very fine: a fair day, but altered to heavy rain in the evening, falling in snow on the mountains, in consequence of which we stopped

---

141 The philosopher and writer Voltaire (1694-1778) bought the château at Ferney in 1758. There he wrote *Candide* and lived the last twenty years of his life.

142 Henri Hentsch (1761-1835) was a Swiss banker based in Geneva.

143 The anonymous political pamphlet *Reflections on the Conduct of the Allies* (1821) denounced the suppression of the 1820 Neapolitan revolution by the military intervention of the European powers, which re-established an absolute monarchy in the kingdom of the Two Sicilies. The pamphlet called on British statesmen to be worthy of their illustrious forebears and to support the cause of freedom and liberty in Europe. The author concluded (pp. 9-10): 'I could mention one illustrious youth, who, descended from a long and renowned ancestry, has already obtained a distinguished academic honour, and who seems destined to shed fresh lustre on his hereditary rank by his personal merits. But I forebear to dwell on this topic, lest I should offend the modesty I respect.'

144 Possibly the Anglican minister, pamphleteer and life-long Whig, Samuel Parr (1747-1825).

at Tourtemagne where we found a comfortable Inn [the Hotel Soleil], not the Post, and were very well here. Heard a wonderful account of three fir trees enclosed by the road side. Our Postilion first said that those English had found them very curious, had embraced each other, *se sont fait mille caresses, et sont restis ici vingt quarter heures* ['made a thousand caresses, and stayed twenty four hours']. Afterwards we heard an English Countess had gone up there and had a grand fête, had stayed there 24 hours, and bought and enclosed the trees, and our informant added that some other English had offered 500 Francs to have the trees cut down, but the Commune refused. There are, however, some plates upon the trees which would explain the whole.

[September, Friday] 14th. Set out in good time, but were stopped at Brig for want of horses. In consequence of which we took a walk to a little village called Artars where there is an old castle and some of the most beautiful country I ever saw. Set out from Brig about 3 o'clock, having been detained six hours. It is here that the great work of the Simplon begins.[145] The road is certainly very wonderful and the scenery magnificent, but as a work of art I own I think that the Mt Cenis is more extraordinary.[146] The galleries[147] so much talked of disappointed me in particular, and are not to be compared with the passage pierced through the rock near the Echelles de Savoie [on the Cenis Pass]. As it was getting late I walked the last stage over the Simplon, and got in at quarter past nine, an hour before the carriage. It was a wild cold windy night, with a bright moon at intervals. I am not sure that I did not see the mountain in this way to its full advantage, but the silence and solitary desolation were quite awful, particularly before and after the Barrière. The sound of a dog barking in the valley long below me was quite a comfort. The Inn at Simplon very comfortable and warm. There is nine months winter here and even in the three summer months there is frost most nights. It is now so cold that in the rooms not warmed by stoves one's teeth chatter with the chill.

Saturday 15th. Set out from the Simplon and the change of weather, sky, climate was instantaneous. I never was so sensible of the superiority of

---

145 The Simplon Pass, crossing from the Lepontine Alps to the Pennine Alps and connecting the Swiss canton of Valais with Domodossola in Piedmont, rises to a height of 6,636 feet. At Napoleon's order a route was built between 1801 and 1806 across the Simplon Pass, requiring the construction of 611 bridges, ten tunnels cut through the rock, and terraces to support the road.

146 The road over the Alpine Cenis Pass in Savoy, built by order of Napoleon between 1803 and 1810.

147 Tunnels hewn out of the rock at points along the road. The galleries were sketched by J. M. W. Turner in 1819.

Italian climate, and G. is in triumphant raptures. The descent on Domodossala is very striking and the country continues beautiful to Baveno, with the exception of one or two swampy valleys. The approach to Feriolo is charming and the beauty of the Lake [the west shore of Lago Maggiore] is beyond anything I should have conceived. We crossed over from Baveno to Laveno [on the east shore of the lake] and on our way stopped at the Isola Madre, the largest of the Borromean Isles. It is a sort of pleasure house belonging to the Count Borromeo who <u>lives</u> in the Isola Bella. It is laid out in the old style of stone slopes and terraces, planted with evergreens botanically arranged, and with a number of Pheasants half wild half tame. The house was built, or rather begun, for it is not yet finished, by a Count Borromeo who was a General in the service of Maria Theresa, and died here. His camp bed, his picture, and four others representing his principal exploits are religiously preserved. The Queen had hired this place for the summer, but abandoned it on some huff with the Milanese about Pergami.[148]

The wind got up very high and we reached Laveno late at night, with some trouble, but no danger. The Inn seems tolerably good and the people civil, but the *vini squisiti* [exquisite wines] which appears on the sign we have not found. The Boatmen are a merry race and did nothing but laugh and make us laugh. They cut various jokes about the *Costipazione* [Constipation], as they call the Constitution, a *gravissimna malaltia* [severe illness], of which many had died and of which the *guerigioni è pronta ma un po'penosa* [healing is ready but a little hard]. There was a proverb they quoted, which amused me much. It was this:

> *Nel Mill 'ottocento vent 'uno*
> *Comande nessuno*
> *Nel Mill 'ottocento venti due*
> *Comandano due.*[149]

Alluding to their two present kings.

Sunday 16th. Hired a boat and rowed over to the Isola Bella, the palace of the Count Borromeo. It is handsome enough in the old-fashioned style of terrace above terrace all raised artificially. The expense is said to be incalculable, but it cost less from troops being employed, as the house was laid out under the Count B. who was Viceroy of Naples from Spain.

---

148   During her exile from England, Queen Caroline of Brunswick appointed Bartolomeo Pergami as her principal servant. She lavished titles on him and it was widely assumed that they were lovers. This accusation was a central part of the case brought against her by George IV in his attempt to secure a divorce.

149   'In 1821 no one commands. In 1822 they command two.'

The gardens, however, cost £2,000 a year for repairs and the whole is on a similar scale. The pictures are moderate, but there are one or two good ones of Luca Giordano and one of Bassano,[150] which want cleaning. There is a colony of fishermen who have their nasty huts under the windows of the house, and who refuse an offer of double the value of their houses and new ones built, and will not leave the Island. We admired this independent sort of family pride, till our boatman gave us a worse solution: that at present Count Borromeo maintains all their old sick people, and they say he would not do so if they were further off. The refusal is the more ungrateful as he employs them all, and has the means of forcing them to go by applying to Government, but is too humane to do so.

In coming back we stopped by Pallanza, the effect of which is better from the Lake than nearer. The Boatman told us, in answer to our enquiring whether it was the custom to sing and dance in an evening that it had been, but was now forbidden by the Government!! Walked in the evening up the Chesnut Woods behind the town.

Monday 17th. Set out for Locarno and Bellinzona. The Lake very beautiful all the way up, but about the Islands is the best part. Cannobio is very prettily situated, but the hills are a little bare. From Magadino [at the mouth of the River Ticino] took a Char to Bellinzona,[151] a pretty town and a comfortable Inn at the Aquile.

Tuesday 18th. Returned to Laveno. Had a breakdown in the morning from our rickety char wheel breaking into 20 pieces, but no mischief done. A very agreeable excursion and well worth the trouble.

---

150 Jacopo Bassano (1510-1592).
151 Bellinzona, on the River Ticino, was dominated by three partly ruined castles, formerly the residences of three Swiss bailiffs deputed to govern the district.

VOLUME 4

Milan—Naples

19 September 1821 to 5 May 1822

Wednesday September 19th. We finally left Laveno for Varese, deter-
mining to be guided by circumstances as to staying there or going on
to Lugano. Our day was glorious, and the view back upon the mountains
of the Lago Maggiore was superb. When, however, we came above the
Lake of Varese we found a prettyish but very tame Lake with no features
to make it interesting except the distant view of these same mountains,
not so the view about the town. On the higher ground towards the left
the views are charming, and especially the Monte Sagro, with its large
irregular line of chapels offers a beautiful and striking prospect. At
Varese we had a violent dispute with the Postmaster, which ended in
his complete discomfiture before his own arbiter the Officer of the
Gendarmes, and in our taking *Voiturier* horses. Passing by the Monte
Sagro the new road goes up a steep hill and descends again into the
Valgana. It might have been carried along the Vale, but the entrepreneur
being some Signor di Milano who had campagne on the hill it was
carried thus for their accommodation. The road, however, to do them
justice, is admirable. The Valgana is barren and dreary, and not bold
enough even for that style of beauty, but when you leave it, and reach
the top of the hill arriving down on Ponte Tresa, the beauty of the scene
which opens upon you is beyond description. I think this is the most
beautiful thing we have seen in Italy or anywhere else. Groves of chesnut
trees, white villages scattered here and there, ground beautifully tumbled
in all sorts of shapes, two reaches of the Lake [Lugano] gleaming beneath
your feet, and separated by a bold and rocky promontory, and in the
distance the white Church of S. Salvador perched upon its towering
mountain, such is the descent on Ponte Tresa, the boundary between
Austria and [the Swiss canton of] Ticino. On the Swiss side of the

wretched bridge[1] is a turn among houses, all but impracticable. Apparently left to make the road more difficult from a remnant of mistrust of their neighbours, which I think ought to have prevented their making this road, as well as the one from Como. From Ponte Tresa to Lugano the road is very beautiful, but more particularly the part which comes down the hill upon the latter town. As we walked in the evening along the new road it put us both in mind of the Strada Nuova and Naples and Vesuvius in miniature. The town and mountain behind it here in effect very like. The inside of the town is dirty and the Inn but very moderate.

Thursday 20th. As our boatmen took us in the morning to Porlezza, apropos of the place of execution, they gave us an account of their government and politics, upon which they seemed tolerably well informed. They said the Council of I forget how many were changed every six years; that they elected by ballot, and that every man who possess 200 Swiss Francs (300 French or about £12) were allowed to vote. They said it had frequently been discussed in the Council whether or no they should give themselves to Austria, that some of their upper classes were in favour of it, but that the lower were one and all determined to die rather than yield to them. They said that the Milanese gave as much as 8 to 10,000 Francs for substitutes to serve in Italy, for 8 years, but this I cannot believe, though he added he had had the offer made to him, and on my asking with some surprise if he had refused the offer, he said *Lo, Signor! Morriei di fame puittosto che entrare nel servizio Imperiale* ['Lo Signor! I would starve rather than enter Imperial service']. He said their own elders had just been made to go into the Canton of Fribourg, which are also by ballot.

Our excursion on the Lake was pleasant enough and we returned well satisfied to Lugano, though the mountains about this Lake are too barren and the effect of the Lake altogether inferior to Lago Maggiore.

Friday 21st. Set out for Como. The road is pretty as long as it keeps along the Lake, which it crosses by a ferry, but when it leaves it the country changes for the worse. The first view of Como is of very second rate beauty. The hills on the right are pretty, and an old Tower (of Baradello[2]) in the distance stands well on the summit of a high green hill. But the hills on the left are bare without boldness and the town, situated in a swampy plain, is too large and covered with red tiles, which have a very ugly effect. Within it is but paltry. We did not like the Angel

---

1   A wooden bridge with stone pillars that was rebuilt with stone in 1846.
2   The surviving fabric of Castello Baradello.

and drove to the Couronne, situated out of the town and comfortable enough. Como seems full of Austrian and Tyrolean troops and one hears nothing but drums and bugles. The Cathedral is very handsome in its style, which is a sort of mixture of Gothic and Italian, which I rather like.[3] We could not get where we wanted on the hills, because all the paths into and through the vineyards are now shut up on account of the approaching vintage: but we found one beautiful point of view on the hill immediately behind the Villa Adelaide.

Saturday 22nd. Having found out that Comte Frederic Confalonieri[4] is here we called on him this morning, and finding him still in bed at ½ past 11 we left the book and a note, and took a boat to the Queen's Villa, the Villa d'Este, or as it is called here the Villa d'Estra.[5] On going to it one passes by a piece of deformity lately built by in a swamp by General Pino[6] with little painted red battlements, etc. in a style that outTwisses Twiss.[7] The Villa is a fine looking house, but now going to ruin. It has been fitted up at immense expense and I think with bad taste, except the Theatre which is beautiful. The gardens are horrible and the celebrated grotto in vile taste. The Adam and Eve, fig leaves and all, are now in the house. Upon this point of the evidence I am not quite convinced. If the statues were in the round room, it is just possible a man about one corner of the ceiling of the other room might by stooping down see one of the niches, but if the statues were in the further room, he could not by any possibility see either of them. Our *custode* was a stupid fool and rather insolent. The upper rooms could not be seen, as there was an express order against it. In the further part of the grounds appears General Pino's taste again in a multitude of walls, towers, fortifications, etc. looking as if they were made of red and white pasteboard.

Sunday 23rd. We were to have set off today for Cadenabbia, having made our agreement last night with the boatman, who after asking 20 francs a day, agreed to take 12, but besides that the morning looked

---

3   Como Cathedral, constructed between 1396 and 1521, was largely made of marble.
4   The Italian patriot Conte Federico Confalonieri (1785-1846), a member of the Carbonari, was responsible for inciting the insurrections in Lombardy in 1820-21. He was imprisoned by the Austrians in December 1821 and exiled to the United States in 1835.
5   Queen Caroline of Brunswick bought the Villa d'Este in 1815, where she lived with Pergami amid scandalous rumour.
6   Domenico Pino (1760-1826), born in Milan, was one of Napoleon's generals. After participating in the Peninsular War and Russian campaigns, he was given command of the army of Italy. He retired to Lake Como in 1815 and died there eleven years later. His wife, the ballerina Vittoria Peluso, inherited the Villa d'Este from her father.
7   Possibly a reference either to the travel writer Richard Twiss (1747-1821) or the drama critic Francis Twiss (1759-1827).

threatening. We received a very civil note from Comte Confalonieri asking us to dinner today, in consequence of which we determined to stay. Walked up to the old tower of Baradello, which is still entire, though the old fortifications of it are of course ruined. The only entrance was by a bridge to a door halfway up which still remains, and there is the entrance to a *souterrain*, where they say three roads branched off underground, one to the city and two others to different villages, but I suspect exaggeration here. Day cloudy and bad, and I fear our weather is going to break up just when we want it fine. Another week of it would not much signify. Just returned from dining at Comte Confalonieri's where we had a pleasant party enough; he is a remarkably agreeable man, and she is very well.[8] A comical medley of people, as the Prima Donna of the Opera and another Singer dined there, and the General-in-Chief of the North of Italy called in the evening. A horrible night and no hopes for tomorrow.

Monday 24th. Dark cloudy day—walked among the hills, but driven down by an approaching thunderstorm. Just got home in time. We shall, I think, certainly set out for Milan tomorrow as there little chance of settled weather.

Thursday 25th. Contrary to all our expectations today has been a beautiful day. In consequence of which we set out upon our Lake excursion. The first part of the Lake of Como is too much covered with Houses and trim Villas. All is artificial and the Villas themselves look too much like Boxes. Torno is, however, very pretty. After turning the point the Lake widens and on the right is the Villa called Pliniania, not because it was the residence of Pliny, but because there is a very singular fountain there, which forms the subject of one of his letters and which he describes as ebbing and flowing three times a day.[9] It continues to do so to this moment. Succeeding naturalists have been as little able to account for the phenomenon as he was. The only difference between his account and the actual state of the case is that these ebbings and flowings are not *certis monumentis*[10] (which I think is his expression) but irregularly, except that it is three times in the 24 hours. It is at present built over with a detestable grotto, and the house is stuck under a rock, facing north, and never seeing the sun. At 100 yards off would be a beautiful situation for a villa. The cascade is in its way fair enough. That is, as a

---

8   Conte Confalonieri married Teresa Casata (1787-1830) in 1804.
9   Villa Pliniania was built on the shore of Lake Como in 1573 by the governor of Como, Giovanni Anguissola, and was named after the Roman writer Pliny the Younger (AD 61-114), who came from Como.
10   A quote from Pliny the Younger's *Epistulae*.

thread of water falling down 200 feet, but it cannot compare with a very beautiful one a little higher up called the Orrido di Nesso: which you don't see till you come close to it, but when you do it forms a perfect picture, being crossed by two bridges and the hills between which it falls beautifully speckled with trees and houses. The Villa Balbianello, built by Cardinal Durini, is beautifully situated on the promontory of Lenno, commanding a very fine view both ways.[11] The house is now to sell, by Government, who, it is said, ask from 12 to 16,000 Francs for it. The late owner, named I think Sporra, having been convicted of Carbonarism, their property has been confiscated.[12]

Arriving at Cadenabbia, or Cà di Nabbia, that is in old Italian change house or halfway house, the first thing we went to see was the Villa Sommariva [now called Villa Carlotta]. The situation of it is splendid and possesses every advantage of natural beauty. But we could not help remarking that the present proprietor was a man of no taste and had done everything he could to spoil it.[13] For instance, grubbing up the old chestnut trees of a beautiful wooded knoll and making serpentine walks bordered with rows of plantains and acacia; obtained possession of this house [in 1801] by sending the Countess Bigli a note to demand within 24 hours a particular sum, saying if it could not be paid, he would take her house instead, and these conditions she was obliged to accept. His income is now supposed to amount to about 500,000 Francs a year. Being separated from his wife, he allows her 25,000 and to his only son, a Colonel in the French service, whom I should think he was not on very good terms, 10,000 more. The remainder is all laid out on his house, his grounds, pictures, statues and, as I said before, with very little taste. It is a great pity that he has not a room more worthy to receive the splendid frieze which Thorvaldsen is finishing for him at Rome.

Friday, the evening drawing on and not a very fine sunset, we determined not to ascend the promontory but go to the Villa Melzi.[14] This is

---

11   Villa Balbianello was built in 1787 by Cardinal Durini (1725-1796).

12   The villa was in fact owned by the Italian republican nationalist Luigi Porro-Lambertenghi (1780-1860), who inherited it from his uncle Cardinal Durini in 1796. Under Porro-Lambertenghi's ownership, Villa Balbianello became a centre of republican activity and a meeting place for the Carbonari. In 1820 Porro-Lambertenghi was forced to leave for Belgium.

13   The proprietor during Stanley's visit was the banker, politician and art collector Giovanni Battista Sommariva (1760-1826). A man of humble origins, Sommariva had amassed a large fortune as Napoleon's representative in Milan. He was a patron of Canova and Thorvaldsen, and carried out extensive modifications to the buildings and grounds of the Villa Sommariva.

14   Built on the shore of Lake Como between 1808 and 1810 and designed by Giocondo Albertolli, the Villa Melzi acquired the popular name of the Pearl of Lake Como. Staying there in 1810, the French novelist Stendhal described it as affording the most beautiful view in the world after that of the Bay of Naples.

by far the most beautiful of all the Italian Villas I have seen, uniting the beauty of Italian architecture and an Italian climate to the comfort of an excellent English country house. It now belongs to a young man of about 23, to whom it was left with the Dukedom by his uncle the late Duke of Melzi.[15] This was a gentleman who I should rather think feathered his nest also at the expense of the country under the French, having filled the office of *Guarda Sigillo*, where he made a great deal of money. The young man has not been long married and in possession of an income of 400,000 Francs a year. There is nothing very remarkable in the way of painting or of sculpture in the house, except some very good busts, chiefly of the Bonaparte family, but there is an air of comfort, luxury and taste combined very different from the *parvenu* air of the Sommariva *ménage*. In fact the Melzi's are an old family of nobles, originally I believe Spanish. In the garden at one end is a private Chapel, where there is a monument to the late Duke, and at the other end a good group of Dante and Beatrice, the former figure stiff and not good, the latter light, easy, graceful and expressive.[16] To add to the conveniences of this Villa there is a *strada carrozzabili* to Milan, an advantage not to be despised.

In returning home our boatmen entered into a comparison between the French and Austrian government. Formerly, they said, the people had hardly any taxes, and in particular the stamp duty *carte bollata* was unknown. The French laid on heavy duties, levied contributions and conscriptions, and oppressed them in every possible way. The return of the Austrians was hailed with delight, but, instead of relieving them as was expected, they have continued precisely the same system as the French, not taken off a single grievance, and even continued most of the same persons in office. They are all discontented to the highest pitch and want an opportunity to break out, but with all their own troops in Hungary, and forty thousand Hungarians and Austrians in Milan itself, what can they do?

We returned about 7 to our Inn, where the people are remarkably civil and the house tolerably comfortable.

Wednesday 26th. Went today further up the Lake, which, however, I think inferior in point of beauty to the others, being more barren and presenting fewer objects to catch the attention. We went up as far as Rezzonico, which commands a magnificent view very nearly to the top, and walked some way above an old town which stands near, from whence there is a fine superior view. In returning our boatmen pointed out the

---

15   Francesco Melzi d'Eril (1753-1816), who also held the title duke of Lodi, was, under Napoleon, vice-president of the Cisalpine Republic from 1797 to 1802 and grand chancellor of the kingdom of Italy from 1805 to 1814.

16   The sculpture was made by Giovanni Battista Comolli (1775-1831) in 1813.

Sasso Rancio, a tremendous pass, whence the Austrians passed with cavalry and lost many of their horses, which fell into the Lake. Nearly opposite is Bellano, a village which makes annually about 30,000 brenti[17] of wine, each brenta being, if I mistake not, 96 bottles. It is, however, very cold, facing nearly north, while its neighbour Varenna looks due south, which gives rise to the proverb.

> *Se vuoi pevar li penco dell inferno,*
> *L'eslati a Varenna, a Bellan l'inderno.*

They have a vast number of these proverbs, of which some are very good and some very moderate, as for example on the same Varenna, a little mercantile place on a rock.

> *Varenna è situate sopra un scopio:*
> *Del mio non ho, del tuo non vaglio,*
> *Ma suppose chi o viver voglio.*

There is another which says *Il Lago di Como è quasi un nomo*—of which they make the Lake of Lecco and the corresponding branch the two legs, and the two woody knolls at Bellagio the *coglioni* [testicles]. This, however, they dare not say to any inhabitant of Bellagio.

On this promontory stood the two villas of Pliny, and for situation nothing can be conceived more beautiful. The proprietor, however, is not a man of good taste and have done a good deal to spoil it. It might, however, with very little alteration be charming as it has the finest view of the whole Lake. In coming down we passed the Villa Giulia, being a large staring house, with a straight vista on each side to the Lake, not a tree near it and on the Cadenabbia side being nothing more than an immense ditch cut artificially between two stone walls to let in a view of the Lake at a quarter of a mile, which after all it only does to the upper stories.[18] We afterwards refreshed ourselves by walking in the gardens of the Villa Melzi and returned to Cadenabbia.

Having seen my Servant with some peaches I asked him what he had given for them. He said he had 13, which were beautiful, and he had given the woman 10 Sous (5d) and might have had them for 5. She afterwards brought him a large packet of figs, for the whole of which he gave 5 Sous more, and she kissed his hand, calling him *Vostra Excellenza.*

---

17 A Milanese measurement of liquid volume: one brenta equals 75.6 litres.
18 The Villa Giulia, completed in 1806, was built by Count Pietro Venini and named after his wife.

Tuesday 27th. Went down to the Lake of Lecco, as the other division of the Lake of Como is called, meaning to take horses from Lecco and return to Como. The voyage is uninteresting enough, the mountains being very bare and the Lake monotonous. Bellano stands well enough, and Lecco itself is not amiss. It has a handsome stone bridge which was destroyed by the French, but since rebuilt. At Lecco the Inn keepers great rascals and *d'accord* together. So not being able to agree about horses or carriage we returned to Cadenabbia.

Friday 28th. Returned in good time to Como, met no less than 8 families going to Cadenabbia. Met some of the Douaniers on the water, à propos of which our men told us that the Contraband system was carried on to a great extent in connivance with the Officers: but that all English goods were absolutely contraband and could not pay duty. Another proof of the obligations we have to our wise Ministers and their Austrian friends. Dined at Como and got to Milan in the evening, where we dined again. The Inn quite full and moderate rooms.

Saturday 29th. The first day at Milan was devoted to regular sightseeing. The beauty of the Dome I had no conception of. It is the most perfect specimen of Gothic architecture, where it <u>is</u> Gothic, that I ever saw in my life. The façade is Italian and, therefore, its effect bad, but all the rest is superb, except that the highest point of all strikes me as being too sharp, tall and pagodaish. When on the roof, the effect of the minarets and spires all around is amazingly striking, and the carving on some of them seemed to me good. We went to the top to take a panoramic view of the city, which is much larger than I had expected to find it, but not so well built and very irregular. The statues in the inside of the Cathedral appeared to me too large for the building, at the very extremity they appear gigantic. From the Duomo we passed to the Museum, the only collection of pictures in Milan. The room is splendid, but the pictures, except three or four, are not very good. There is a superb Guido, St. Paul arguing with St. Peter, and a very fine Salvator, but damaged. I think these are much the best. There is also a good Vandyke, Marie de Medici. From the Museum we went by the Piazza d'Armi and along the present road to the intended Arch of Triumph, which would have terminated the Simplon Road. The design is very noble and would have [been] a grand termination to the work, but at present it is only completed to one third of its height, and though the Emperor of Austria[19] has signed an order for completing it, it is not to be expected that it will be carried into execution at least for the present. The magazines upon the spot are full

---

19   Emperor Francis I (1768-1835), who reigned from 1804 to 1835.

of stone already cut, medallions, prepared statues finished and only waiting to be put up. The chief defect of the plan appeared to me a deficiency of width in the centre arch, but possibly this is occasioned by the scaffolding which still remains. The expense still remaining to carry it in to execution is estimated as 2 million Italian Lira, about £85,000. The Piazza Dormi which the road was then to have crossed is a fine spacious plain, serving for reviews and military exercises, and bound sat the opposite end by the old Castle, a large heavy square ugly building, which the road was to have entered, and which would therefore probably have been altered. On the left of the plain stands the Arena: an oval building of immense size, open at the top, and in fact presently resembling the old Roman Amphitheatre. It contains a large portico on one side serving for the Viceroy and Court when they assist at the Games, the rest being nothing but ranges of grass banks, which were I believe to have been covered with stone. At one end is the Scuderia, where the chariots enter for the race, at the other the principal entrance, very simple, handsome and classical, the frieze adorned with ancient chariots in bas relief, etc. The arena is capable of being floated, and a Naumachia [a staged naval battle] was represented there on the occasion of the K. of Rome's christening. After passing the Castle, the road was to have gone in a straight line, pulling down some bad streets, to the Dome, which would have been a noble ending. From hence we finished our long day's walk with a visit to the Villa Bonaparte, at present the residence of the Viceroy,[20] but fitted up chiefly by Eugène de Beauharnais, when he was here as Viceroy.[21] It is altogether a beautiful <u>small</u> palace, charmingly fitted up in the <u>best sort</u> of French taste. The garden, an English Garden as it is called, is very paltry.

In the evening we went to the Scala,[22] a magnificent theatre, and I think handsomer, though apparently smaller, than the S. Carlo at Naples. It is besides ill lit and the most noisy I ever was in.

Sunday 30th. Windy nasty day. Went, however, to the public gardens where the military band were playing, and the people were assembled. But it was a bad day and the collection was moderate. Sent my letters to Conte Crivelli and Conte Cicogna, the latter is not in Milan.[23]

---

20   Giulio di Sotto was viceroy of Milan and Lombardy from 1818 to 1830, having been appointed by the Austrians.
21   Eugène de Beauharnais (1781-1824) was Napoleon's stepson and viceroy of the kingdom of Italy from 1805 to 1814.
22   La Scala opera house, built in 1779.
23   Ferdinando Crivelli (1767-1856) and Francesco Cicogna (1748-1823), both of prominent Milanese families.

October 1821

Monday October 1st. Went to see the famous Cenacolo by Leonardo da Vinci.[24] It is certainly very much damaged, but not as much as I had expected. The head of our Saviour is particularly beautiful, as is a figure leaning on the table in the right hand corner. Dined with Comte Crivelli, a good-humoured rather agreeable old man, if he was not very like General Ross.[25] Our party was of 12, the Duke Visconti, the Governor, the French Consul, Lord and Lady Kinnaird, and some other persons whom I did not know.[26] We had a rather agreeable dinner and I was received quite *a bras ouverts* [with open arms]. Nothing could exceed their civility. Theatre in the evening.

Saturday 6th. The weather has today broken up and I imagine the wet season is now setting in. On coming out of the Theatre I met Labouchere to my great astonishment.[27] We stared at each other some time, neither of us being sure of the other, but when we were our greeting was most cordial. Yesterday I went with him to lionise him and afterwards to see the Imperial Palace, which is full of fine rooms, but nothing else to see except some paintings of Appiani, whom I think very bad.[28] He dined with us yesterday and told me a great deal of English news, which I had not heard before. Just as we had done dinner Agar Ellis came in.[29] He is, I believe, on his way south, but I do not know. We all went to the Italian Comedy which I thought very bad. Today I dine with Labouchere and am afterwards to be presented at the Casino di Nobili by Comte Crivelli. The Casino was rather pleasant, though it is a bad institution, birth being alone an introduction to it and there being no power of excluding a noble or admitting one who is not so. Billiards, cards, etc. are played, but no games of chance. Ladies are admitted and sometimes

---

24   *The Last Supper* in the convent of Santa Maria delle Grazie.
25   Presumably Robert Ross (1766-1814), a British general who served in the Napoleonic Wars and the War of 1812 with the United States. He was killed in the battle of Baltimore in 1814.
26   Lord Kinnaird married Lady Olivia FitzGerald, daughter of the 2nd duke of Leinster, in 1806.
27   Henry Labouchere (1798-1869) was a contemporary of Stanley's at Christ Church, Oxford. In 1826 he became the Whig MP for St Michael, and then MP for Taunton in 1830. He served in the governments of Lord Grey, Lord Melbourne and Lord John Russell.
28   Andrea Appiani (1754-1817), who painted a fresco depicting Apollo and the Muses in the dining room of the royal palace.
29   George Agar-Ellis (1797-1833), Whig MP for Seaford and a man of letters, was another contemporary of Stanley's at Christ Church, Oxford. In 1822 he married Lady Georgiana, daughter of the 6th earl of Carlisle, and in 1832 he was raised to the peerage as Lord Dover.

come. I played two games of billiards with Comte Crivelli and won. In the evening Comte Cicogna very civil, going to his campagne, but returns on the 15th.

Sunday [7th]. Wet day. Lord Clare and Mr Sneyd arrived.[30] Ellis gone to see Como.

Monday 8th. Written to Hammersley and Hentsch about my lost letter of credit.[31]

Tuesday [9th]. Found said letter. From hence till Friday nothing particular. Opera almost every night. D. of Leeds arrived Monday. Dined there on Wednesday, Ellis and Dr Ciceri.[32] On Thursday 11th dined with Comte Crivelli, who almost a request that I would send him from England some English gunpowder, which I promised whenever I had an opportunity.

Saturday 13th. Clare and Sneyd dined with us yesterday, before which we walked to the Church of Chiaravalle. This was a very celebrated old convent, but why people go there now I cannot conceive as there is no appearance of beauty, or anything to see in the Church. Today they are gone to the Lake Como, Ellis is gone home. Went this morning with Brecknock and Rice[33] to see the body of St Carlo Borromeo,[34] dressed in his robes of state with the face exposed, in a magnificent tomb covered with silver in the most beautiful workmanship, the whole shrine composed of the same materials and of crimson and gold embroidery: the case in which is kept the body is of rock crystal, with an upper case of solid silver, and in every direction in this splendid pageantry the eye is struck with Humilitas in gold letters.
   'And the Devil smil'd, for his favourite Vice was Pride, that Ap'd Humility'![35]

---

30   John FitzGibbon, 2nd earl of Clare (1792-1851) succeeded to the title in 1802. He had a passionate attachment to Lord Byron while he and Byron were schoolboys at Harrow. 'Mr Sneyd' was Ralph Sneyd (1793-1870) of Keele Hall, Staffordshire.

31   Hugh Hammersley (1774-1840) of Hammersley, Greenwood and Brooksbank, a bank based at 69 Pall Mall. In 1840 the bank was acquired by Coutts and Co.

32   Dr Ciceri was a prominent physician in Milan. He had attended the severely wounded Colonel Brown in January 1821.

33   George Pratt (1799-1866) was styled earl of Brecknock from 1812 to 1840 when he succeeded his father as 2nd Marquess Camden. Thomas Spring Rice (1790-1866) was a Whig MP who served in the governments of George Canning, Lord Goderich, Lord Grey and Lord Melbourne. He became comptroller general of the exchequer in 1835 and was created Lord Monteagle in 1839.

34   Carlo Borromeo (1538-1584), a cardinal and archbishop of Milan, was buried in Milan Cathedral and canonised by Pope Paul V in 1610.

35   A quote from the poem 'The Devil's Thoughts' by Samuel Taylor Coleridge (1772-1834),

Went to the Scala this evening, found the D. of Leeds not yet gone. He sets out, however, early tomorrow morning. Rice and Brecknock set off on Monday and we shall follow on Tuesday. Meantime, among the arrivals here, are Lady Lismore and Standish (F.H.), whom I called on yesterday and who seems a greater fool than ever. We have also been honoured by the presence of Mr and Mrs Rowley and Lord and Lady Weymouth, with her sister![36] They are all, however, gone I believe south.

Tuesday 16th. Left Milan, a gloriously fine day. The Milanese a very curious country from its irrigations, as you often see water in four or five different levels in one field. Rice prohibited within five miles of the town. Apropos would not rice grow on our moss lands in Lancashire when it is too wet for other crops? The great shrines of the irrigations are at Pavia, but we did not stop to see them or the Certosa, which is very rich in fine marbles, but contains nothing else.[37] Pavia is a very fine town, but a little on the decline. From hence the country becomes a little more like what indeed it is, Piedmontese. Towards Novi it seems flat and swampy, but it was getting night and we could not well see. A new road from Genoa to Parma will be open next month, going by Tortona and thereby nearly ruining Novi. Inn at Novi the Genossa tolerable.

Wednesday 17th. The road from Novi execrable and I think not the least pretty except for the first part of the Castello as you come on the River Lemme, till you begin to descend the hill to the town very properly called Campo Morone, being thickly studded with Chesnuts the whole way. G. suggested and I think with probability that the Bocchetta [Pass] may be a corruption of Boschetto [a grove of trees]. The people are a very fine race and show a great deal of costume. In short, they are more Neapolitan than any other Italians I have seen except perhaps about Como, which they much resemble. There seems an immense quantity of traffic along this road, all on mules. I am sure I am not exaggerating when I say we met at least five hundred today. From Campo Morone we coast the river the whole way to Genoa. Here the new road to Parma branching off, which will, therefore, avoid the tremendous hill of the Bocchetta, the descent from which by the way reminded me strongly of that from Mont Cenis upon Susa.

The first view of Genoa is superb indeed. It seems amazingly strong

---

which was first published in September 1799.

36   Thomas Thynne, Viscount Weymouth (1796-1837) was the eldest son of the 2nd marquess of Bath. Against his family's wishes, he married Harriet Robbins in 1820.

37   The Certosa is a monastic complex north of Pavia built between 1396 and 1495. It was founded by Gian Galeazzo Visconti, 1st duke of Milan, as atonement for his murder of his uncle and father-in-law.

and the line of the bay is beautiful, hardly, indeed, inferior to Naples, except that there is something bleak and chilling in the hills which back it, which does not remind one of the warm and glowing atmosphere of Naples. We took a stroll along the Docks before dinner, which we have just dispatched and the waiter in returning held the following dialogue. *Commanda huite alto sta sera? Grazie, sta sera minite Perla colozine domattina?*—being duly informed—*Ah, Capito! Molto bene! Derugue, augouand Coro un a fibissima nolte, ho l'onor deun lor servo rumiblissimo!*—accompanied with very appropriate action. I did restrain my laugh till the man had shut the door, when it exploded violently. Tomorrow we begin our peregrinations through the town.

Thursday 18th. After a night's rain, with the most violent and tremendous thunder and lightning I ever heard, we set out in a horrible wet day to see Palaces, Churches, etc. Our first visit was the Church of St Syr [San Siro], a magnificent building inside, with splendid colouring of marble. The outside has nothing to boast of; the façade is only just finished, and though not handsome is composed of white marble. The Palazzo Brignole (Palazzo Rosso) contains some very beautiful pictures. The best seemed to me a portrait by Bordone,[38] quite superb, a Christ bearing the Cross, two or three portraits by Vandyke, a Holy Family, Guercino,[39] and a portrait by Titian. This Palace seems tolerably well kept up. The [Palazzo] Carrega we wished to have seen, but could not gain permission, it is said there are some good pictures.

The Palazzo Durazzo [also known as the Palazzo Doria] gives one a sad idea of the decaying state of Genoa. The Palace is let to the King, but the old grey-haired servant, the image of the old butler at Wolf's Cray, would not acknowledge this for the honour of the family and only said that when the King came he was always *allozziato qui*. The gallery of pictures, which was very fine, has nearly disappeared also and there remains scarcely anything but copies and daubs. My old friend here rather overdid his part, pointing out the pictures *Tha opervi Signor, questo è un quadro veramenti superbo—me veda quanto è bello questo*. Accounting for the loss of a Paul Veronese, which I since find was bought last year, I believe by Lord Templeton, he said, *Sono state molti combiamento, era que è vero, ma dove l'hau masso adesso, io non Sapici din precisamente. Ha venduti alcuni quadri il Signor Marchese, none è vero? Ma*, with the Italian shrug, *cose si dire, ma caro lei, ne pa tauti*, as if making his Master's excuse. The Terrace commanding a view of the Harbour is magnificent, of black and white marble; but evidently like

---

38 The Venetian painter Paris Bordone (1500-1571).
39 Giovanni Francesco Barbieri (1591-1666), known as Il Guercino.

the rest going to ruin. To satisfy the old man's family pride, however, I praised everything and rather increased my usual *buona grazia* at parting.

The University is just opposite, but it is now shut up and occupied by troops. Genoa, however, still angry, at least the privilege of being free from Austrian troops, and of being garrisoned by only 5,000 Piedmontese. The old Church of St Laurent [also referred to as Genoa Cathedral] is very curiously built, both without and within. It is composed entirely of black and white marble alternately: the outside is in a sort of bastard Gothic, and the aisles within are separated from each other by a double row of arches one above the other. The famous Sacro Catino[40] we could not see till tomorrow. The guidebook gravely tells you that the best critics are in doubt whether this is really the dish out of which our Saviour [shared] the Passover with his disciples. It is composed of a solid Emerald!!!!

The Palazzo Ducale contains a noble staircase, and the small salon is very beautiful, but the great Sala di Consiglio of the old times of Genoa is, I think, one of the finest rooms I ever saw in my life.[41] Its marble statues were destroyed by the revolutionary fury in 1797 and have been replaced by casts. In the Palazzo Serra [di Cassano] there is one remarkably beautiful salon, not very large, but splendidly and very handsomely furnished and well worth a visit. In the afternoon walked along the quays and to the end of the Mole, then round then line of batteries which seem immensely strong on the S.W. side of the city. Rice and Brecknock dined with us and staid till ½ past 11! Such a visitation was never inflicted. They are neither of them bright, but the latter is the stupidest man I know. He never once opened his mouth except to yawn.

Friday 19th. After settling with *Voituriers*, Felucca [a small two-masted ship] people, Police, etc. for setting out tomorrow, we went on with sightseeing. Genoa appears to me the place on the whole Continent where there is the most imposition attempted and practiced on foreigners; where there is a greater number of people without regular employ and who consequently are a nest of Harpies who seize, on all sorts of pretences, on strangers. One can hardly believe that any government authorises a fixed and exorbitant tariff for *facchini* [porters] to load and unload strangers' carriages, and does not permit them to dispense with their attendance: but so it is and I saw the printed tariffs myself. It is said it was attempted to be suppressed and nearly caused a revolution.

Our first visit was to the *Sacro Catino*, of which we had heard so

---

40   The Sacred Bowl allegedly used by Christ at the Last Supper, which was brought to Genoa by Crusaders in 1101.
41   The Sala is made up of fifty-six columns and pilasters of broccarello marble, with yellow marble pediments.

much. Great, therefore, was our disappointment at seeing a large bowl
of green glass, broken into 20 pieces in the removal from Paris in 1815,
and which they have the impudence still to call an Emerald!! We went,
in a very bad humour, to the Palazzo Durazzo, where we found among
several good pictures two or three beautiful Vandykes, particularly a child
represented as young Tobias with the Fish, and two Spagnoletti, a little
overcharged but very beautiful Heraclitus and Democritus. There is also
a Magdalene said to be by Titian, a duplicate or a copy of the one in
the Barberigo in Venice. In the Palazzo Caregga, to which we obtained
an admittance today, there are very few pictures, but almost all good of
the Masters. Among them are one or two Guercinos and Caravaggios.

On our way to the Church of [Santa Maria Assunta di] Carignono
we passed that of St Stephen,[42] where there is a notable picture of the
martyrdom of St Stephen by Raphael and in part Giulo Romano, at least
so they say. At any rate it is a splendid picture and I think pleased me
as much as any we have seen. It has, however, been retouched by David,[43]
having paid its visit to Paris. The Church of Carignono is a very fine one
and commands a magnificent view of the city and country. It owes it
origin to an odd circumstance. A Lady of the Sauli family was in the
habit of attending Mass at a neighbouring Chapel and one day sent to
beg that, as she was late, they would defer it a short time. The answer
was if she wished to have Mass at her own time she must have a Church
of her own. On which, out of pique, she built this, which is said to be
on the model of St Peter's at Rome. I own I could not see the resemblance
in any one point. There is a good picture St Peter and St John healing
the paralytic, by I think Piola,[44] but I am not sure. We returned by the
splendid Ponte Carignono built by one of her descendants,[45] leading to
the Church and joining the hills by a row of arches far above the highest
houses.

Our carriage went off about four with a fine breeze and will arrive
tomorrow morning.

Saturday 20th. Set out on a beautiful morning with a *Voiturier* for Sestri.[46]
The whole of our drive today of nine hours to Sestri is very beautiful,
particularly the sea views. Porto Fino and the Bay of Rapallo are, I think,
as fine as almost anything I ever saw, and when this road is finished it
will be much the best entrance into Italy. Our Inn at Sestri [the Hotel

---

42 The thirteenth-century Church of San Stefano.
43 Jacques-Louis David (1748-1825).
44 Domenico Piola (1627-1703).
45 Domenico Sauli commissioned the bridge, which was built between 1718 and 1724.
46 Sestri was a favourite sea-bathing place located on an isthmus at the foot of a wooded
    promontory.

de l'Europe] but very moderate. We were not, therefore, sorry to leave it in good time, accordingly.

Sunday 21st. We set off on mules at 6 o'clock and arrived at Spezia about five in the evening. The first part of the route is too wild, bleak and barren, but there is some very pretty country and the descent on Spezia is glorious indeed. Certainly in no country but Italy do you see the sea shore as you see it here: bold, rocky and picturesque in outline, and yet covered with beautiful woods to the very water's edge and everywhere covered with the most luxurious vegetation, and, as here, with vines, olives, figs and oranges, and the whole lit up by the sky which is unrivalled. From Spezia to Magra there is nothing very striking. The Inn at Sarzana [the Albergo di Londra] is comfortable enough, but on Monday 22nd we were called at ½ past four, meaning to go off immediately; such a morning I never saw, torrents of rain and a high blustering wind, in consequence of which all sorts of delays were made by the people to save themselves from setting off before daylight. We did, however, set off with the lamps lit just before it broke, about ½ past 5. The rain never ceased the whole day, and when at 8 at night we got to Prato, the last post before Florence, we were told that the river had burst its banks, and that in one place there was six feet of water in the road. This we should have believed, if the conclusion had not been that we must stop the night there. But we no sooner heard the word Locanda [a simple hotel] than we suspected exaggeration, and ordered the horses, saying we would try; and after some grumbling and swearing we got there. Prepared as I was for exaggeration, I own I had not expected to find it a complete lie, as it proved; and while we were anxiously looking out for this dreadful place, we found ourselves at past ten at night at the gates of Florence, wet through, for the rain had not only soaked the oilskin cover of the trunks, the trunks themselves and everything in them, but the oiled leather apron of the carriage, the roof and sides of it, and great part of our clothes. We drove to Schneiderf's,[47] but could not be received, and at last got admitted at the N. York, which has been newly fitted up since last year, and seems comfortable.[48] We got a very good supper, having eaten nothing all day, but some dry bread, or rather which ought to have been dry, in the carriage, and got to bed at ½ past 12.

Tuesday 23rd. Employed all morning in drying our clothes and books, which have suffered severely. Wrote to Mr Frieborn and Gasparo. Walked

---

47   A private boarding-house in the Palazzo Schneiderf, Florence.
48   The Hotel de New York on the Lungarno Arno.

to the Casino and reading room, where I found no news and a comical set of people and dined quietly at home.[49]

Wednesday 24th. I am sure the pleasure of a second visit to almost any town is much greater than the first. On the first there is always so much to see that one has not the time to admire: one can never depend upon the reports of others and one is obliged to wade through an ocean of trash to know what is really worth seeing. Books too and prints give an exaggerated ideas of everything. One goes with high-raised expectations and one meets with disappointment. On the second visit one knows what one has to see; one goes where one chooses and every object unites to the charm of novelty the renewal of an old acquaintance. I am sure these remarks will apply to Rome as well as Florence and these were my feelings on going into the [Uffizi] Gallery this morning. On some of the pictures, as well as the statues, I have changed my opinion since last year, for instance, the Guido in the Tribuna, which I now see to bear his weak manner and more Carlo Dolci-ish.[50] I was wonderfully struck too with the inferiority of the very fine copy of the Laocoön[51] to the original much more so than I was with the superiority of the latter when I first saw it.[52] The group or rather the Statues of Niobe and her Children too disappointed me on second sight, though the Mother and one daughter are wonderfully fine.[53] It was, however, a very great pleasure to see gain the glorious St John, the Fornarina, the Leonardo di Vinci, the Sybil, the two Correggios, the Annibal Caracci and the Andrea del Sarto,[54] with many others. I am, however, ashamed to say how little admiration I feel for the Venus di Medicis. One knows it is perfection and that one <u>ought</u> to be in raptures, but I cannot and it is a 'damming proof' against me that surrounded by the Arrotino,[55] the Wrestlers,[56] and the pictures I hardly looked at the Goddess.

We met Sir W. Drummond, Miss Fanshawe, and Lord and Lady Charleville[57] in the Gallery, and an execrable crew of English. Miserable day, cold and raw.

---

49   The Casino di Firenze on the Via Ghibellina was a club supplied with English, French and Italian newspapers.
50   Carlo Dolci (1616-1686).
51   A Trojan priest in Greek mythology.
52   The original of the ancient Greek statue of Laocoön and his sons is in the Vatican, Rome.
53   The third-century BC Roman marble statue of Niobe and her youngest daughter.
54   The Florentine painter Andrea del Sarto (1486-1530).
55   The first-century BC Roman statue known as *The Blade Sharpener*.
56   A Roman third-century BC marble copy of a lost Greek bronze statue.
57   Charles Bury, 1st earl of Charleville (1764-1835) was a fellow of the Royal Society and the Society of Antiquaries, and president of the Royal Irish Academy from 1812 to 1822. He married Catherine Dawson in 1798.

Thursday [25th]. Dined with Sir William Drummond, nobody but himself, his *cara sposa* [dear wife], and Comte and Countess Moutti.[58] Our Inn keeper has just brought me in to look over the manuscript of a book he is publishing as a Guide of Italy and Sicily dedicated A. S. A. Anna Countessa and Princessa Cowper, *nata* Gore.[59]

Friday 26th. I hear of nothing but people going to Rome, and horrible murders between there and Naples. I am afraid we shall find hardly anybody at the latter place. Lady Dillon[60] is opened mouthed about a change of ministry, but I do not believe a word of it. Lord W. Russell, however, says he is certain that Lord Londonderry has not been spoken to by the King upon his journey. We rode today towards the Pratolino, but it was cold and unpleasant.

Saturday 27th. Dined with Lord Rendlesham. She is very much altered and looks unwell. Thelluson and his wife are said to be always quarrelling and not to be well with Lord R. They certainly were not mentioned nor do they dine there tomorrow. They have been married a year, and each thought the other a great fortune and made no settlements. They prove to have £5,000 a year. Another marriage which has taken place within a few days is likely to get more happy. My <u>friend</u> Trevor[61] has just married a Miss Daisy Irvine without or rather against his father's consent, who has in consequence stopped his allowance, and he has the power of cutting him off at his death with £300 a year. He is now living with his stepfather here. He wrote an admirable letter to his Father, merely alleging he might have done worse, and quoting Weymouth, Rowley, etc. I know him well and am not, therefore, surprised to hear the way one and all speak of him here at Florence.

Our party yesterday consisted of Lord and Lady Charleville and Miss Fridall, Col. and Mrs Pallier, Mr Dawkins, the English *chargé d'affaires*, and an Italian, whose name I do not know. Apropos, I must put down a mistake of Comte Moutti's in English as he told it himself. Talking of some lady, he said she was big. He was told he ought to say in the family way, and asking what that meant literally, was told in *via di famiglia*. Remembering

---

58 Possibly the French adventurer Nicholas de la Motte (1755-1831), whose claim to the title of comte was dubious.
59 Hannah Anne, Countess Cowper, née Gore (1758-1826), was the widow of the 3rd earl of Cowper, who died in 1789.
60 Henrietta, Lady Dillon, who married the 13th Viscount Dillon in 1807.
61 Arthur Hill Trevor (1798-1862), son of the 2nd Viscount Dungannon, was a contemporary of Stanley's at Christ Church, Oxford. He was a Conservative MP from 1830 to 1843 and succeeded his father as the 3rd Viscount Dungannon in 1837. As the holder of an Irish peerage, he was not precluded from membership of the House of Commons. In September 1821 he married Sophie 'Daisy' Irvine.

this, and not the English, he retranslated it the next time, 'She is in Family Street!' This he swears to. In the evening we called on Lady Alvanley, who with 'her girls' is on her way to Rome. She was in high force; she told us too to our great astonishment that the Talbots were returning, and that the old Margravine is going to England, it is supposed exiled from Naples. I am glad to find Sir W. à Court will still be there. Lady à Court is coming out immediately. We dine with Lord R. again tomorrow.

Sunday 28th. Dined with Lord Rendlesham, Lord Blantyre,[62] Bradshaw, Dawkins and ourselves. Not so agreeable a dinner as yesterday. Went to see the Pergola[63] and found Sir W. Drummond and Romilly,[64] did not stay long. Lady à Court and Sir H. Lushington[65] returned on their way to Naples. I am glad of it, as it ensures Sir William's stay there. He would not thank me for this.

November 1821

Thursday 1st November. We set out on a fine bright morning, just before sunrise, for Naples. The first part of the road, which I had heard so much abused, struck me as rather pretty, quite in the Florentine style of beauty, though it gets a little monotonous. We got to Siena about 3 and finding our carriage was broken, determined to have it repaired, and then go on all night. We dined, therefore, and went up to the Cathedral,[66] the front of which is glorious in the barbarous Gothic style, covered with ornament and yet not having the effect of being overloaded. In the inside too there are some very curious inlaid figures of Saints, Sybils, etc.[67] The Cathedral appears to have suffered greatly, I believe in the earthquake of 1798, and I should almost think that what remains was only one of the original cross. In returning to the Inn we passed by a singular V-shaped Place called, I think, Piazza del Campo, where Mass was celebrating in the open air being the high feast of *Tutti i Santi*. We got off from Siena about ½ past 6 and at daybreak next day found ourselves just on the top of the mountains of Radicofani. The town seems finely situated, and appeared at that hour to command a view of a magnificent Lake, which, however, as we descended proved to be nothing but mist, in which we were

---

62   Robert, 11th Lord Blantyre (1775-1830). He was accidently killed in Brussels during the revolution in 1830.
63   The Opera House della Pergola, built in 1738.
64   Joseph Romilly (1791-1864), fellow of Trinity College, Cambridge.
65   Sir Henry Lushington (1775-1863).
66   The Duomo is situated on the highest point of the hill of Siena.
67   Mosaics on the floor of the nave.

completely enveloped. From hence to Rome the country is chiefly uninteresting, with the exception of the town of Acquapendente, whose
situation is very picturesque and the Lake of Bolsena, which is not amiss.
We arrived at Rome about one in the morning, and were glad to get into
the Hotel de Franz, having tried three others. The Duchess of Devonshire
is not returned, but she is expected every day. I have little doubt she has
been scheming to get Mr Foster[68] sent to Naples: we hear too she has
been spreading all sorts of unfavourable accounts of our business at
Benevento. *Peu n'importe* [Whatever]. We were detained the whole of
Saturday Nov. 3 at Rome for Passports, and were just able to get off in
time to reach Velletri[69] at 10 at night.

Sunday 4th. We set off at six in the morning and arriving in good time
at Mola and the Inn keeper being very extravagant in his charges we
went on to St Agata, where we slept at a Vituerino Inn, not uncomfortable. Our Postilions flew with us the last stage, and once we stopped
thinking the wheel was on fire. They asked us very sharply why we did
not think of that at the Post. On arriving at St Agata this was explained.
The last post is the only one where there is now any danger and we
passed it just at the dangerous time, but without any accident.

Monday Nov. 5th. All the little towns between St Agata and Naples are
fuller than ever of Austrian troops. We got to Naples at three o'clock,
just in time to escape a tremendous thunderstorm, which with hail, rain
and wind lasted all night and very much disguised *la belle Napoli*, where,
however, I am very glad to find myself.

Tuesday 6th.   Dined with Sir W. à Court quite *en famille* as he says,
which we found to mean with Borel, the Prince of Hesse, Mr Anderson
the Vice Consul, and Mr Bingham his Attaché.[70] In the evening General
Haugwitz[71] and Prince Butera came in. It is said, but not ascertained,
that Carascosa has been shot in a duel by a Roman officer.[72] It is also
said that the affairs of the Greeks are going on better, and from Sir W.'s

---

68   The diplomat Augustus Foster (1780-1848) was the duchess's son by her first marriage
     to John Foster (1747-1796).
69   Velletri, on the lower slopes of Monte Artemisio.
70   Richard Bingham (1801-1872), diplomat and a younger son of Lord Lucan, had become
     infatuated with Lady Lismore while in Rome. Later, when Lady Lismore arrived in Naples,
     they began an affair. Bingham was cited in the subsequent divorce proceedings brought
     by Lord Lismore against his wife in 1825-26.
71   General Eugen Haugwitz (1777-1867) had been military commander of Naples from 1815
     to 1817 and returned in 1821 with the Austrian army.
72   General Michele Caracosca (1774-1853) had led the Neapolitan army alongside General
     Pépé against the Austrians in 1821.

language it is clear to me that there has been a revolt in Corfu. The Margravine is decidedly banished and never to return, and they say that a general order has been issued to refuse her passports for entering the Kingdom again. Went Mad. Ficquelmont's box at the [Teatro dei] Fiorentini, and had a most pressing invitation for Friday.

Wednesday 7th. Dined with Maberly at the Villa di Roma, which is not as good as it was. Went to the Fondo,[73] but saw nobody. Mad Ficquelmont's box contained a large party and I was much amused with a scene between Catherine [von Tiesenhausen] and her intended.

Thursday 8th. Occupied all morning lodging hunting. Letters from Mary and Charlotte with accounts of the new Dining Room which must be horribly ugly.[74]

Wednesday 14th. Dined at Sir W. à Court's, having been presented to Lady à Court the day before. I do not admire her.[75] She is rather too 'gentle and juvenile, curly and gay in the manner of Ackermann's dresses for May.'[76] Our party were M. Doubril the Russian Minister and his wife, Mad. Nugent,[77] Lady Acton,[78] Comte Ludolf, General Haugwitz, Maberly, an Englishman whom I did not know, Mr Fontenay, Lord W. Russell, Hornby and myself. I did not think it particularly lively, though I was well placed by Comte Ludorf, who is a gentlemanlike and an agreeable man. In the evening the *Femme Jalouse*[79] was acted at Mad. Hitroff's Theatre at the Barbiga, but not acted very well. Prince Torella,[80] Countess Catherine and Mad. Hitroff were good. The others I thought all bad. There was a Ball after, which did not begin till near two o'clock. Mrs Otway is very angry that we did not dine with her on Friday last

---

73   The Teatro del Fondo, which was built in 1778 as a miniature of Teatro San Carlo and renamed the Teatro Mercandante in 1871.

74   Stanley's grandfather, the 12th earl of Derby, built the huge new state dining room at Knowsley Hall, designed in the neo-Gothic style by the Liverpool architect John Foster (1786-1846) in 1820-21, in preparation for a visit by King George IV.

75   Maria Bouverie married Sir William à Court in 1808.

76   Rudolph Ackermann (1764-1834) published a very popular periodical describing the latest fashions.

77   Madame Nugent was the wife of Irish-born General Laval Nugent, who was serving in the Austrian army.

78   Mary Anne, Lady Acton (1784-1873) was the widow of Sir John Francis Acton who died in 1811.

79   *La Femme Jalouse* (1780) was a verse comedy by Pierre Choudard, pen name De Desforges (1746-1806). It was based on the English comedy *The Jealous Wife* (1761) by George Colman (1732-1794), which in turn was partly based on Henry Fielding's novel *Tom Jones*.

80   Giuseppe, Prince Torella (1787-1856), had served under General Pépé in defence of the Neapolitan revolution.

and we had a good scene with her on calling this morning. Sir W. and Lady Drummond are arrived, both looking very juvenile indeed. They are in the Franca Villa and Lady Drummond says, with an air of satisfaction, that it is very uncomfortable, but very magnificent.

Friday 16th. Set out to Capri, got nearly there, but the weather got so bad that we returned in time to escape a wetting—a complete Scotch mist, or as they have the impudence to say *brouillard Anglais*.

Sunday 18th. A good deal surprised in taking a quiet ride by the Lago d'Agnano to see before us about 20 people on horseback, and I do not know why, I said this looks like English Hunters going to cover. I wish we could see the hounds. When, to my astonishment there appeared a pack from behind an old building, and I saw two whippers in, and heard an English Halloo! We rode up and found they were Prince Petralla's Hounds, set up in the English style, and all come from England.[81] They were out at exercise and go in about a fortnight to St Agata where they have a regular kennel and hunting establishment, and astound the country people not a little. The Italian rider's attempts at leaping afforded us some good fun.

Monday 19th. Dined at Sir W. à Court's, full dress, previous to going to Court. Met only Borel, Mad. de Fontenay, and Blasiel. The Court very dull and not very full. The circle being made the old King comes round, speaking to the Ministers, and receiving presentations, then the Prince follows, then the Princess and lastly the children, whose mock dignity was admirable.[82] Sir William was most graciously received, and the King came back to him to talk to him about his Chasse [shooting party], and a long story of 3 of his calves which the wolves had killed. He finished as usual with Elbene, adesso Andrians tutti al Teatro, which we did. A new ballet, horribly bad, but it was not etiquette to miss it before the King, so it survives.

Tuesday [20th] Dined with the Duke of Leeds. A very agreeable dinner, but nobody there except old Borel. Went in the evening with Carmarthen[83]

---

81 On a visit to Naples in 1825, the young Henry Fox observed that Prince Petralla and his friends had an Anglomania with regard to their horses, carriages and dress, and in their frequent use of 'damme, dammed' and 'God dammed'. *The Journal of the Hon. Henry Fox (afterwards Fourth Lord Holland)* (London, 1923), p. 203.

82 Prince Francis (1777-1830). He was duke of Calabria from 1778 to 1825, when he succeeded his father as King Francis I of the Two Sicilies. He married Maria Isabella of Spain (1789-1848) in 1802, when she was aged thirteen. Their children included Luisa Carlotta (1804-1844), Maria Cristina (1806-1878) and Ferdinand (1810-1859), who succeeded his father as King Ferdinand II of the Two Sicilies in 1830.

83 Francis Osborne (1798-1859), who was styled marquess of Carmarthen from 1799 to 1838, when he succeeded his father as 7th duke of Leeds.

to the San Carlino, where we saw a tragedy <u>divinely</u> acted, amid roars of laughing, and a good farce afterwards.

Wednesday 21st. Dined sorely against our will with Mrs Otway Cave, and had a more agreeable dinner than I anticipated, chiefly foreigners, M. Jetzer,[84] du Blaisel, not the French, Bredy, old Mr Mathias,[85] who I think found himself *de trop*, and Hornby and I. After dinner went to Mad. Hitroff's and were most graciously received, M. de Fontenay, [Baron] du Blaisel <u>the other</u>, and the Sardinian Minster came in—the latter seems a great fool, and M. de F. amused me much by the determined way in which he talked him into silence. Lady à Court's in the evening was very full and I did not think very good. There was a bad set of English and too many of them. Presented to Lord Suffolk at his request.[86] He seems a very extraordinary man, goes out very little into society, and does not seem fond of it when he is there. He is lodged in the same House with us.

Thursday November 22nd. Received a cargo of letters, announcing Mary's intended marriage with Wilton.[87] This has surprised me a good deal, and though I see no positive objection, I confess it has not pleased me entirely. I would have wished something superior for her, but after all one cannot choose for one's friends, and she might have done much worse. I fear, however, they have been a little hasty. While I was reading the letters Lord Suffolk came in, and George soon after, to whom, of course, I could not show the letters till Lord S. was gone, and I flatter myself I behaved incomparably. Wrote three letters, one to Maria, one to Lady Derby,[88] another to Wilton. Well! As the marriage is to be, they have my warmest wishes for their Happiness! The badness of the day prevented me going to Capri as I had intended with Maberly!

Friday 23rd. Dined with Sir W. Drummond. Our party were Sir W. Gell, Lord W. Russell, Maberly, Fairfield, Hornby and I. She [Lady Drummond]

---

84   Captain August von Jetzer (1789-1862) of the Austrian military command.

85   Thomas Mathias (1754-1835), author of *The Pursuits of Literature* (1794). He had previously served as the queen's treasurer and librarian at Buckingham Palace, but left England in 1817 to live in Naples until his death.

86   Thomas Howard (1776-1851), formerly styled Viscount Andover, succeeded his father as the 16th earl of Suffolk in 1820.

87   Lady Mary Stanley married Thomas Egerton, 2nd earl of Wilton (1799-1882) in November 1821. He was an expert horseman—he established the Heaton Races in 1827—a keen yachtsman and a composer, but also a womaniser. The social hostess Lady Waldegrave took to referring to Wilton as 'the wicked Earl' and the Stanleys blamed Mary's illness and death in 1858 on Wilton's semi-public affairs. Angus Hawkins, *The Forgotten Prime Minister: Achievement, 1851-1869* (Oxford, 2008), p. 193.

88   The actress Elizabeth, née Farren (1762-1829), who married the 12th earl of Derby in 1797.

is more insufferably vulgar than anything I ever saw, and disgusts me more and more every time I see her. She has a thoroughly vulgar mind as well as manner, and talks of nothing but her house, her clothes, her money, etc. Met Sir J. Egerton[89] in her box and made acquaintance with him, which does not seem worth the trouble. Afterwards in Lady à Court's box between whom and Lady D. there is a cordial hatred. Madame Ficquelmont's in the evening. Met the Miss Lushingtons there, who seem nice unaffected girls and one of them rather pretty.[90] They were with the Duchess of Leeds.

Our weather is horrid, fogs, clouds and rain: the prelude to the rainy season which I wish would set in in earnest. I find on Wednesday night there was a slight shock of an earthquake felt in Naples. So many people felt it there is no doubt of the fact, but it did not disturb me; and I only remember being awoke that night by the rats making an most extraordinary scampering over my head. G. and I interpret the rats over a bed—that W. [Lord Wilton] will change politics on his marriage. We received the news of it the next morning. Looking back I find my journal of the proposal day (Saturday 27th) is full of nothing but unlucky marriages. *Nullum sit in omni pondus*! [There should be no weight in it all!]

Sunday 25th. Last night there was again a slight shock of earthquake, as I am told. All these warnings are considered here as certain preludes to an approaching eruption, particularly as the mountain is more than usually quiet, and I hope therefore we shall not leave Naples without seeing the splendid sight. The S. Carlos was unusually empty on account of Marquis Sampieri's new opera making its reappearance.[91] Mad. Ficquelmont too with a large party is gone to Paestum. Sir W. Gell, who was in Sir W. Drummond's box, was very amusing. Lord Ellenborough is arrived at last. I am sorry for it! I have just been reading K. Craven's book, but I own I am not charmed with it.[92] His account is but meagre and not very well written, and still worse printed. My landlord has just been in with a request that I would allow him to open a door in my room communicating with another suite of rooms, that he may tell some German officers who wish to take them that they all belong to me, preferring not to let them at all to letting them to the Germans.

---

89   Sir John Egerton (1776-1825).
90   Miss Maria Lushington (b. 1800) and Miss Louisa Lushington (b. 1801), daughters of Sir Henry Lushington.
91   The composer Francesco, Marchese Sampieri (1790-1863), whose opera *Valmiro e Zaida* was premiered at the San Carlo opera house in September 1821.
92   Richard Keppel Craven, *A Tour Through the Southern Provinces of the Kingdom of Naples* (London, 1821).

Monday 26th. Lady Ellenborough arrives and brings news of Mary's marriage, of which, however, I have not heard a word from anyone else. Ball at the Academia tonight which was <u>very</u> dull, no Ladies there. Came home at ½ past one.

Tuesday 27th. Up at 7 to see the *prove generali* [dress rehearsal] of a review to take place tomorrow, but I was disappointed. Dined with Sir W. à Court, Lord W. Russell, Borel, another Dutchman, Bingham and I—a dull dinner, and Lady à C out of humour. Opera at San Carlo. Another earthquake last night. Being in bed only 5 hours I was out of luck not to feel it.

[November, Wednesday] 28th. Today the review has taken place and was certainly a fine sight, and it did not appear to mortify the Neapolitans the least to see 15,000 Austrians reviewed on their Champ di Mars, where Murat reviewed his troops, and lately their own disbanded army was assembled. An Austrian soldier who stood near me was in raptures, dancing about and crying *Vassa Vin Tu! Fahzl jibjl! Turb ir felön, misl mzorpi?* The old King was there and looked very well on horseback, much better than I ever saw him before. He was received in perfect silence from the whole immense multitude. Lady à Court's in the evening. A Ball and a tolerably good one.

Thursday 29th. A letter arrived this morning begging me to return to England—written an answer to excuse myself. I think my grandfather cannot seriously wish it on such slight grounds. S. Carlo in the evening.

Friday 30th. O-o, o, o, o, o, except Mad. Ficquelmont's.

December 1821

Saturday December 1st. Dined with Carmarthen at the Albergo Real. A Ball in the evening at Blaca's and a very good one. Staid till 2, when Bingham and I vainly endeavoured to get some supper at all the Trattorias.

Sunday December 2nd. Went to Church for the first time since I have been abroad—very agreeably surprised. The service is performed very decently, though not remarkably well, and I shall certainly continue to go. We hear today that Frimont has had bestowed upon him a present of £40,000, with the title of Prince of Antrodoco.[93] Such an insult was

---

93   This title and money was conferred by King Ferdinand I of the Two Sicilies.

never put upon any nation as this title. I wonder he is not ashamed of accepting it. As to the King, he has no sense of shame at all, and it does not therefore so much surprise me. It has, however, made some little sensation among the foreigners. No letter today. I am glad of it. I dread a recall to England. Opera at San Carlos. Nobody there but Lady à Court.

Monday December 3rd. The finest day I have seen since I left Naples in June, with a sun so hot I can hardly bear it on my balcony. Tried a horse meaning to buy him, but did not like him. Dined with Sir W. à Court. A party for Lady Ellenborough who kept us waiting till ½ past six. Sir H. and Lady Lushington, who tells me she was a great friend of Mrs J. Hornby's, Carmarthen, Bingham, Mr Vyner, Mr G. Baring, Mr Throckmorton, Borel, Fairfield, Hornby and I. Borel tells me he shall be returned home much about the time we go through the Low Countries. I shall have great pleasure in seeing him there again. Staid late and did not go to the Academia, which I have no doubt was very dull. My German master arrived for the first time today. I like what I have seen of him, except that he flummerys me exceedingly.

Tuesday 4th. Received an invitation for Mrs Arbuthnot's whom I do not know, through Sir F. Falkiner[94] whom I hardly know, for her Ball this evening. Shall not go. Opera, nobody there, the Laws, all of them without Lady Ellenborough, Lushingtons, Sir W. à Court and Mrs Smith. Very bad opera, Sampieri's new one. It is said that the King had forbidden the representation as being so bad, King Bulaja said he wanted to hear it, and it was given. I hope he is satisfied.

Wednesday 5th. We shall have a dull dinner at Sir W. Drummond's. I hear the Ball last night was but moderate. My fears for dinner amply verified. Our party was Lady and Sir F. Acton,[95] Sir J. and Lady Egerton, General de la Tour,[96] more commonly known by the name of the Marshal de Saxe, Madame Falconieri and her son, Lady Lushington, Sir Henry being ill, Mr Mrs and Miss Douglas, Abbé Campbell, Hornby, Bingham and I. Quite dreadful. I made love to Lady Egerton in self defence against the tide of nonsense which D. was pouring into my other ear. Young F. is insufferable. Lady à Court's in the evening a relief and I believe I made a great fool of myself there. Staid till one.

---

94   Sir Frederick Falkiner (1768-1824).
95   Sir Ferdinand Acton (1801-1837).
96   Possibly General Marie de la Tour (1768-1850).

Thursday 6th. No letters today, thank God! I hope, however, that they will not have opportunity under the idea that we are on our way to England, which I am rather afraid of.

Saturday [7th] down to dinner at 8, up at ½ past 10. Stupid and bad dinner, Bingham, Carmarthen, Borel, old Mathias. Played at Billiards at the Academia.

Sunday 9th. Lady E. hoax. Dined with Lady Drummond, an agreeable dinner, Mr and Mad. Preville, Mad. Zapara, Jetzer, Prince Butera, Prince Taxis,[97] de Bredy, Mr Throckmorton, Abbé Campbell, General Haugwitz, Hornby and I. Everybody still indignant and still talking about Frimont's grant.

Tuesday 11th. A Ball at Mrs Risse's and a good one. The Turk there and made a great love to by all the women and men. Came away very late.

Wednesday 12th. Dined with Lady Ellenborough to meet Borel, hoax dinner, an agreeable dinner, Carmarthen, Lord Rosehill,[98] Romilly, Hornby and I. Lady à Court's in the evening. I cannot affront Mrs A. She has introduced herself this evening, but I shall take no notice of her and see what she will do.

Thursday 13th. S. Carlo in the evening, Lord Ellenborough, Lushingtons, Sir W. à Court. Supped with Standish, home at 6 in the morning. Have not done such a thing since I left Oxford I believe.

Saturday 15th. Dined with the Duke of Leeds, the Duchess, Lady Charlotte, Borel and Sir H. Lushington. S. Carlo in the evening for the last time as the Novana[99] now commences and until after Christmas Day everything is suspended. Bought a horse today for 120 ducats, of a gentleman, having been asked 180. One and all Neapolitans are alike.

Monday 15th. An interview by appointment between the Duchess of Leeds, Lady C. Osborne,[100] Mrs and Mr Stanley, bought my margaritini [Venetian coloured glass] after much bargaining. Dined at Lady à Court's. He was not there having gone to a Chasse with the King. They say it will excite great jealousy, that he is the only one of the *corps diplomatique*

---

97 Karl Alexander, 5th prince of Thurn and Taxis (1770-1827).
98 William Carnegie (1794-1874), styled Lord Rosehill prior to succeeding his father in 1831 as the 8th earl of Northesk.
99 Marking the nine days before Christmas.
100 Lady Charlotte, daughter of the duchess of Leeds.

asked. Our party was a bad one, all English, and I flatter myself I behaved incomparably. Seated between Mrs Gordon and Lady Griselda Tickell. The party were Lady à C., Borel, Lady Newburgh,[101] Lady Dolly Ayr and Mr Ayr, Mr and Lady Griselda Tickell, Mr O'Hara, Brecknock, Bingham, Hornby and I. We had, however, very good fun discussing them all when they were gone.

Tuesday [16th]. Sir W. Gell sent us his manuscript of travel in the Morea to read and criticise.[102] We shall very soon set up for established critics, having just had a translation of Horace from Sir William Drummond. Gell's book is very amusing and gives a good idea of the habits of the people as far as a stranger can form an opinion of these. There is not otherwise a great deal of information in it, but it is very amusing and the stories are well told. Dined with Bingham, Brecknock, and went to the Academia.

'*Und fo flosner tiräg, vry vonman*', or very near it, for it is now the last day of the year, and for a fortnight I have written nothing in my journal for lack of matter. Let me see what has happened. We have dined with the Drummonds, à Courts, Egertons and Ellenboroughs, who, by the bye are going away. Theatres just open again. Balls beginning. My horse, I fear, will turn out a roarer,[103] if not broken winded. Fairfield has won Sir J. Falkiner's carriage and I am deputed to sell it for him. We heard yesterday the news of the day, that the Grand Signor has been murdered.[104] As he is the last of his race it is now a fine time for the rebels and rioters. Apropos the accounts from Ireland are horrible. The changes in our cabinet have excited some astonishment here, particularly Canning having succeeded in getting the Admiralty. It is said Prince Leopold[105] is coming out here the 16th for the Carnival. Prince Liechtenstein is just arrived.[106] We dine tomorrow with Lady Drummond for New Year's Day and I mean to have some very good fun. Hyppolite is arrived. I went to the Opera on purpose to tell her, but she was not there. I am in great despair at parting with my servant, getting a new one is such a bore!

---

101 Lady Newburgh was the wife of Vincenzo, 6th Prince Giustiniani and 'de jure' 6th earl of Newburgh (1762-1826).
102 Sir William Gell's *Narrative of a Journey in the Morea* (London, 1823), which describes his visits to the Peloponnese and the Greek and Turkish communities there.
103 A horse whose breathing emits a loud hoarse sound.
104 Benderli Ali Pasha, grand vizier of the Ottoman Empire from March to April 1821, was executed on the order of Sultan Mahmud II (1785-1839).
105 Prince Leopold of Saxe-Coburg (1790-1865). After a distinguished military career fighting Napoleon in the Russian imperial cavalry, he married Charlotte, princess of Wales, in 1816. In 1831 he became King Leopold I of the newly created state of Belgium.
106 Johann, prince of Liechtenstein (1760-1836).

January 1822

Tuesday January 1st 1822. Employed all morning in having visiting cards, according to the established custom here. Dined with Lady Drummond and had, as I expected, rather a stupid dinner, Sir F. and Lady Falkiner, Sir J. and Lady Egerton, Jetzer, Bingham, Lord Rosehill, Mr Mundell, etc.

Wednesday 2nd. Gloriously fine day. Rode on the Strada Nuova. Very sorry, though not surprised to hear of the arrest of Confaloniere and Baron Freschi at Milan. What their crime is, or whether anything is proved I do not know. It is said the circumstances have come out upon the Turin trials which have led to this arrest. Dined with Mr and Mrs Gordon (Burn) and met Mr and Mrs Smith, General and Mrs Eustace,[107] the two prettiest English women in Naples, as they are reckoned. I think Mrs S. has it hollow. Col. Dalton dined there too, the *aidevant jeune homme*. Lady à Court's in the evening and agreeable enough. Young Law hard hit by Lady C. Osborne. I have suspected it some time and am sure tonight.

Thursday 3rd. Lady Drummond's splendid Ball, not a bad one, staid till 3 o'clock, but played whist most of the time.

Friday 4th. A very stupid dinner at Lady Ellenborough's, the à Courts, Borel, Lord Rosehill, Bingham, Colonel Dalton and I. Not much more lively at Mad. Ficquelmont's, but did not last quite as long.

Saturday 5th. A very bad day, played billiards in the morning, dined at the Albergo's and went to a whist party at Sir J. Egerton's. The chief topic of conversation the supposed rape of Miss Arbuthnot, who found her maid's lover by mistake in her bedroom the other night. She cried out, but malicious people say not till <u>after</u>. The maid trounced off and very full of stories against her *quondam* mistress.

Sunday 6th. No Church, Mr Turner being ill. Vile day.

Monday 7th. Still a bad day. Dined at Sir W. à Court's, not a very lively dinner, Duke and Duchess of Leeds, Lady Charlotte Osborne, Lord W. Paulet,[108] Bingham, Romilly, Col. Dalton, Capt. Jackson, Mr Ricketts, Mr Newman and I. Academia in the evening. Better than usual, but not good. It certainly is not the fashion this year.

---

107 Possibly General William Eustace (1783-1855).
108 Possibly Lord William Paulet (1804-1893), son of the 13th marquess of Winchester.

Tuesday 8th. Bad day. Rode on the Strada Nuova, dined at the Albergo, went to S. Carlo, and afterwards to the Duke of Leeds's where we played whist till very late. Borel's despair and superstition, and Mrs. Bligh's madness quite enchanting.

Wednesday 9th. Heavy rain. Vesuvius covered with snow nearly to the Hermitage, and smoking away—a curious effect.

Sunday 13th. Determined to set out tomorrow morning with Bisse[109] to Cisterna [di Latina] to meet Edsell from whom we have heard today that he shall be there tomorrow. Mad. Ficquelmont's Ball tonight, a very good one, and a good many of the English there, in spite of their consciences.

Monday 14th. Set out with Bisse, very fine morning, in his Charabanc. Reached St Agata about five o'clock, having had a breakdown at Capua. Dined at Prince Petralla's hunting box and saw his hounds, among which there are some nice looking ones. Went on to Nola to sleep. On arriving there we hear that Brigands, of the large band of 20, commanded by Don Pietro Paolo de Redis have seized an Austrian Colonel and a Sergeant Major for whose ransom they demand 20,000 ducats. This will bring the Austrians down upon them and seems to me a rash measure.

Tuesday 15th. On reaching the Portella we found the Brigands were within a quarter of a mile of the road, and had just sent down a message to the Commandant of the Terracina with a letter from the prisoners, by a peasant whom they seized and sent: and whom we overtook and carried to Terracina. Bisse had some conversation with the Commandant and says Frimont's orders to the troops are not to return till they have rescued the Colonel and exterminated the Brigands. Very fine talking: we shall see what they do: Arrived at For tu Ponti and found the party there snipe shooting. Joined them for a little while, but did nothing. Found our lodgings at Cisterna as uncomfortable as anything could be, but could not grumble having made up our minds to rough it. Bisse and I slept in the dining room and the other four in two rooms adjoining. Our party was altogether a very agreeable one and we had no disputes or disagreements. Our weather very fine and sport good on the whole. !st day's total 48 Woodcocks and a Chevreuil [roe deer]. My total for 8 days 40 Woodcocks, 8 Snipes, one Wild Boar and some Chevreuil, besides a few ducks, etc.

On returning by Terracina we found that the Brigands were surrounded

---

109   Thomas Chaloner Bisse (1788-1872), who had served in the 1st Dragoon Guards from
        1809 to 1812.

by a cordon of above 2,000 troops, all Austria with the exception of 500 Romans. The Colonel was still in their hands, but was released the day after, the Brigands having all escaped and been paid *sotto mano* [secretly] 6,000 ducats of ransom. Three soldiers killed and wounded. Saw Jetzer at Terracina. Wrote to the Major who commanded begging to be allowed to serve in the ranks, as they expected a brush and we wished to see the nature of the service. Were too late with our request, but a good deal astonished on arriving at Naples to find it had been regularly transmitted as an offer of service to Frimont, who complimented Bisse on it. Jetzer talked a great deal of nonsense about it. Our last four days were at Bisse's Casino, about four miles to the right of the Portitia on the road to Naples. It is nothing but a square tower with three rooms upstairs, but altogether the accomodations are much better than we got at Cisterna. We christened him Robinson Crusoe, and he had an excellent man Friday in the shape of Raffaello. The small band of nine Brigands were in his woods as they always are, but we were never less than four and well-armed, so that they did not venture to attack us. Returned to Naples with Bisse and Edsell on Saturday evening January 26th. Dined at the Albergo Real, etc.

Monday 28th. Dined with Lady Ellenborough. Dullish dinner as usual. I was seated between Anne and Eliza. On recollection this was on Tuesday. Went afterwards to San Carlo—Mrs Smith's box.

Monday 28th. Dined with Lady à Court, Bingham, Brecknock and du Blaisel. Sir W. at great Minister and Bankes dinner at Rothchilds. Blacas the Magnificent sent to say he had toothache.

Wednesday 30th. Dined at the Duke of Leeds's, the à Courts, Bligh, Brecknock, Borel, Mr Moore, Sir H. Lushington and I. Well placed between Lady à Court and Lady Charlotte. Lady à C's in the evening, her last party, staid <u>very</u> late.[110] All the Austrians are very angry about report of the Brigands and deny the troops are recalled. I held my tongue, but Bisse is very imprudent. Douglas very foolish in expressing his joy at the à Courts going and his own consequent greatness. I am <u>very</u> sorry for it, but it will not make much difference to me as I must go soon myself. What would I give for six months more!

Thursday January 31st. Dined with Sir William à Court, last party, a sweep, and therefore dull. I was between Lady Lushington and Bingham. I did very well, went away early to set a good example and took them

---

110 Sir William à Court was posted as British envoy to Spain in 1822.

away with me. I am sure I was thanked for it. S. Carlo, Sir W. Drummond and Sir H. Lushington.

February 1822

Saturday February 2nd. Rode as usual with Bingham. Dined at Sir W. Drummond's and had a bad party—all men. Dietrichstein,[111] Jetzer, Letizia, Colinfiano, Sir J. Falconer, Anderson, Capt. Hamilton, Hornby and I. A quarrel between Diet. and Col. I thought they would have fought, but it passed off. Went to the Opera. Sir W. à Court took me to Lady Acton's Ball, a child's masked Ball, and pretty enough. Home about 12.

Sunday 3rd. The *passeggiata* [leisurely walk or stroll] in the Toledo[112] dull enough, but begins to be better than it was; it cannot compare, however, with the Carnival in Rome.

Monday 4th. Bingham's quarrel with [Prince Andrea] Pignatelli goes on and must, I should think, come to something serious, if the latter is not a coward, which I suspect he is. Dined at Sir J. Egerton's. Dull party. Whist in the evening.

Tuesday 5th. Sir G. Talbot and Sir W. Gell dined with us at the Albergo Real; Opera in the evening. Sir George gives a sad account of the way Lady Westmoreland is going on, quarrelling with everybody. She is quite crazy and I am, therefore, sorry for her. It is now certain that Foster coming here as Minister. The Duchess [of Devonshire] has played her cards well and played off the King and Consalvi like a profound politician.

Wednesday 6th. At length the quarrel has come to a challenge, but there is so much shuffling on the part of Pignatelli that I hardly yet think it will come to anything. I have scarcely escaped being Bingham's second, which I was to have been if we had not found Captain Arnold at home. He was gone out, but we sent to the Duke of Leeds's and hit upon him. Passed a very uncomfortable day. There is a dispute about weapons, but all the Austrians give it in favour of Bingham's right to pistols. Dined at Mr Smith's, Col. and Mrs Kenah, Bligh, Mr Moore and myself. Opera in the evening, where too much was said about the duel.

---

111 Franz Joseph, prince of Dietrichstein (1767-1854), was a prominent Austrian noble.
112 The Via Toledo, one of the main thoroughfares of Naples.

Thursday 7th. At three today they went out. Pignatelli's second had left him in consequence of his ungentlemanlike conduct, and when he came to the ground and he refused to fight with pistols and submitted to be called a coward and told by the second that Bingham would take every opportunity of insulting him, and report his conduct in the most public meetings of Naples.

After the affair went to the Toledo, but hardly got there when a child ran under my horse's legs. All the people called out *E morto—andate—* wishing me to make my escape as a Neapolitan would have done. Of course, I got off to see if the child was hurt and gave myself up to the Police, who are very strict on these occasions. I was detained four hours, but as the report of the child whom I saw there was very favourable, I did not so much mind it. I was at length allowed to go, Sir H Lushington answering for my appearance. While there I saw some other cases tried and was once taken for the Head of the Police by the Plaintiff and the Defendant, who began to plead their cases before me. I was prevented dining with Sir W. à Court who waited for Brecknock and me above an hour. Went to the Festino at S. Carlo, which was very dull. Supped with Bingham, Brecknock, Arnold and Carmarthen at the Albergo Reale.

Friday February 8th. The brother of the child has been down with me this morning. He brings a bad account. On which I sent up Boskelly the surgeon, whose account is doubtful. I am to send him again tomorrow, when he will be able to tell me more about it. Dined at the Duke of Leeds's, Borel, Brecknock, Lod. Blantyre, Bingham, Bligh, Mr Moore, Arnold and I. I had a <u>very</u> agreeable dinner. Ball at Lady Ellenborough's, very agreeable too. Staid late.

Saturday 9th. Dined with Brecknock, Borel, du Blaisel and Bingham. S. Carlo.

Sunday 10th. Toledo in the morning in the carriage with Brecknock and Arnold: a great many people and better than it has yet been. Fondo and the Festino at San Carlos, very good, suppers and card parties in the boxes and swarms of masks. Staid till 5 o'clock and left the House full. Went to supper at the Albergo Reale, which was full also, with Bingham and Brecknock.

Monday February 10th. The finest day that ever was seen—an English summer day. Dined with Lady Ellenborough, sat between Freddy and Lady Charlotte. All pleasant people and yet a dull dinner and longer than anything that ever was seen, à Courts, 4 Leeds's, 6 Laws, Borel, P. of Hesse, P. Butera and I. S. Carlo and Academia in the evening. The latter very full and good. Pignatelli was there and not Bingham which I was sorry for. P. was dancing; Arnold, Brecknock, Carmarthen and I got immediately opposite to insult him, but he would not look. After all it was not worthwhile. Came away about one. Great preparations making in the garden to celebrate the Emperor of Austria's birthday tomorrow, a temporary chapel building and all the troops to be drawn out. What is to take place except a Mass I know not.

Saturday 23rd. <u>Rome</u>. What a change has taken place since I last wrote in my journal and how little did I then think that I should now be dating here it from here. What passed in the week I know not. Saturday 17th the à Courts left us and about half an hour after they were out of the house the Porter appeared in the Drummond livery: this disgusted all Naples. At the opera in the evening. Duke of Leeds's box. After it was over, the Duchess, who had been out of humour, suddenly exclaimed: 'I said nothing during the opera, but I <u>hate</u> having people in my box all night.' I was literally stunned, but at the same time very much offended, and said 'I am only sorry your Grace did not tell me so earlier. I have <u>now</u> the honour of wishing you a good evening', and rushed out of the box, found my carriage, and when I got home was violently ill. Next morning, Sunday, I had come to the determination of leaving Naples immediately, for I can only interpret the Duchess's speech, 'I do not approve of your attentions to Lady C. if you mean nothing', and though it is too late to fly for my own sake, I cannot in honour stay, knowing that I am not in circumstances to propose. Passed a wretched four days, during which I sedulously avoided all the Duke's family, except to take leave of them, which I got through to my own astonishment. Refused two invitations to meet them at dinner and set out for Rome on Thursday. Arrived at Rome on Friday night, found the à Courts still here and delivered letters to them, but as they set out this morning I suppose I shall not see them. Seen nobody but Bingham and Brecknock, the former tells me he shall not return to Naples, but join the à Courts at Madrid.

Sunday 24th. Crowds of people and a mob of acquaintances, but very dull. Dined with Brecknock. Found lodgings 43 Bocca di Leone and move into them tomorrow.

Monday 25th. Dined with the Talbots, large party, Lady Abercorn[113] (who sent four men one after the other to say she wanted to be introduced

---

113 Lady Anne Hatton (1763-1827), who married the marquess of Abercorn in 1800. He predeceased her in 1818.

to me at St Peter's yesterday), Lady Sandwich[114] and her daughter, Col. and Mrs Ponsonby, Sneyd, Vincent, Bradshaw, Bingham and I, and M. la Marre. Appony's in the evening. Bad set of English and very dull.

Tuesday 26th. A visitation from Otway in the morning, introduced to Mr Neville. Called on the Margravine, but found her *poco bene* [not very well] and was not admitted. Got into my new lodgings, which I like tolerably well. Dined with Lady Alvanley, Lord G. and Lady Georgiana Quin who is delightful,[115] Mr Vincent, Col. Gordon,[116] Sneyd and myself. Dullish dinner and bad party at Mrs Bold's yesterday.[117]

Wednesday 27th. Rode with Brecknock to the new excavation. Very civil young Englishman, some young artist I conclude, staid some time. Dined with Lady Westmoreland, who is much madder than ever. A very odd party, Lady Walpole, Mr and Mrs Crauford, Bradshaw, Lord Suffolk and Lady Elizabeth,[118] and myself. Cradock and the Ladies came in the evening. Went away early.

Thursday 28th. Dined at home. Asked Edsell, Mills, Childers, and St John[119] to dinner. Two of the party are going to Naples.

March 1822

Friday 1st March. Dined with Ld. Kinnaird, Ld. and Lady K., Mr and Lady C. Fitzgerald, Lord Carnarvon,[120] M. Lamarre, M. Bertholdi, Bingham and one or two more. Dullish dinner. Was to have gone tomorrow

---

114 Lady Louisa, née Lowry-Corry (1781-1862), who married the 6th earl of Sandwich in 1804.
115 Lord George Quin (1792-1888), son of the 1st marquess of Headfort, and his wife, Lady Georgiana, daughter of the 2nd Earl Spencer. They married in 1814.
116 Colonel Charles Gordon (1790-1835), younger brother of the 4th earl of Aberdeen.
117 Mary Patten Bold (*c.* 1770-1835). She inherited Bold Hall in Warrington, Lancashire, from her aunt, and was the widow of Peter Patten Bold, whom she married in 1790. Her husband, who possessed estates in Lancashire and Cheshire, was an MP from 1797 to 1818. He died in 1819.
118 Lady Elizabeth Howard (1803-1845), eldest child of the earl of Suffolk.
119 The Hon. Ferdinand St John (1804-1865) was a son of the 3rd Viscount Bolingbroke. In 1789 Bolingbroke caused a scandal by having an affair with his half-sister Mary Beauclerk, and leaving his wife and children for the Continent. In the 1790s he entered a bigamous marriage with Anne, Baroness von Hompsech, and died in Pisa in 1824. His son Ferdinand St John lived a life of leisure on the Continent, publishing *Rambles in Germany, France, Italy and Russia in Search of Sport* in 1853.
120 Henry Herbert, 2nd earl of Carnarvon (1772-1832). He succeeded his father to the title in 1811.

with Neville and Bingham to the Chapel at Ostia, the former being ill we thought better of it.

Saturday 2nd. Refused Sir G. Talbot on account of the Chasse, dined with St John and prevented him from going to Naples.

Sunday 3rd. Down at St Peter's, nobody there. Bingham gone to the Chasse with Lemarre. Saw the new arm of the Vatican, a fine room with many faults, the pavement superb, the way of lighting ugly, but not bad. Steps up to one of the windows very mean and paltry contrivance. Dined with Brecknock and went to bed early!

Monday 4th. *Grande partie di Chasse* [large shooting party], eleven guns, which ended in the *cacciatori* killing two Chevreuil. Not a boar seen. Did not return until ½ past nine. Supper at Mills's.

Tuesday 5th. Rode with St John, dined with Ld. Carnarvon—Ld. Suffolk, and Lady Elizabeth, Ld. Kinnaird, Lady Walpole, Mr Vincent, Mr Sebright and myself. A dullish dinner, but pleasanter in the evening. Came home and went to bed without going to Blacas or Lady Westmoreland's.

Sunday 17th. Rome has afforded little to note in my journal. I have been dining out almost every day, but with the same round of people. Few parties in the evening and the mornings passed chiefly in riding with the Bolds.[121] Miss Bold [Mary] is infinitely better than she was, and I have good hopes that her life may be prolonged. Clare is much in love with her and I wish this may do: as also little St John with Fanny [Frances Bold]. He and I are living together and I find him a very agreeable companion, and with a fund of spirits which never fails. He talks of next year going to Vienna and I hope to be able to accompany him. Dined with Lady Alvanley, not a very agreeable dinner. Mrs Bolds's in the evening, but nobody there except the <u>regulars</u>.

Monday 18th. Disappointed at receiving no letters from England or Naples; wrote to my Grandfather. Dined at home and went nowhere.

Tuesday 19th. Received the intelligence of the defeat of Ministers on the question of the two junior Lords of the Admiralty. Glad to find that the country gentlemen are beginning to <u>think</u>, though the question in itself

---

121 Mrs Bold was travelling with three daughters: Mary Patten Bold (1795-1825), the eldest, Frances Patten Bold and Anna Maria Bold. Her second eldest daughter, Dorothea Patten Bold, had married Sir Henry Houghton in 1820.

is of no great importance. Dined with Lady Ruthven, Count and Countess Stackelberg,[122] M. de Hahn, M. de Stackelberg, Marquis Sommary, Vyvyan, Bradshaw, Sneyd, Medici and myself. A small party in the evening and agreeable. Staid lateish and did not go to Blaca's.

April 1822

Sunday April 7th. My journal has again been suspended for a good while and I think little has occurred very interesting. The Pope is in so bad a state that he has not been able to officiate at any of the ceremonies and, in consequence, there is, I believe, no Benediction, which would otherwise be going on at the moment. The Austrians are very anxious, but I know not for what reason, that the Pope should live till September. I do not know what difference this will make in their designs. There was a report that he was actually dead, but Borel, whom I saw yesterday, says this is not true, but he is only kept alive by Tokay [a sweet white Hungarian wine] which Appony sends him. The Austrian plan is said to be this. There are in the Conclave two parties, very nearly even, at the head of one of which is Consalvi, and of the other I believe Cardinal Pacca:[123] the Emperor wishes to keep these balanced and to force the Conclave to remain sitting for a great length of time. This being a scandal to all good Catholics, he then claims and always has claimed the privilege of interfering, to put an end to scandal, and nominates his own brother the Archduke Rudolph:[124] but I can hardly think this plan will succeed.[125]

A change of ministers at Naples is confidently expected. The Abbé Campbell, an old government spy, is come here under a pretence of being sent for by Lady Bute,[126] which I know to be false: he is constantly closeted with Medici, and I believe there is little doubt that their conversations turn upon the return of the latter to Naples in the room of Circello.[127]

I dined yesterday with Lady Ellenborough and had a rather agreeable party, though G. says it was very stupid. The Laws, Prince of Hesse, Borel, du Blaisel, Col Bock a Russian, Lord Rosehill, a Mr Telip, G. and I. A party in the evening and staid till 12 o'clock: too late for Lady Ruthven.

---

122 Count Ernst von Stackelberg (1766-1850), a diplomat of Estonian birth who represented Russia at the Congress of Vienna.
123 Cardinal Pacca (1756-1844).
124 Rudolph, archduke of Austria (1788-1831). He was also archbishop of Olomuc and was made a cardinal by Pope Pius VII in 1819.
125 Pope Pius VII lived until August 1823, when Cardinal Annibale della Genga (1760-1829) was elected to succeed him as Pope Leo XII.
126 Lady Maria North (1793-1841), who married the 2nd marquess of Bute in 1818.
127 The marquis di Circello.

Sunday April 14th. Little or nothing happened this week. The old Pope, instead of being dead, performed Mass himself last Sunday in his private Chapel, and is said to be recovering. It is said that there will be a great Congress at Florence in the month of September next, which will account for the anxiety of the Austrians for the preservation of his life.[128] Made acquaintance this week with Prince Sapieha, a Pole, and a friend of St John's.[129] He seems a very gentlemanlike man and a fine open manly character. I have seen a good deal of him in the last week and like much what I have seen. He talks of making, with St John and me, the tour of the Abruzzi, which I hope he will do. Dined the other day with Old Margravine, met nobody but Gell, Capt. Scurth, Vyvyan and Lady Hardy, who seems as lively a person as ever I happened to meet. The old Lady is very much aged, and has got yellow rouge which does not improve her beauty. Clare and Sneyd gone to Naples and everybody else going away. Lady Ruthven went away the other day.

May 1822

Aquila, Sunday evening, May 5th. Just arrived across the mountains from Rome, with a little time to resume my unhappy journal. The last fortnight has been occupied by a very agreeable and very amusing excursion to Albano with the Bolds, Bradshaw, St John and Sapieha, from which we returned to Rome on Tuesday last. On Thursday May 2nd set out again from Rome in rain late in the day after a thousand difficulties, and arrived at Tivoli at 7 o'clock, long before our guide and saddle bags. We, therefore, took a doubled bedded room, put the table between us and dined in bed. Friday 3rd a beautiful day. Set out in good time, halted at Vicovaro, and soon after left the Subiaco road, over the steep and dreary mountain of the Spiaggia, descending the other side arrived at an ugly plain bound by a fine Amphitheatre of mountains, and after crossing the plain, arrived at Carsoli, a miserable little town on the edge of the hills, very prettily situated. The last two miles upon the old Valerian Way, but not distinguishable. At Carsoli we were received at 4 o'clock by the Signor Capitan, a plain vulgar shrewd countryman of about sixty years old, with a host of brothers and sons. He received us, however, most hospitably, but never could escape from one or another of them. As fast as one left the room another came in, and to all our reiterated entreaties that they would not

---

128   At the Congress of Laibach in May 1821, Austria, Russia and Prussia agreed to hold a congress at Florence the following year. In the event, it was held at Verona between October and December 1822.

129   Eustachy Kajetan, Prince Sapieha (1797-1860). The princes of Sapieha were an historic Polish noble family.

give themselves so much trouble we had no answer but *'signor, é il mio dovere, angi mi piacen'* ['Sir, my duty pleases me']. The case was, therefore, hopeless and I talked Italian incessantly to relays of people for six hours and a half, not having any time to eat till ½ past 10. When it did come, however, it was certainly very good, but crammed down our throats plate after plate by our host, who was a fine specimen of <u>savage</u> hospitality. Hospitality, however, it was, and that to the greatest extent, though the manner was, perhaps, not the most agreeable. I made him very happy by a present of an English razor, which will be the pride of his heart, in consequence of which he appeared very well shaved next morning, which he certainly had not been for a month. Next morning, Saturday 4th, on our thanking him, he told us it was he who had to thank us for the honour *tanto poco da lui mentato* ['without a lie'].

Saturday 4th. The first part of our ride along the Valerian Way very beautiful, along a rich narrow mountain valley, the hills covered with fine timbers to the very top. At Colli it becomes more mountainous and rugged: at Rocca di Cerra we first caught sight of the main object of our journey, the Lago Fucino.[130] It required, however, above six hours ride to reach it. The approach to the Lake is rather disappointing, the mountains around it not being sufficiently high. It is, however, a very fine expanse of water, and quite the *vitrea Fucinus unda*.[131] We were received in the house of the Cavalieri Don Aurelio Mattei at Razzano, a neat little village something in the Swiss style. Our host and hostess were far superior to those at Carsoli, and their house really a good one. They were, however, both of them exceedingly full of ceremony, especially to My Lord, Mr Jones playing honourable Companion to perfection. Their civility and hospitality, however, were beyond anything. On our expressing a wish to see the Emissary that night, as we wished to set out again next morning, he immediately ordered out his carriage and sent for a gentleman of the place who performed the office of Cicerone, accompanied by whom we set out for this extraordinary work.[132] The main channel is no longer visible, as from the movements of the Lake it begins a mile from the present shore. During the last 24 years the Lake has risen extraordinarily. So much as to increase its circumference about ten miles, by which, of course, many persons have been ruined

---

130 Between 1862 and 1875 the lake was completely drained and the area turned into fertile farmland.

131 A quote from Virgil's *Aeneid*: 'Fucinus with a glassy wave.'

132 Because it had no natural outlet, Lago Fucino experienced dramatic changes of water level. According to Tacitus, the Roman Emperors Claudius and Hadrian constructed an emissary, an open or subterranean channel, through the mountain between the lake and the River Liris.

and even several villages overwhelmed. It has, however, gradually sunk for three years and the old proprietors are some of them already in possession again. The main channel of the Emissary being thus covered, all that is now visible are the *conicoli* [drain openings] and the *pozzi* [wells or shafts], of each of which there about seven, the two upper ones accessible for about 400 paces. The *conicoli* are almost 8 feet high by six or seven wide, cut into the solid rock, and are sloping passages opening into the mountain perpendicularly one above the other, for the purpose of descending into the great canal. The *pozzi* are merely circular openings cut perpendicularly for the purpose of admitting light and air and going through all the *conicoli* to the great canal. Each *conicoli*, after going a certain way, divides into two passages of different elevation in order to reach the great canal at different places. At the other side of the mountain the great canal itself is accessible for about 460 paces. It is even said the King has an idea to restore the Emissary to its original purpose. He has already laid out large sums upon it, but the work is suspended, the present estimate of expense to come in about £30,000. It appears to me quite evident, whatever the increase of the Lake may have been for the last few years, that it has at some time been much beyond its present limits, and I see no reason for supposing that the Emissary has not in some measure answered its purpose, and that the increase of the Lake has been perhaps more rapid from the stoppage of the Emissary.

On our return to the house we went out to walk with our host, returned about 8 o'clock, and found to our horror the whole town assembled and a regular card-party; as we did not understand the Italian cards it was very lively, the whole party being engaged, with the exception of ourselves. About 11, however, when our patience was nearly exhausted the party broke up and we got some supper and were then ushered by our host and hostess through a suite of seven rooms to our bedrooms, magnificently furnished, damask beds, silk hangings, etc. etc. I thought they both intended to sleep with us, but fortunately neither of them did so.

Next day, Sunday May 5th, they were ready to receive us at the door of our rooms after we had breakfast, and we took a most ceremonious leave, the Master of the house having the good taste to urge our setting out immediately, having an unfortunate rent in my nether garments behind.

Bologna—England

5 May to 29 July 1822

I took the opportunity of backing out of the room and thus escaped the observation of the Lady. The gentlemen followed us downstairs, saw us mount our horses, kissed us, and we set out. The ride for six miles along the Lake is very pretty and the road is very *carrozzabile* [capable of being driven in a carriage], running along what appears to have been the original boundary of the Lake, by the distinctly marked bank of round polished gravel stones as well as the flatness of all the land between for a considerable space. This road reaches to Celano, a prettily situated town with a castle [Piccolomini Castle] above it placed on a rising ground at the foot of the steep and craggy mountains, which on this side begin to border the Lake. Up one of these we began our ascent between snow mountains, the Avellino on the left and the Majella on the right, the latter, however, not visible. The views back upon the Lake from this ascent are very beautiful and the Lake itself is seen to much more advantage than from below. After a steep ascent of at least two hours we reached Carcolo [presumably near Ovindolo], a small town perched up at the very summit of the hill. The road is in most parts good and I have no doubt might be rendered *carrozzabile*. After passing Carcolo we travelled over a nearly dead flat, covered with fine pasture, closely resembling the pastures on the high Alps, and at this time of year in all its Spring beauty, covered with a profusion of wild flowers of all sorts. Among which we remarked what I believe to be a variety of the common heart's ease [pansy] perfectly yellow, intermixed with others entirely blue. As, however, I am not a botanist I may perhaps be only showing my ignorance. After near five hours riding at a foot's pace we reached Rocca di Mezzo, a poor wretched village with a building in it calling itself an

Osteria. The interior of which would have made a fine subject for Wilkie[1] to paint or Walter Scott to describe. I am sorry I cannot do justice to the long dark room, propped on sundry irregularly placed pillars, with tables scattered up and down, the fireplace in the middle, but no chimney, the smoke finding its way: unfortunately for us through the window we occupied, the rafters, walls, benches all black with it, and last and not least—the company! consisting of about 25 ill-looking Abruzzo peasants, the three women of the house, the priest, half-a-dozen dogs, cocks and hens *ad infinitum*, and our voiturier. In the midst of all this good company behold us seated at a long board calling itself a table, one or two more boards calling themselves benches, with two black loaves, a couple of bottles of wine, a dozen eggs *arrostiti da bere*, as the expression for a soft-boiled or soft-roasted egg, and some marinara [tomato sauce], or dried skate with oil and vinegar. For all of which we paid 48 grana, about 10d. While our horses were baiting [being fed], I could not resist an opportunity of assembling all these good people and, telling St John what would happen, I pulled out a pack of cards, though it was Sunday morning, and we began picquet. In five minutes the whole room, priest and all, were gathered round us; not the least shocked for the Italians play from morning to night, but from curiosity to see a game they did not understand played with cards they did not know, and here would have been a perfect picture, the expression of faces was admirable.

After leaving the Osteria we passed through a scrubby oak wood among rocks, reckoned a dangerous place for robbers. Here the winter still prevailed; not a leaf on the trees except here and there a withered one of last year and the grass hardly beginning to shoot. Soon after leaving this wood the Vale of Aquila opens upon us, for beneath us hills and mountains lay below at our feet, and the whole scene before us was richness, fertility and variety, while above us all was decay, desolate and uniform. Three hours of steep descent brought us to the high road from Naples, and half an hour more to the town of Aquila: beautifully situated, not as it before appeared to us, in the plain, but on a tolerably high and steep hill, ascended, however, by an easy and beautiful road. The city is handsome in appearance and seems thriving, but I am told its population is rapidly on the decrease. We went to the Croce d'Oro, a very moderate Inn, but such a relief from the excess of hospitality we had just escaped from, as cannot be conceived and only remembered by those who have been in similar circumstances. At Aquila we were obliged to present our passports within half an hour of arrival, and met with an Office Clerk who was all impertinence till we told him we were English, and all cringing servility afterwards.

---

1   The Scottish painter Sir David Wilkie (1785-1841).

Monday May 6th. Left Aquila and taking a wrong road too much to the right made a detour of about 7 or 8 miles. We at length, however, found our road and began to ascend the pass of Introdocco, a long and tiresome business: for the country thus far not very beautiful, and the day was scorching. At the top of the ascent or a little beyond it we stopped to bait at the place the Neapolitan Army had fortified, and might have defended against the world.[2] The road from Cittaducale ascends the hill in a single zig-zag, nearly amounting to a straight line, for at least 500 yards. On each side are very steep mountains all but impracticable to light troops, and which were to have been lined with Neapolitans. As it approaches the pass itself the hill on each side becomes perpendicular to the height of, I should think, sixty feet or more, leaving merely room for the road, and a house built in the side of the rock: immediately opposite the mouth of the pass is a knoll where the road takes a sharp turn, and where the Neapolitans had prepared a battery. Further back, on a higher hill overlooking the other, was a second battery, and the house in the pass was loop holed for musketry and one gun. In spite of all this, and many other points during the whole pass which is upwards of two miles long and might have been defended inch by inch from the Castle of Borghetto upwards, the Neapolitans, after the skirmish at Rieti, did not even halt in the pass and the guns of the higher battery were fired by the Austrian army for the first and only time. The single house is an Inn, and under a walnut tree opposite we found a muleteer sitting, having just dined. On our dismounting he offered us his bottle and glass which, of course, we accepted and much pleased at our preferring dining *al fresco* to the house. We had omelette, bread, cheese and wine, and paid 4 pauls. The people of the place spoke with great contempt of the Neapolitans. Indeed, the whole of the Abrazzi consider themselves as a totally distinct race of beings, and look on their southern neighbours with infinite contempt. They are generally speaking remarkably civil to strangers, at least we found them so on every occasion when we had anything to do with them. Nothing can surpass the beauty of the descent of Introdocco, by the castle of Borghetto and along the vale to Cittaducale, and indeed to Rieti. The views vary every moment and the richness and fertility of the valley and even of the mountains far exceeded my expectations. Reached Rieti after a fatiguing day of 13 hours, and found so miserable an Inn that nothing short of absolute necessity would have compelled us to stay in it. We left early next day.

---

2   General Pépé had hoped to resist the Austrian advance at the Introdocco Defile in 1821, but his Neapolitan troops abandoned the position following the initial clash at Rieti.

May 7th. Reached Terni in good time happy to rest from our fatigues, though we were amply repaid for our trouble. We had just done dinner when Sir George and Lady and Miss Talbots arrived and assisted us to pass our evening very agreeably.

Wednesday 8th. Went over with St John to see the celebrated bridge at Narni. I had seen it before and I own I think the second view disappointed me, though it is a noble ruin. The Bolds arrived in good time. Sapieha arrives tomorrow.

Thursday 9th. S. arrived in the morning and we employed the day in visiting the Cascade, near which we discovered a curious old bridge since I was last here, having been buried in rock. Hornby arrived this morning, but went on to Spoleto.

Friday 10th. Rode the first two posts to Spoleto where we breakfasted, and making a push reached Macerata at night.

Saturday 11th. To Sinigallia, a good Inn.[3]

Sunday 12th. Arrived at Forli [at the foot of the Apennines] in good time.

Monday 13th. Bologna. The [Hotel Il] Pellegrino, not being able to get in at the S. Marco. Found it very comfortable and staid three days there with the Bolds, seeing the Gallery,[4] the [Palazzo] Marescalchi (with which I was much disappointed on second sight), the Churches, and old Crescentini. Found the old Ox at dinner and sat with him while he chewed the cud. He seemed glad to see us and kissed us most tenderly. My conscience reproaches me for not calling upon old Cardinal Spina.[5] It is said, by the way, that he is likely to made Pope.

Friday 17th. Left Bologna and arrived early at Ferrara, a wretchedly decaying town, said to contain about 22,000 souls. Visited the Library[6] and saw the curious MS. of Taso, Ariosto and Guarini, with a jewel of a *custode* to show them.[7] He ought to have been born, and I think was,

---

3   The inn was called Locanda della Formica.
4   The Accademia delle Belle Arti.
5   Cardinal Giuseppe Spina (1756-1828).
6   The Biblioteca Comunale Ariostea, which held 80,000 books and 900 manuscripts.
7   The poet Torquato Tasso (1544-1595), whose most celebrated work was *Gerusalemme liberate* (1581); the poet Ludovico Ariosto (1474-1533), who is best known for his epic romance *Orlando Furioso* (1516); and the dramatist, poet and diplomat Giovanni Guarini (1538-1612), whose most notable play was *Il Pastor Fido* (1585).

at least a century ago and in his way was perfection. In one of the pages of *Orlando* Alfieri obtained permission to write his name, which he has done *Victtorio Alfieri vide & venerò*, with the date. The old Ducal Palace of Ferrara [Castello Estense] a gloomy old building, moated all round, and containing nothing remarkable. In the hospital of St. Anna they show a wretched cell, almost underground, in which they pretend that Tasso was confined, but I believe this <u>at least</u> doubtful. One cannot conceive the intellect of any one standing such a confinement in such a prison, and under gaolers, if they were as bad in Tasso's day as they seem now.

Saturday 18th. Reached Padua in very good time. Aquila d'Oro a good Inn.

Sunday 19th. Visited Santa Giustina, S. Antonio and the great Hall [in the Palazzo della Ragione], and came on to Venice. Found it quite full, but got in at the *Gran Brettagna* and took some rooms for Mrs Bold for tomorrow.[8]

Monday 20th. Mrs Bold arrived. There has been some comical work at Bologna and on the road. St John has at last come to a sort of explanation, which ended as it was sure to do, and as I told him long ago it must. The consequence is he is, of course, very wretched and I think he has not done wisely to come here at all. I am sorry for him, but it could not be otherwise.

Went this morning to the Accademia, the Titian, Tintoretto's St Mark are glorious and there are many others very fine; a Paris Bordon, a very good Leandro Bassano, a Paul Veronese, a Pordenone, and one by a painter whom I never heard of before, Rocco Marini, but whose style I like much.[9] One or two Churches, the Place S. Marco, dined early and went to the Café, etc. etc.

Tuesday 21st. Went over the old Ducal Palace [the Doge's palace]; we could not, however, see the whole of it as the modern Inquisition of Austria was sitting. A considerable number of the Noble Milanese were tried and condemned about a month ago; condemned to death, but reprieved by special favour and their sentences changed to ten or twenty years of solitary confinement; and some even for life! They were exposed to the whole multitudes assembled in the Piazza S. Marco, which was nearly full, stripped of their own dress and clothed in common felon's dress, and so conducted to prison. One of the Borromeos bought the

---

8   La Gran Bretagna was a small hotel on the Grand Canal.
9   The Venetian painters Paris Bordone (1500-1571) and Leandro Bassano (1557-1622); Giovanni Antonio de' Sacchis (1484-1539), who was known as Il Pordenone; and possibly the Venetian painter Antonio Maria Marini (1668-1725).

favour of 20 years banishment at half a million of florins. At least such is our *Laquais-de-place*'s story. True or not I cannot tell. The prisons of the Inquisition are more horrible than anything that ever were seen and I never shall forget the impression: the sight of them made my blood run cold. There was blood on the walls of one or two where prisoners had been strangled and one or two wretched inscriptions '...*sarà l'ultimo... di una povero morenrius e onesta famiglia*' ['... the last . . . of a poor sickly and honest family']. I did not see those Lord Byron mentions.

Went to the old Church of S. Mark, but did not see much of it, as I met the Bolds there. Had a long conversation with Miss Bold, whose marriage with Sapieha is almost definitely settled, but not announced.[10] I knew from herself that it was nearly so at Bologna, and I think then gave her, on her asking for it, my candid opinion on the subject. Of him personally I think very highly and she says, as she said then, that it was for him to choose, but that she never would give up her own country. The whole of her fortune will, I suppose, be settled on her, as he has declared he will never touch a shilling of it.[11] This is handsome and as it should be. I do not know what Mrs Bold and her sisters say to it, as they do not know I have heard anything of it. Clare and Hornby's speculations amuse me much, though I am shocked at my own hypocrisy in discussing probabilities with them on this subject and on that of St John, with whom they see there is something amiss. But I must do so to keep Miss B's secret. Dined with the Bolds and went to the Opera.

Wednesday 22nd. The Accademia and the Palazzo Barbarigo, where there are some very fine pictures, particularly of Titian, but in such a state that it is melancholy to see them. Afterwards to the fine old Church S. Giovanni e Paolo. Opera in the evening, the Bold's box as usual.

Thursday 23rd. Went with St John to see the glorious work of the Muraglia seven miles in length, the boldest work I ever saw.[12] After this I should like to see the Plymouth Breakwater, which I imagine superior even to this.[13] We returned with a brisk wind in time to see the Manfrin Palace where there is a splendid collection, a Rembrandt portrait, a Titian head of Ariosto, a Pordenone *tableau de famille*, two or more good Giorgiones, a good Guercino a very good Carlo Dolci, and a Repose in

---

10   Mary Patten Bold married Prince Sapieha in Florence in December 1822. She died in Rome of tuberculosis in 1824.
11   Mary was heiress to her mother's significant wealth.
12   The Muraglia is the extensive stone wall protecting the Venetian lagoon.
13   The Plymouth Breakwater was built between 1812 and 1814 to provide a safe anchorage for the British Channel Fleet.

Egypt by Ludovico Carracci, I think the flower of the collection and they in tolerable preservation.

Friday 24th. St John was to have gone, but did not. Went to see the gold chain manufacturing process, which is curious. The bars of gold, being reduced to wires, are flattened by passing between two rollers. They are then wound tight around a wire and this being withdrawn and the gold corkscrew thus formed being cut longitudinally, the links of the chain are made. They are then put together one by one, dipping each in gold dust, melting the ends of it in a little lamp and pinching them together to make the ends. The charm is then cleaned and polished and ready for sale. The last operation is ruinous to the eyes. The workmen are obliged to wear magnifying glasses and cannot work for above five or six years. To join on the beads alone of a *braccio* [arm] of chain takes 18 hours and yet they are sold at 18 francs the *braccio*!

We dined at the Bolds and had a very *triste* parting. I am sorry to leave them, as I like them much, especially Miss Bold, whose marriage with Sapieha is certain, but not announced.

Saturday 25th. Set out from Venice. Sapieha ordered his gondola and came with me; we had a long conversation upon his future prospects. Miss Bold had told them that she had spoken to me at Bologna and I told him exactly what I had said to her, not concealing from him that I had set before her the objections to the match, at the same time that I had spoken highly of him personally. He took it very well, thanked me, and said that my advice being asked, I was bound in honour to do what I had done. We parted very good friends and I shall be very glad to meet him again wherever it may be. Reached Padua early.

Sunday 26th. From Padua to Verona, where we found Clare arrived just before us, having come all the way from Venice.

Monday 27th. Went to the Giusto Gardens, from which there is a fine view of the city. The gardens themselves might be beautiful, but are spoilt by being laid out with straight walks and trim cypresses. There is a curious winding path that leads up to the perpendicular rock to a little cool summerhouse at the top; from whence the view is very fine. Verona is a busy handsome town, without many remarkable buildings, but wide good streets and a great air of cleanliness and comfort. There is a good altarpiece in the Church of S. Georgio in the part called Veronetta, by Paul Veronese, which was carried to Paris.[14] It is, however, so hid by wax

---

14   Paolo Veronese, *The Martyrdom of St George* (1564).

lights and the trumpery of the altar that it is difficult to see it. The Coliseum of Verona is glorious. There is little remaining of the outer wall, but the whole interior with all the *vomitories* [entrances through the banks of seats] etc. is perfect. Part of it, however, is modern, but not distinguishable from the ancient. There is a detestable little wooden theatre erected in the very arena, to the disgrace of all good taste on the part of the Veronese. Apropos of theatres, I forgot to mention that of Vicenza, built by Palladio on the model of the ancient ones, entirely composed of wood and *scagliola* [imitation marble]. It is reckoned very beautiful, but I confess it disappointed me. The range of columns which go round the back of the seats in a semicircle is a beautiful piece of architecture, but the whole theatre strikes me as disproportionately high and the slope of the benches too steep, which gives an appearance of confinement and flatness to the whole building.

Tuesday 28th. Made an excursion with St John to see the promontory of Sirmio [on Lake Garda], still called Sermione. We went to Desenzano and there embarked. The promontory is very picturesque not unlike, on a small scale, that of Bellagio on the Lake of Como. The Lake from SW to SE is flat or tame: but towards the north the mountains become very bold and fine. The Lake itself is 18 miles in length from E to W and in the middle just opposite Sirmio runs up a long defile into the Tyrol of 46 miles in length. Sirmio itself is quite *pennisularum insularium que ocellus*,[15] which expression, by the way, is exactly descriptive, for the narrow neck which joins it to the mainland is so low as to be hardly distinguishable, so that Sirmio has more the appearance of an island than a peninsular, and may be said to belong to both. On the very northern point stand some ruins which they call Catullus's villa. I pleased myself by imagining they were so, without examining too closely and, instead of going to the subterranean grottoes, took a delightful bathe in the Lake. We did not return to Verona till 12 at night; and missed seeing the Bolds, who are arrived. We woke up Sapieha, however, before he went to bed.

Wednesday 29th. Verona to Trent [Trento]. Went to see the Opera. The House is, I think, the prettiest I have seen in Italy, the decorations in very good taste, very light and neat. The singing was moderate, though there was one woman who was not bad.

Thursday 30th. From Trent to Brixen, 14 hours, a fine trial of patience.

---

15   A reference to a poem by Catullus (84-54 BC), who lived in a villa on the promontory.

Friday 31st. To Innsbruck, ditto, not to mention several squabbles with Post Masters and Post boys, whose insolence is beyond anything. St John and I <u>walked</u> all the last stage and without hurrying beat the carriage by a quarter of an hour, almost all downhill.

June 1822

Saturday June 1st. In taking a walk met Sapieha coming into the town, who told us the Bolds would be here tonight. Called on him afterwards, but thought we were received rather coolly. He told us he would call on us in the evening, but never came. Met Mycielski there on his road to Berlin, but only for a moment. The Bolds arrived in good time, but did not see them. Sapieha never came. Concluded they were tired, till we found out next day—Sunday 2nd—that Mycielski was with them all night. We are both sure that S. is jealous of my being consulted and they offended at our not calling, he not having mentioned our request.

A glorious and beautiful country all the way to Wallersee; walked almost all the way. Very uncomfortable little Inn and got very tipsy with four bottles of wine for 4 florins.

Monday 3rd. Reached Munich. An ugly country, nothing remarkable after the first post. Very well at the Cerf d'Oro.

Tuesday 4th. Gallery, English Garden, etc. Sent off a letter to Miss Bold explaining our not calling and St John another to S. upon a subject of more consequence. A very unpleasant conversation with St John in the evening which, however, ended in my opinion of him remaining what it was. It had been long on my mind and has been a great relief to have it over.

Wednesday 5th. To Schleissheim, an enormous palace and enormous collection, no doubt very curious, but for one who is no connoisseur hardly worth the trouble. Some good Salvator Rosa's in his bold manner, but not in a good state. A German sentimental Comedy in the evening, very lachrymose and dull, but I understood much more than I expected.

Thursday 6th. A great procession being the Fête de Dieu and one of the best I have seen. The Bavarian regular troops seem very fine and their musketeers beyond ridicule. The people very orderly and very ugly. A play in the evening, but of what sort God knows, neither Tragedy, Comedy, Melodrama, Opera or Ballet, but a little of all, and called Puziosa.

Friday 7th. No letter from the Bolds or P. Sapieha. I think we shall stay till Monday, and we must hear by that time. A letter arrived by Estafette [courier] this evening, to me and not to St John, to which I was, therefore, bound to answer, taking the whole business on myself as I was bound to do. He is very angry and I am not sure that it may lead to something unpleasant. Had St John answered the letter it must have done.

Saturday 8th. Carried my letter over myself to Steinhornig and there sent it by Estafette to Wasserburg, where I expected him to be. Waited until 12 o'clock at night, when I receive an answer he was not come. Returned to Munich at 6 in the morning.

Sunday 9th. Took a long ride on some wretched Munich hacks. Sapieha arrived in the evening, having received my letter. After a short conversation we remained good friends. He has, I think, behaved very well, having shown the whole correspondence to Miss Bold, whom it partly concerned: they arrive tomorrow and our *rencontu* [meeting] will be awkward.

Monday 10th. Went to the Gallery. On our return we found the Bolds arrived; they having set out at five in the morning horribly frightened and evidently expecting a disagreeable termination. I thought I was received well, but St John very coldly. Went out riding and very near killed our horses chasing 3 hares and a Chevreuil. We had a two mile run over the plain with the latter till he beat us in a thick fir wood. Returned and dined with the Bolds. Walked in the English Garden afterwards. But as I was entirely with F., I do not know what the rest think of my conduct. Whatever they think, they pretend to be quite satisfied. But it is too much their interest to be on good terms with me, for me to give implicit credence. God forgive me. I am getting very suspicious!

Tuesday 11th. Left Munich for Augsburg. Three Moors as before, but it did not strike me as so good an Inn. Spoilt by the stay at Munich which is excellent.

Wednesday 12th. An ugly country all the way to Ulm, a little poor town on the Danube. It surely cannot be the one which Mack gave up in 1806 [sic.], for it is not strong and commanded by heights on two sides.[16] At present there is a fair going on, and having not found rooms in the great Inn, we have got 5 in another. 3 Salons, in two of which St John and I

---

16   General Karl Mack von Leiberich (1752-1828) was commander of the army which opposed Napoleon's advance into Bavaria. At Ulm, in October 1805, he surrendered his entire army of 25,000 men to Napoleon, and two months later, following the battle of Austerlitz, he was convicted of cowardice and stripped of his rank.

had beds put up. Mine was the Ballroom, with 28 windows in it, *lustres* [candlesticks], etc. In the morning we were asked if we staid, because if we did, the Ball fixed for that evening should be put off!! We begged we might not derange anything and accordingly, Thursday 13th, set out through an ugly country, which, however, improves gradually and becomes even prettyish about Stuttgart. The entrance into the town is really handsome, but it seems a *triste* and very desolate town. The Inn, the Köenig von Würtemberg, but moderate.

Friday 14th. Went to see the [Ludwigsburg] Palace which is very handsome without and prettily furnished within, though the rooms are not handsome and some of them are in bad taste. There is in one of them an admirable picture of Frederick the Great which must be his living image. The present King[17] does not live in the Palace, but comes over from his country house a league off at seven o'clock every morning for the transaction of business. From the Palace we went to the collection of pictures which, however, having found to be entirely of the old German School we were leaving when we met Blane and Edwin Lascelles[18] on their road to Vienna. Went with them through the King's Stables, magnificent buildings, with a wretched set of several hundred fat horses. Returned to their Inn, having made an ineffectual attempt to see the sculptor Dannecker.[19] Found Henry Lascelles who is very wretched at Miss Greville's talked of marriage with F. Leveson and very anxious to get to Vienna where he expects letters to say whether it is certain.[20] Ran after them and jumped into their carriage without stopping them, over the doors one on each side. Made them carry us to the Baths, where they left us and whence we returned through the English Garden, pretty enough, but not comparable to the one at Munich.[21]

Saturday 15th. Country neither ugly nor pretty to Carlsruhe, a very pretty little plaything town, in the shape of a fan, street houses, palace and all to match, and very pretty, but not the least like a capital. Here, however, the Grand Duke lives I dare say very comfortably and the forest behind

---

17   King Wilhelm I of Württemburg (1871-1864), who succeeded his father in 1816.
18   The Hon. Edwin Lascelles (1799-1865) was a younger son of the 2nd earl of Harewood.
19   Johann von Dannecker (1758-1841).
20   Henry Lascelles (1797-1857), who succeeded his father as 3rd earl of Harewood in 1841, and Harriet Catherine Greville (1803-1866). Lord Francis Leveson-Gower (1800-1857), a younger son of the marquess of Stafford, became 1st earl of Ellesmere in 1846. He was a friend and exact contemporary of Stanley's at Eton and Christ Church, Oxford. He and Harriet Greville were married at St George's, Hanover Square, on 18 June 1822.
21   The English Garden at Ludwigsburg Palace was established by King Frederick I of Württemburg during the 1790s.

his Palace is very handsome.[22] My servant was so anxious to see some relation of his at Strasburg (he says his sister, but I suspect his wife) that I could not refuse him, and accordingly, Sunday 16th, we went there. Road good, but detestably ugly. Lodged in a tolerable Inn, the Esprit. The French Douaniers [customs officers] very strict and we, therefore, only took two *sacs de nuit* [night bags], which they searched from one end to other. In spite of which, Auguste managed to smuggle some things over.

Monday 17th. The Cathedral of Strasburg is a noble building, handsomer, however, without than within, as the Choir, I believe the oldest part, quite spoils the effect of the interior. The tower is very high and grace-ful.[23] I think the view from the platform disappointed me; as did also the monument of Marshal Saxe[24] and of Professor Schöpflin in the Church of St Thomas's. Opposite the latter, however, is a monument of Professor Koch which struck me as very pretty, a female figure reclining against a tomb, the attitude graceful and easy.[25] The Collection of pictures under the direction of Guérin[26] at the Meinu [a district on the outskirts of Strasburg in the 1820s] is very inferior and his own famous picture is in the very worst style of French taste. I do not remember the subject, though I have a confused idea of a figure in the foreground which makes me guess it to be Cain and Abel.[27]

The town of Strasburg has very few handsome buildings and there seems nothing to detain one above a day. The Catholics and Protestants are nearly equally divided, the former having 6 Churches and the latter 7. There is a pretty building with a garden called the Orangerié outside of the ramparts built for Josephine.[28] The garden is a semicircle enclosed by a shady walk of oriental planes. The plan will serve as a hint for the dairy at Knowsley.

Tuesday 18th. Left Strasburg. On the road (why <u>here</u> I cannot understand nor can anyone tell me) is the monument of General Desaix.[29] I did not

---

22   Louis I, grand duke of Baden (1763-1830), who succeeded his uncle in 1818.
23   Until 1874, Strasbourg Cathedral was Europe's tallest building. An enraptured Goethe described it as the 'sublimely towering, wide-spreading tree of God'.
24   Marshal Maurice de Saxe (1696-1750). The monument was made by the French sculptor Jean-Baptiste Pigalle (1714-1785).
25   Johann Schöpflin (1694-1771), professor of history, law and rhetoric at the university of Strasbourg, and Christoph von Koch (1737-1771), professor of constitutional law and history, also at the university of Strasbourg. Both professors taught Goethe, and Koch also taught Metternich. Koch's monument was sculpted by Landolin Ohmacht (1760-1834).
26   The French painter Pierre-Narcisse Guérin (1774-1833).
27   Possibly Guérin's painting *The Death of Cato* (1797).
28   Joséphine, née de La Pagerie (1763-1814), first wife of Napoleon and first empress of the French.
29   Louis Desaix (1768-1800), the French general who seized victory out of defeat for Napoleon

think it anything remarkable, though I had heard it much praised. Reached Heidelberg, through Carlsruhe, about ½ past 10. Found a very comfortable Inn, the Court of Baden.

Wednesday 19th. Made a short excursion up the Vale of the Neckar, which is well wooded and pretty enough, but I think hardly repays one or two hours' drive. Returned by the Wolfsbrunnen, which are a set of *bathe mineral* I believe, one above the other, like a flight of steps coming down between two wooded hills of only second rate beauty. On arriving, however, at the old Castle of Heidelberg we are amply repaid for our trouble by finding I think the most beautiful view I ever saw. It was partly blown up by the French troops under Louis the 14th, and has remained in ruins ever since. The old Church, however, and the Ritter Saal were not destroyed, till they were burnt by lightning 54 years ago last Monday. The shell of the building is all that is left. The architecture is that of James 1st's time, Tudor Gothic, richly ornamented; we found there an artist who is engaged about a work, which will be very beautiful, representing the different carvings about the building, some of which are beautiful. We bought of him some prints of the Castle, and had his great work been finished I think I should have been tempted. The stone is precisely the same as Knowsley and the windows as nearly together as those of the West Front, which, I am therefore convinced, might be altered in this style if it were worthwhile. We left Heidelberg and travelled across a frightful country, flat, without a tree, and seas of corn, along the banks of the Neckar to Mannheim. This town was destroyed by Louis 14th and has since been built with great regularity and beauty. The streets are wide, very clear, and at right angles; so that from almost every corner one sees the whole extent of the town. The principal street is planned up the middle with a broad alley of trees which have a good effect. The Palace, formerly the residence of the Electors Palatine and since of the Kings of Bavaria till ceded to Baden in 1803,[30] is an enormous building in this shape . . ., but except its size has not much to recommend it. From its size alone, however, it becomes one of the finest palaces we have seen and far too good for the Grand Duke of Baden, particularly as he never lives in it, as he has his family Palace at Carlsruhe. No one lives there, but the Dowager Stéphanie,[31] niece of Joséphine, to whom it must be a sort of prison. The ramparts behind the town are turned into a garden, which for its extent, which is very *bonné*, is not amiss. The inside of the Palace we intend seeing tomorrow. One wing has been

---

at the battle of Marengo (1800). Desaix was killed at the moment of his triumph.

30   It was in fact ceded to Baden in 1802.

31   Stéphanie, grand duchess of Baden (1789-1860), was the widow of Karl, grand duke of Baden (1786-1818).

gutted completely by fire. When I know not, but believe during the last bombardment of '94.

Thursday June 20th. Did not see the Palace <u>having got up too late</u>. We went on a day's drive through just the same country as before yesterday. Seas of corn, dead flat, and no trees, till after crossing the river at Oppenheim, and leaving the next post, Gross Gerau, we enter an immense forest called the Frankfurter Wald, which relieves the eye at first, but soon becomes as monotonous as the plain we had left. Immediately on quitting this we come to Frankfurt, a handsome town with good streets and many fine houses, giving the idea of just what it is, an opulent mercantile town, very much in the style of Liverpool, but improved. A number of new houses are building and the town seems thriving. The Weidin Busch a good Inn, immensely large and with a noble Salle, in which there is a *table d'hote* every day of from 40 to 60 persons, never less than 40.

June 21st. I have often been disappointed by Guide Books and reports, but never so much as today. Went by the directions of Schrieber's *Rhine*[32] to see 1st the Cathedral, and was a little staggered on finding a very mean paltry building in the form of a Latin Cross and evidently of no higher antiquity from the style of the architecture than the 14th century at the earliest. Schrieber says 827. The Pfarrheim is certainly handsome and certainly the corner buttresses, but this is of the 15th century and never has been finished. Hence to the Braunfelhof or Exchange. As paltry a one as ever I saw and this surprised me the more as it is a great commercial town. My *Laquais-de-place* then begged me to the Römer Saal, a building in which Emperor Joseph was crowned.[33] I first saw a fine room enough, now used as a Library, but nothing very striking in it: and on saying this cannot be <u>the</u> fine room you talk of, he said 'Oh no!' and took me to a little square room, about 25 feet, and told me that was it. Wishing the Emperor Joseph joy of his coronation I went to the Saalhof or residence of the Carolingian Kings. This is, I believe, a magazine [a military storehouse], for having penetrated through some houses to an archway, my guide told me so and added that was all I could see. My last object of curiosity was the old Palace of the house of Thurn and Taxis. When I arrived at it he told me that there was nothing inside, and if there was I would not see it, for an Austrian General lodged there. The outside is a commonplace looking red house, with a great

---

32   Aloysius Wilhelm Schrieber (1761-1841), court historiographer in Karlsruhe, published a
       number of travel guides to the region. In 1818 he published his *Handbuch für Reisende
       am Rhein*.
33   The Holy Roman Emperor Joseph II (1741-1791). He was crowned in Frankfurt in 1764.

gateway, a court, *il predterra nihil*. To wind up all, I was taken round the ramparts, or about half the *quondam* ones, along a very tolerable promenade and so back to my Inn, and so blessing Mr Schrieber, Historiographer to the Grand Duke of Baden, and hoping his histories are more veracious and not so flattering as his Guide Books.

I got in my carriage, and went to Mayence [Mainz] passing by a little village called Höchst, which seems entirely composed of an old Chateau, now divided into small houses, with a long iron railing before it. It has no pretentions to architectural beauty, but has been and still is striking from its size. The road to Mayence is flat and ugly, and it is only from Hockheim that it is prettyish from the number of vineyards. The junction of the Main and the Rhine is fine, and the united streams form a noble river, crossed by a bridge of boats joining Cassel and Mayence. The latter has an imposing appearance seen from the river. It belongs to the Duke of Hesse Darmstadt, but is now garrisoned provisionally by 8,000 Austrians and Prussians, half of each. The Cathedral is very ancient and (though built of red stone or rather I believe of brick and plaster columns) very handsome. It has, according to Mr Schrieber rightly, suffered in the revolution. That is, it has lost half of the roof and the towers at one end. The convent adjoining it has been entirely destroyed and the corridors of the Cathedral itself have been deprived of their ornamental stonework, which adorned all of their arched windows, three of which still remain to show how beautiful the whole must have been. In this corridor are several old monuments, the most remarkable of which is that of Heinrich Frauenlob, the poet of the 13th century, who was carried to his grave by the women of Mayence.[34] The monument of Fastrada wife of Charlemagne was transported to this Church from another, which is burnt down as an inscription under the old one proves.[35] Out of the new gate, on the Mannheim road, between the river and the Citadel, is a new garden just laid out as a public promenade, which promises to be pretty enough.

June 22nd. Went early in the morning to see a collection of pictures, but thought them very moderate. A large landscape by Philippe de Champaigne one of the best.[36] They give great names to them all, but it seemed to me very ill applied. From Mayence we took the Post road and great was our horror on finding that it did not run even within sight of the Rhine, till we reached Bingen. There, however, it comes down upon it and for the remainder of its course hardly ever loses sight of it. Little as I expected

---

34 The influential Middle High German poet Henrich Frauenlob (*c.* 1250-1318).
35 Fastrada (765-794) was the third wife of Charlemagne.
36 Philippe de Champaigne (1602-1674).

of the Rhine, I confess I was disappointed, but we are spoilt by coming from Italy and the Tyrol. The hills are mostly round, tame and destitute of trees, and the chief beauty of the scenery consists in the old ruined towers, which are here and there scattered about and always picturesquely placed. I should say that the scene immediately about St Goar, with the ruins of the old Castle of Schönberg (from which the Marshal Schömberg took his name)[37] immediately above it is the most striking. We slept at a little Inn at Boppard, clean but not good, and the next morning,

Sunday June 23rd, breakfasted at Coblenz. The situation is fine, on the confluence of the Rhine and Moselle (*ad confluentis*) and the ruined Castle of Ehrenbreitstein, or the Broad Rock of Honour, on the other side of the Rhine immediately opposite the town. The streets and buildings appeared very ordinary and we made no stay. Almost immediately after leaving the town, passed in a cornfield the plain tomb of Marceau and soon after that of Hoche.[38] The country is here flat and ugly, but mends again near Andernach and becomes pretty enough, till we pass the Siebengebirge and the Castle of Drachenfels. It is then very uninteresting till we reach Cologne, a large, old, ugly town, where we slept at the Mainzer Hof, or rather were to bed, for there was such a noise in the house that sleep we could not. We had meant to stay a day here, but changed our minds, and therefore Monday 24th. Went out to see the Lions, with a son of Dr Dorati, whom George knew at Brussels, acting as our Cicerone. He is here as a German student and the account he gives of the want of discipline and malorganisation of the University makes me cease to wonder at the name German students have acquired all over Europe. Boys of 14 are admitted, are quite their own masters, at liberty to change their Professors when they like, and as each Professor's salary depends on the number of Boys whom attend his lectures, of course they are dependent on their scholars, and their only aim is to curry favour by indulgence. They have secret political societies and political clubs—boys of 14!!!—and every member of the University on entering takes an oath to stand by the others in everything they do, good or bad. The consequence is they have had the military called in against them more than once. Our Cicerone, whom I did not admire, took us to one or two

---

37   Marshal Frederick Schomberg (1615-1690) was second in command to William of Orange when he landed in England in 1688. He was made the 1st duke of Schomberg in 1689, and was killed at the battle of the Boyne in 1690.

38   François Marceau (1769-1796), a French general, was killed in battle aged twenty-seven. The tomb Stanley mentions is a small simple pyramid. In 1889 his ashes were transferred to the Panthéon in Paris. In 1796 General Louis Hoche (1768-1797) led the failed French attempt to invade Ireland and join up with the nationalist United Irishmen to bring British rule in Ireland to an end.

Churches. The most remarkable of which are the Church of St Peter, where there is a beautiful picture of the Crucifixion of that Apostle by Rubens, who was baptised here on St Peter's day. On the other side is a wretched copy by a German artist. There is nothing else in the Church worth notice, except that in the ruined convent adjoining Marie de Medici closed her life. The Cathedral, though unfinished, is a very fine specimen of Gothic architecture, but it is not above half completed and of course never will be. In the rest of the town there appears little or nothing to see, and our Inn being bad we left Cologne about one and travelled through an ugly country over new-made gravel roads, to Aix la Chapelle [Aachen], where we arrived about nine, and went to a new Inn, apparently very good, the Hotel des Etrangers.

Tuesday 25th. The town, so far as I have yet seen it, seems handsome, as far as cleanliness and good wide streets can make it. The Cathedral is in the form of one of the old Roman Baptisteries, with a choir tacked on to one end. The circular part is as old as the time of Charlemagne, who was buried here, and whose bones they religiously preserve as well as his chair of white marble. His body was found embalmed sitting in the chair by Frederic Barbarossa, who removed it and stripped the gold from the chair, and placed the latter in a gallery where it still remains, and has served as the coronation chair for many of the Emperors. The French respected this chair and left it where they found it. The Porphyry pillars which were brought by Charlemagne from Jerusalem they carried to Paris, but they have since been returned. In the Hotel de Ville, in the Salon where the Congress of 1748 was held,[39] there is a picture representing it, but the old man who showed it us could not name the portraits. There are other portraits of the several Ambassadors, but none by good masters or of very distinguished persons. Here also the Congress of 1815 was held, but there is not here any picture representing it.[40] Though I believe one exists. There is a portrait of the King of Prussia, a striking likeness.[41] We find here the Queen of Sweden with Prince Oscar who are lodged opposite and whose presence will bring crowds to the Baths this year.[42] It is said the Queen of the Netherlands is coming, but I should

---

39   The 1748 Congress of Aix-la-Chapelle brought an end to the War of the Austrian Succession, an eight-year-long conflict between all the major European powers.

40   Stanley is in fact talking of the October 1818 Congress of Aix-la-Chapelle, which was attended by Britain, Austria, Prussia, Russia and France. The purpose was to agree on the withdrawal from France of the army of occupation and to renegotiate French reparations. This congress therefore concluded the agreements made at the Congress of Vienna in 1815.

41   King Frederick William III of Prussia (1770-1840), who succeeded his father in 1797.

42   Désirée, née Clary (1777-1860), who married King Charles XIV of Sweden in 1798, and Prince Oscar (1799-1859), who succeeded his father as King Oscar I of Sweden in 1844.

think this doubtful.[43] The second view of the town is not so favourable as the first. Walked up to a hill behind it, where there is a good view of the country around. On the side of the town it is rich varied and well sprinkled with trees; on the other sides bare and ugly enough. The ramparts of the town destroyed and the ditch filled up and planted as a promenade all round, but not yet finished.

Forgot to mention an anecdote which amused me at Cologne. In the town is a fountain on which the Prefect, a zealous Frenchman, put the inscription *à Napoleon le Grand—l'an 1818 mémorable pour la guerre contra les Prusses*. On the passage of the Prussian army the General saw this and on the other side engraved *Préfectual de . . . Vin et par nous . . .*

Wednesday 26th. Left Aix la Chapelle, in German Aachen, and arrived at Liege, in German Luttig. The situation of the town is good, upon the side of a hill, the river running through it in several small branches, but the houses and streets are mostly mean, with the exception of the Palace which formerly belonged to the Bishop, and is very handsome, in the Moorish style of architecture, <u>something</u> resembling the old Palace at Venice, and surrounding four sides of a court supported on Arcades. The drive along the river is generally very pretty scenery, especially between Huy and Namur, being rocky and well wooded, but a vast quantity of the wood has lately been cut down. I suppose by government, which has for the time considerably impaired the beauty of the country. We reached Namur.

Thursday 27th. A late breakfast, having set out at 4, in order to get to Brussels. From Namur the road is hideous passing over a flattish open country and crossing the centre of the line of Waterloo. We had not time to stop and examine it, as I mean to make it the object of a day's journey. The immediate environs of Brussels are much better, but the town has for the present been much altered for the worse by levelling the high rampart, on which were some fine old trees and from whence there was a fine view of the whole city. The present Boulevard which they are making all round the city <u>will</u> be handsome. The people all say they are *comme à Paris* and therefore *tout a qu'il y a De plus beau*. Saw the Blundells as we drove into the town; Mrs B. did not know me. The Flanders being full, established at the Hotel d'Angleterre, not uncomfortable.

---

43   Frederike, née Wilhelmine (1774-1837), who married King William I of the Netherlands in 1791.

Friday 28th. Settling accounts, looking over clothes half the morning. Received a number of letters from England. I am sorry to hear the proposal actually made by the Liverpool people to bring me in without a contest has been refused, but I do not know that it is all over yet. We shall have some conversation on that subject when we return. Walked about the town a good deal. The town hall where Charles V abdicated[44] is a fine old building and the Cathedral or Church of St Gudula is [a] very handsome Gothic Church, though its two towers are quite ruined. Walked in the Park and the States House which was burnt is rebuilding, and makes or would make a noble termination to that side of the square. Wrote a long letter to my father which I find I may carry myself as the Post does not go out till Tuesday. Dined early and drove in the Abbé verti. Theatre afterwards. One or two tolerable actors, but stupid play and worse opera.

Saturday 29th. Was to have gone with Blundell to Lachen, but a bad day and sore throat prevented me; so I staid at home and to amuse myself took a dose of salts.

Sunday 30th. Rode to Waterloo and went over the whole of the ground, which enables one to have a very good idea of the operations of the day. From our guide, old Lacosti, I think we got nothing very new or very interesting. Dined quietly with Blundell.

July 1822

Sunday July 28th. After a month's interval I resume my journal, as well as I can remember what has happened. Monday July 1st. Dined with Blundell again, but not quietly, and met a party of near 100 people in the evening of whom I knew not one. Introduced, however, to plenty, among others Lady C. Lemon, Lady Lansdowne's sister.[45]

Tuesday July 2nd. Left Brussels and arrived without accident though late at Ypres.

---

44 The Holy Roman Emperor Charles V (1500-1558), who abdicated in 1556 and retired to the monastery of Yuste in Spain.
45 Lady Charlotte, née Fox-Strangways (1784-1826), daughter of the earl of Ilchester, who married Sir Charles Lemon in 1810. She was sister to Lady Louisa (1785-1851), who married the marquess of Lansdowne in 1808.

Wednesday 3rd. Very unwell and to mend it upset in dining off the Champré onto the China de terre. Got, however, early to Calais and there took to my bed.

Thursday 4th. Passed in bed.

Friday 5th. Got over with a bad sore throat, smuggled all my goods and Chattels, and slept at Canterbury. Mrs C. looking very well and I hope their difficulties drawing to a close.

Saturday 6th. Arrived in town. Expected to find my Grandfather in, but he left it yesterday. Found, however, a letter announcing Lord Grosvenor's[46] offer of bringing me into Parliament for Stockbridge.[47] Sent him a note thanking him and accepting the offer with the condition that I should follow my own inclinations in voting. He called in the evening and was everything I could wish. Confined to my room by Liversay till Friday 12th. Several people called, but I saw none except Clare, who spoke of Miss B.'s marriage with Sapieha. He wishes it to be supposed he was not in love with her. *Crid al Judas* ['Raise Judas'] or as Phipps[48] would translate it, 'tell that to the Marines'.

Saturday 13th. Went down to Eton. Got leave for Charles and Bot. and asked young Egerton and Hopwood to dine. C. and B. looking very well, the latter much grown, but very plain.[49]

---

46   Robert Grosvenor, 2nd Earl Grosvenor (1767-1845) of Eaton Hall, Cheshire. He developed the London Grosvenor estate, built Grosvenor House, and established himself as one of the wealthiest peers in the country. He was created marquess of Westminster in 1831.

47   The small borough constituency of Stockbridge, 16 miles north of Southampton, was created in 1563 and returned two MPs to the House of Commons. In 1820 the two MPs elected for Stockbridge were Joseph Foster Barham (1759-1832), who owned sugar plantations in Jamaica and was a partner in the West Indian merchants' Barham and Plummer, and his eldest son John Foster Barham (1799-1838), who was noted as an accomplished equestrian and good shot, but an idle MP. Joseph Barham's ownership of extensive property in Stockbridge, including Stockbridge House, and his building of a new town hall gave him effective patronage of the constituency, in which, in 1822, there were approximately ninety-three qualified freehold voters. In the same year, due to a sharp decline in the value of his West Indian interests, Joseph Barham indicated he wished to step down as MP. He sold his Stockbridge property to Lord Grosvenor, which carried with it control of the constituency. The protracted negotiations that accompanied the sale eventually resulted in Grosvenor paying a total of £81,000 for the estate, including £38,000 for the political interest.

48   Phipps Hornby (1785-1867), George Hornby's uncle and a distinguished naval officer.

49   Charles Stanley (1808-1884), Stanley's fourteen-year-old brother, who followed him to Eton; William Tatton Egerton (1806-1883), who became 1st Baron Egerton; and Edward Hopwood (1810-1891) of Hopwood Hall, Lancashire.

Sunday 14th. 3 Egertons, Hopwood, Wilbraham, C. and B. to breakfast.[50] Called on Keate and Hawtry, the former very civil, did not see the latter.[51] Returned to London and dined with Lord Grosvenor *tête à tête*, that is with his ward Mr Leach who goes for nothing. Found in my absence the Duke and Duchess of Somerset had called upon me.[52]

Monday 15th. Received a note from Ld. Lansdowne[53] asking me to dine on Sunday (yesterday) with an Opera ticket for Saturday. Sunday, again received an invitation for Saturday. Declined as I expect to leave Town on Wednesday. Called on B.[54] Wednesday. He begged me to postpone going out of town as he thought of resigning immediately, but I said I should know more tomorrow.

Thursday 18th. Called on Ld. L. who again asked me to dine on Saturday which I accepted, and in half an hour refused owing to a note from old Barham, again putting off his resignation. In consequence I set out for Lancashire immediately.

Friday 19th. Arrived at Knowsley. The Derbys at Heaton.[55] All the party well and looking well.

Monday 22nd. The Derbys returned from Heaton, he a little gouty but looking well and she is not as ill as I had expected. A very warm reception from both, and both evidently pleased with their visit at H.

---

50   Philip Egerton (1806-1881), a contemporary at Eton of Charles Stanley and Edward Egerton, who became the 10th Baronet Egerton, and Edward Bootle-Wilbraham (1807-1882), younger son of the 1st Lord Skelmersdale. Bootle-Wilbraham's older sister Emma (1805-1876) married Stanley in 1825 and so became the countess of Derby in 1851.

51   John Keate (1773-1852), headmaster of Eton from 1809 to 1834. He was a harsh disciplinarian and classical scholar who encouraged the oratorical skills of his pupils. Edward Hawtry (1789-1862) was appointed an assistant master at Eton in 1814 and became headmaster in 1834.

52   Edward Seymour, 11th duke of Somerset (1775-1855) and his wife Lady Charlotte Douglas-Hamilton (1772-1827), daughter of the 9th duke of Hamilton. They married in 1800.

53   Henry Fitzmaurice, 3rd marquess of Lansdowne (1780-1863), who succeeded his brother to the title in 1809.

54   Joseph Foster Barham (1759-1832).

55   Heaton Hall, near Manchester, was the country seat of Lord Wilton (1799-1882), who married Stanley's sister Lady Mary in November 1821. The house was remodelled in the Palladian style by James Wyatt in the 1770s.

Tuesday 23rd. Called at Orford[56] and Winwick.[57] All looking well except James, who has grown fat and bloated. Brought George back to Knowsley.

Wednesday 24th. Arrived a summons from old B. in consequence of which I shall set out for Stockbridge on Saturday.

Thursday 25th. Went with my Father to Heaton, good house and will be much improved, grounds beautiful. Mary's manner just as usual. Has lost nothing of its warmth and very little altered: dotingly fond of him and I think he is of her. Lady Grosvenor very fond of her and a pleasing person, warm in her manner to me, but I am sure she <u>could</u> freeze one to death.[58] On the whole I think better of the *ménage* than I did, though my opinion of him remains unaltered.[59]

Friday 26th. Returned to Knowsley. Walked out with guns with H. and Phipps. New plantations coming on well, except Moss, part of which has quite failed and must be replanted.

Saturday 27th. Set out for Stockbridge and arrived at Hockley without adventure.

Sunday 28th. Arrived at Andover, where I hear there is to be a contest for Stockbridge. I have, in consequence, sent off a message thither to Mr Jones, who of course is arrived there, and expect his answer every hour. Said answer arrived very late at night, and very satisfactory.

Monday 29th. Arrived at Stockbridge about ten. Drawn into the town and, to my astonishment, found them all in orange and blue ribbons. I find these were Barham's colours, and also Lord Grosvenor's, as well as ours; this is singular enough. We find there is an opposition, but nothing

---

56   Orford Hall, in Warrington, Lancashire, was the residence of the Hornby family. The grounds were known for their rare plants and trees. There was also a hothouse in which pineapples, coffee, tea and sugarcane were grown, and an orangery where citrus fruits were cultivated.

57   Lord Derby was patron of the living of Winwick, an extensive parish located 3 miles north of Warrington. The Revd Geoffrey Hornby (1750-1812), who had married Lady Lucy Stanley (1751-1833), sister of the 12th earl of Derby, was rector of Winwick until his death in 1812. He was succeeded as rector by his second son, the Revd James Hornby (1777-1855). Stanley's travelling companion George Hornby was James Hornby's nephew and a grandson of the Revd Geoffrey Hornby.

58   Lady Eleanor, née Egerton (1770-1846), daughter of the 1st earl of Wilton. She married Lord Grosvenor, 1st marquess of Westminster (1767-1845), in 1794 and was mother-in-law to Stanley's sister Lady Mary.

59   As it proved, Stanley's private reservations were not unfounded; Lord Wilton later became known for his inveterate womanising.

very formidable. Our canvass has been very successful and the Election takes place tomorrow, so that I shall get to Knutsford on Thursday, in time for the races.[60] Old B. has been very much out of sorts, but he is now very civil, though the canvass has very near killed him. I dine with him today.

---

60   Stanley was elected unopposed on Wednesday 30 July, upon which he gave a long and eloquent speech to the constituency. Despite the earlier reputation of Stockbridge for venality, no record survives of the 'buying' of votes in the 1822 by-election, although this allegation was a cause of complaint among some Stockbridge voters.

Venice

By the Hon. Edward Geoffrey Stanley
Transcribed and annotated by Alexandra Mayson

Sleep you who wish!—for me, while all around
The pensive moonlight melts on Adria's waves,
   Lulled on her all unruffled breast
   Be mine, with loftiest thoughts possest
To gaze upon the lone, but glorious grave,
When Venice once was Queen, in matchless splendour crowned.

'Tis now, in mystic fullness of delight
That soft-ey'd Melancholy loves to hail
Her own, her fav'rite hour of hallow'd light
And drink the fragrance of this midnight gale.
There is a voice, that walks the waveless sea:—
A voice that whispers in the scarce felt wind—
   A voice that in this magic hour
   Tho' still and small with such strange pow'r
   Of undefined harmony

Speaks to the inmost Soul, that ev'ry vein
Responsive thrills, while in the o'wrought mind
Are kind and wordless thoughts of more than mortal strain.
   The language of a higher sphere
   Beyond the reach of human gaze—
   The voices of the lost, the dear
   That tell a tale of other days

They come—they come—from a perfect Spirit of one
Whose early love my thoughtless Childhood blest.
I feel thy Soul without my panting breast
Speak peace and comfort to thine erring Son.
And if such those which flow for thee
Perchance a bitterer teardrop start,
Forgive the struggles of a heart
Not yet from mortal weakness free.

Or if you would bespangled pole;
The night, the heavenly stillness breathe
No music to thine earthly Soul,
Then cast a glance on things beneath!
Lo before thy wound every eye.

Yes, thou hast heard! thine influence mild.
Best felt beneath the starry night
Breathing soft Melancholy and calm peace,
And bids the crude throb of earthly passion cease:
And Love in many a waking dream beguil'd
Presents the glowing rose and hides the canker blight.

O'er the pensive Soul is thrown
A gradual softer purer tone,
And Love in many a waking dream beguil'd
Presents the glowing rose, and hides the canker blight.
    Bright Visions, must you fade!
    Forever gone! And in your stead
The sad realities of Life remain!
But hark upon discarded strain!—

Poor Child of Earth! It whispers from on high,
Amid a scene so pure, so fair,
Which all around thee the luxurious air
Breathes peace and holy calm, which Earth, Sea, Sky,
    Loud mortal, what art thou?
    Lo beofre thy wandering eyes
    A mighty Latin.

And worlds and worlds, that grow the starry brow
Or Heaven's infinitude, would raise
Their choral symphony of mystic praise
    Fond mortal, what art thou!

What are thy petty hopes and fears,
The trivial griefs, the childish tears?
Lo before thy wond'rous eyes
The Queen of nations prostrate here.

Strike on the Harp for Venice—boldly wild
The tones of splendours past shall sing
A moment of her grief beguil'd.
The Ocean Queen shall break her listless dream,
And rous'd awhile, and kindling with the theme
The voice of glory sound through every trembling string.
    Ask no! for not to Slaves belong
Such lofty flights of heav'n born song:

Ah no! extinguished are her patriot fires:
    And while the strangers iron hand
    Lies heavy on her blighted land,
She cannot, dare not hear thy glory of her Song
Strike we the Harp for Venice—sadly slow
The stifled notes shall flow—
Such as of old, their hearts to Sion turning
The wounds of Memory only burning,

Thine hopes hang idly by their side
The Chosen nation bound to Babels listening tide.
For such is Venice now—the rich, the proud,
The free, to whose submission are Tyrants bow'd
Yes now on her the curse of Slavery falls:
"Her house is left unto her desolate".
Her marble palaces, her gorgeous halls
Are taking on the curse of fate

No more resound her gay canals along
The hum of commerce and the careless song—
No joyous sight salutes the gladdened eyes—
No sounds of life relieves the listening ear—
In Venice reigns a deathlike stillness now—
Saves when at times the lonely gondolier
Wakes the dread silence with his warning cry
And o'er the watr'y way glides swift his burnished prow.

And now she is a worse than nameless thing—
Her glory shames her in th' historic page

And o'er her Lions slow declining age
The Austrian Vulture screams, and flaps his folding wing,
Strike we the harp for Venice—once again
Strike we a louder and a bolder strain
Queen of the hundred Isles, arise, awake—
　　Break but the chain which binds thy Sense
　　In helpless hopeless indolence
The strangers yoke shall then be easier far to break!

And this was once th'abode of mirth,
The mast, the carnival of Earth!
Is this where crowding nations came
To see, enjoy, admire, adore?
Whose very air breathed Happiness
And Love and Liberty, and in Excess
Might catch a following spark from
　　Freedoms sacred flame!
　　Such Venice was of yore!
And now…

The captive Ocean serves ye yet—
Your Fathers curb'd his restless waves—
But proud th' indignant waters fret
To think their Lords should now be slaves.
Your winged Lion still surveys
Your now unpeopled Arsenal
And still in mocking line the wall
The monuments of nobler days,
The harness from the Moslem sent!

　　Ne' giorni tuoi felice
　　Ricordati di me! [1]

What! Only in thy happiest days
A thought on me at sun down east!
Companion of thy Summer days
And shrinking from the wintry blast?

1　This can be translated as 'In your happy days / Remember me'. These are also the first two
　lines of a high soprano duet sung by the characters Aristea and Megacle at the end of Act
　1 of Pergolesi's 'opera seria' *L'Olimpiade* (1735), which was regarded as one of the finest
　operas of the eighteenth century. The libretto was written by Pietro Metastasio. Beethoven
　also set the same lyrics to a duet for soprano and tenor at the start of the nineteenth century.

Ah no!—when from this cloud of woes
The darkest dreariest storms descend,
Remember then the heart that glows
With honest pride to call thee—Friend!
But may thy Life a brighter hue
Display without one chequering shade!
Be therein to know they Friends are True
Without grief to need their aid!

Can this be she whose haughty dow'r
Was once the empire of the Sea!
To whom the Istrian bow'd the knee,
The waning crescent own'd her frown

The arms a patriot Monarch sent!
Ah little irk'd the warriors, they
Should e'er become the Austrians prey!
Lo by your Country's Genius plac'd
Even in the Halls their splendour grac'd,
Their arms prison'd, their manly sense
Charmed with its patriot Eloquence—

In deathless glory still look down
Your free Republic's chiefs of old.
And each with an indignant frown
Their now desperate Sons behold
You all, save one! The Doge whose hated name
Serves but to mark the funeral pall of shame

For he betray'd his country—hearken ye
Who in the lap of careless luxury
Your silken fetters clasp, and idly gaze
Upon your country's wrongs—to you they turn,
Those hoary Senators, and bid you learn
That when ye see your Island home become
A stranger's prey, her children's living tomb,
Who rescues not, betrays!

Your black eyes tell of Love alone
A nobler flame ye dare not own—
Yet oft on many a swarthy cheek
I see a purer glow arise—

And oft in many a moistened eye's
Dark lightning nobler feelings speak—

Oh arise the sacred spark! your ancient fame
Speaks with the voice of a thousand years.
Bids you your Island boon of Freedom claim—
Oppression's, slavery's wrongs demand your tears—
Your tears!—yes, mourn as injured nations should
Your country's insults! mourn in tears of blood—

Bath'd by that hallow'd stream once more
Your Lion shall as proudly soar;
Your gay Rialto shall rise
Her Ocean Phoenix rise again:
Of joy and wealth and freedom hear—
Again your lively gondolier
Shall cast Tasso's lofty strain;

In revelry again the nations meet
And mirth and music cheer the wat'ry street—
And clad once more in glory-beaming smiles
Shall Venice yet rejoice thro' all her 100 Isles.

This untitled and undated poem was probably written by Stanley in 1822. In it, he gives his response to and hopes for Venice under Austrian control. It is written at the back of volume five of his European Grand Tour diaries, a few blank pages after the final entry of July 1822.

Ludovico Manin became the last doge of Venice in 1797, presiding over the last days of more than a millennium of *La Serenissima*, the independent republic of Venice. He had only been doge for one year when the city was captured by the French army under Napoleon Bonaparte. It initially fell under Austrian control, administered from Milan. Napoleon then retook control from 1805 to 1814 as king of the Napoleonic Kingdom of Italy. Venice subsequently returned to Austrian control from 1814 to 1866.

Stanley's poem, an example of his self-professed 'poeticising mania', takes up ten pages of his original manuscript diary. Its romantic, melancholic tone is seemingly at odds with the lack of regret he expressed upon leaving Venice in June 1821, although he did return to the city in May 1822. His second visit was marked by confusion surrounding his friendship with Miss Mary Bold. Whether or not Miss Bold had any influence on the poem, its tone and length suggest that Stanley's experience of Venice remained with him after he had left the city. Like his poem of 12 January 1821 inspired by the decay of the Forum at Rome, this poem of Venice's decay and 'slavery' to Austria is manifestly rooted in pathos.

Index

À'Court, Sir William, 1st Baron Heytesbury (1779-1868), 1821: 10 Jan., 14 Nov.; 1822: 30 Jan.

Aachen [Aix-la-Chapelle], 1822: 24 Jun.

Abercorn, marchioness of (1763-1827), 1821: 25 Feb.

Ackermann, Rudolf (1764-1834), 1821: 14 Nov.

Acton, Sir Ferdinand (1801-1837), 1821: 5 Dec.

Acton, Lady Mary-Anne (1784-1834), 1821: 5 Dec.

Agar-Ellis, George, 1st Baron Dover (1797-1817), 1821: 1 Oct.

Aigle, 1821: 23 Aug.

Albani, Francesco (1578-1660), 1821: 22 Jan.

Albano, 1821: 30 Apr.

Albany, countess of (1752-1824) 1820: 10 Dec.

Alcudia, 1st duke of (1767-1851), 1821: 1 Apr.

Alfieri, Vittorio (1749-1803), 1820: 24 Dec.

Alvanley, Lady Anne-Dorothea (1757-1825), 1820: 10 Dec.

Ammanati, Bartolomeo (1511-1592), 1821: 23 Jun.

Ancona, 1821: 19 Jun.

Andermatt, 1821: 3 Aug.

Andover, Thomas Howard, Viscount (later earl of Suffolk) (1776-1851), 1821: 21 Nov.

Anson, Thomas, Viscount (1795-1854), 1821: 11 Aug.

Anspach, Elizabeth Berkeley, margravine of (1750-1828), 1821: 10 May

Appiani, Andrea (1754-1817), 1821: 1 Oct.

Ariosto, Ludovico (1474-1533), 1822: 17 May

Arth, 1821: 26 Jul.

Augsburg, 1821: 15 Jul.; 1822, 11 Jun.

Baden, Caroline of, queen of Bavaria (1776-1841), 1821: 14 Jul.

Baden, Ludwig I, grand duke of (1763-1830), 1821: 19 Jul.

Baden, Stéphanie, grand duchess of (1789-1860), 1822: 19 Jun.

Barham, John Foster (1759-1832), 1822: 6, 15 Jul.

Barham, John Foster (1799-1838), 1822: 6 Jul.

Barnett, Elizabeth (1765-1820), 1820: 29 Dec.

Bassano, Jacopo (1510-1592), 1821: 16 Sep.

Bassano, Leandro (1557-1622), 1821: 26 Jun.; 1822: 20 May

Bassano del Grappa, 1821: 30 Jun.

Baveno, 1821: 15 Sep.

Beauharnais, Eugène de, viceroy of the kingdom of Italy (1781-1824), 1821: 29 Sep.

Beauharnais, Hortense de, queen consort of Holland, duchess of Saint-Leu, 1821: 16 Jul.

Beckford, William (1760-1844), 1821: 19 Feb.

Bellinzona, 1821: 17 Sep.

Benderli Ali Pasha, grand vizier of the Ottoman Empire (d. 1821), 1821: 16 Dec.

Benevento, 1821: 31 May-3 Jun.

Benvenuti, Pietro (1769-1844), 1820: 23 Dec.

Berne [Bern], 1821: 13 Aug.

Bex, 1821: 22 Aug.

Bienne [Biel], 1821: 15 Aug.

Bingen, 1822: 22 Jun.

Bingham, Richard (1801-1872), 1821: 6 Nov.

Bishop, Henry, 1821: 15 May

Bisse, Thomas Chaloner (1788-1872), 1821: 13 Jan.

Blantyre, Robert Stuart, 11th Baron (1777-1830), 1821: 28 Oct.

Bold, Mary (1795-1825), 1822: 17 Mar.

Bold, Mary Patten (d. 1824), 1821: 26 Feb.; 1822: 21 May

Bologna, 1821: 21 May; 1822: 13 May
   Accademia di Belle Arti, 1821: 21 May; 1822: 13 May

Bolzano, 1821: 2 Jul.

Bonaparte, Joseph, king of Naples and Sicily (later king of Spain) (1768-1844), 1821: 24 Aug.

Bonaparte, Joséphine, empress of the French (1763-1814), 1822: 18 Jun.

Bonaparte, Maria Letizia (1750-1836), 1821: 29 Jan.

Bonifacio de' Pitati, Veronese (1487-1553), 1821: 26 Jun.

Bootle-Wilbraham, Edward (1807-1882), 1822: 14 Jul.

Boppard, 1822: 22 Jun.

Bordone, Paris (1500-1571), 1821: 18 Oct.; 1822: 20 May

Borghese, Pauline Bonaparte, Princess (1780-1825), 1821: 25 Jan.

Borromeo, Cardinal Carlo (1538-1584), 1821: 13 Oct.

Both, Jan Dirksz (1618-1652), 1821: 17 Jan.

Bracciano, Giovanni Torlonia, duke of (1754-1829), 1821: 15 Jan.

Brecknock, George Pratt, earl of (later 2nd Marquess Camden) (1799-1866), 1821: 13 Oct.

Brienz, 1821: 6 Aug.

Brig, 1821: 14 Sep.

Brixen, 1821: 2 Jul.; 1822: 30 May

Brougham, James (1780-1833), 1821: 9 Mar.

Brunswick, Caroline of, queen of Great Britain and Ireland (1768-1821), 1821: 19 Jun., 15, 22 Sep.

Brussels, 1822: 27 Jun. to 2 Jun.

Buochs, 1821: 2 Aug.

Buonarroti, Michelangelo (1475-1564), 1820: 17 Dec.

Burghersh, John Fane, Lord (later 11th earl of Westmoreland) (1784-1859), 1820: 17 Dec.

Burgoyne, John Fox (1782-1871), 1821: 31 Jan.

Bute, Lady Maria North, marchioness of (1793-1841), 1822: 7 Apr.

Caccio, Carlo (1782-1873), 1821: 15 May

Cadenabbia, 1821: 23-27 Sep.
  Villa Sommariva [now Villa Carlotta], 1821: 25 Sep.

Calabria, Francis, duke of (later king of the Two Sicilies) (1777-1830), 1821: 15 May, 19 Nov

Calais, 1822: 3 Jul.

Camarthen, Francis Osborne, marquess of (later 7th Duke of Leeds) (1798-1859), 1821: 19 Nov.

Campbell, Abbé (1753-1830), 1821: 30 Mar.; 1822: 7 Apr.

Campbell, Lady Charlotte (1775-1861), 1820: 29 Dec.

Campomorone, 1821: 17 Oct.

Canova, Antonio (1757-1822), 1821: 16 Jan.

Canterbury, 1822: 5 Jul.

Capua, 1821: 14 Jun.; 1822: 14 Jan.

Caracosca, General Michele (1774-1853), 1821: 6 Nov.

Caravaggio, Michelangelo Merisi da (1571-1610), 1821: 9 Feb.

Carbonari, The, 1821: 9 Jan., 1 Mar., 25 Sep.

Carnarvon, Henry Herbert, 2nd earl of (1772-1832), 1822: 1 Mar.

Carracci, Agostino (1557-1602), 1821: 1 Apr.

Carracci, Annibale (1560-1609), 1821: 22 Jan., 1 Apr.

Carracci, Ludovico (1555-1619), 1821: 21 Jun.

Carsoli, 1822: 3 May

Cassia, Baron (1778-1867), 1821: 11 Mar.

Catullus (84-54 BC), 1821: 28 May

Cave, Robert Otway (1796-1844), 1821: 26 Jan.

Cave, Sarah Otway (1768-1862), 1821: 12 May

Celano, 1822: 5 May

Cerva, Pier Antonio (1600-1670), 1821: 26 Jun.

Cesari, Giuseppe (1568-1640), 1821: 6 Jun.

Champaigne. Philippe de (1602-1674), 1822: 22 Jun.

Charles V, Holy Roman Emperor (1500-1558), 1822: 28 Jun.

Charleville, Charles Bury, 1st earl of (1764-1835), 1821: 1 Nov.

Church, General Richard (1784-1873), 1821: 2 Feb.

Ciambino, Luigi Ludovisi, prince of (1767-1841), 1821: 25 Jan.

Cicogna, Conte Francesco (1748-1823), 1821: 30 Sep.

Cimerosa, Domenico (1749-1801), 1820: 27 Dec.

Circello, Tommaso Somma, marquis di (1737-1826), 1822: 15 Jan.

Cisterna, 1822: 15 Jan.

Clare, John Fitzgibbon, 2nd earl of (1792-1851), 1821: 7 Oct.

Colchester, Charles Abbot, 1st Baron (1757-1829), 1821: 17 Jan.

Coleridge, Samuel Taylor (1772-1834), 1821: 13 Oct.

Colli di Monte Bove, 1822: 4 May

Cologne [Köln], 1822: 23 Jun.

Como, 1821: 21-28 Sep.
  Villa Pliniana, Lake Como, 1821: 25 Sep.
  Villa Melzi, Lake Como, 1821: 26 Sep.

Comolli, Giovanni Battista (1775-1831), 1821: 25 Sep.

Confalonieri, Conte Federico (1785-1846), 1821: 22, 23 Sep.

Confalonieri, Contessa Teresa (1787-1830), 1821: 23 Sep.

Consalvi, Cardinal Ercole (1757-1824), 1821: 9, 19 Feb.

Constance [Konstanz], 1821: 19 Jul.

Corradini, Antonio (1688-1752), 1821: 25 Jun.

Cortona, Pietro da (1596-1669), 1821: 21 Mar.

Cowper, Hannah Gore, Countess (1758-1831), 1821: 25 Oct.

Craven, Richard Keppel (1779-1851), 1821: 13 May

Crescentini, Girolamo (1762-1846), 1821: 10 Feb.; 1822: 13 May

Crivelli, Ferdinando, conte di Ossolano, di Luino, delle Quattro Valli (1767-1856), 1821: 30 Sep.

Czartoryska, Princess Izabela (1746-1835), 1821: 11 Mar.

D'Arpino, Cavaliere (1568-1640) *see* Cesari, Giuseppe

Dannecker, Johann von (1758-1841), 1822: 14 Jun.

David, Jacques-Louis (1748-1825), 1821: 19 Oct.

Denmark, Christian, crown prince of (1786-1848), 1821: 28 May

Derby, Edward Stanley, 12th earl of (1752-1834), 1821: 7 May, 12 Sep., 29 Nov.

Derby, Eliza Farren, countess of (1762-1829), 1821: 21 Nov.

Desaix, General Louis (1768-1800), 1822: 18 Jun.

Désirée, queen of Sweden (1777-1860), 1822: 25 Jun.

Devonshire, William Cavendish, 6th duke of (1790-1858), 1821: 16 Jan.

Devonshire, Elizabeth Foster, duchess of (1758-1848), 1821: 15 Jan.; 1822: 5 Feb.

Dietrichstein, Franz Joseph, Prince (1767-1854), 1821: 2 Feb.

Disbrowe, Edward Cromwell (1790-1851), 1821: 23 Jul.

Dolci, Carlo (1616-1680), 1821: 25 Jun., 19 Oct.

Domenichino, Domenico Zampieri (1581-1641), 1821: 22 Jan., 1 May

Domodossola, 1821: 15 Sep.

Douglas-Hamilton, Lady Susan (1814-1889), 1821: 7 Feb.

Dow, Gerard (1613-1675), 1821: 25 Jun.

Drummond, Sir William (1769-1828), 1821: 31 Jan.

Durini, Cardinal Angelo Maria (1725-1796), 1821: 25 Sep.

Ebel, Johann Gottfried (1764-1830), 1821: 22 Jul.

Eboli, 1821: 19 May

Egerton, Sir John (1776-1825), 1821: 23 Nov.

Egerton, Philip (1806-1891), 1822, 14 Jul.

Egerton, William Tatton (later 1st Baron Egerton) (1806-1883), 1822: 13 Jul.

Einsiedein, 1821: 27 Jul.

Ellenborough, Anne Towry, Baroness (1768-1843), 1821: 19 Jan., 9 Feb.
Eliott, George, 1st Baron Heathfield (1717-1790), 1821: 28 Jun.
Eustace, General William (1783-1855), 1821: 2 Jan.

Fabvier, Colonel Charles (1782-1855), 1821: 13 Jun.
Falkiner, Sir Frederick (1768-1824), 1824: 4 Dec.
Fano, 1821: 19 Jun.
Fanshawe, Catherine Maria (1765-1835), 1821: 22 Jan.
Fasolato, Agostino (1714-1787), 1821: 23 Jun.
Fastrada (765-794), 1822: 21 Jun.
Ferdinand IV, king of Naples (1751-1825), 1820: 17 Dec.
Feriolo, 1821: 15 Sep.
Ferrara, 1822: 17 May
  Castello Estense, 1822: 17 May
Ferrari, Francesco (1634-1708), 1820: 27 Dec.
Feretti, Jacopo (1784-1852), 1821: 13 Mar.
Fesch, Cardinal Joseph (1763-1839), 1821: 25 Jan.
Fiano, Marco Ludovisi Ottoboni, duke of (1777-1830), 1821: 17 Jan.
Finoglia, Carlo (c. 1590-1645), 1821: 6 Jun.
Fitton, William Henry (1780-1861), 1821: 10 May
Florence, 1820: 16 Dec. to 1821: 1 Jan., 21 Oct. to 1 Nov.
  Laurentian Library, 1821: 2 Jan.
  Palazzo Pitti, 1822, 3 Jan.
  Palazzo Vecchio, 1820: 17 Dec.
  Uffizi Galleries, 1821: 3, 24 Jan.
Fontana, Cardinal Francesco Luigi (1750-1822), 1821: 18 Jan.
Forlì, 1822: 12 May
Forsyth, Joseph (1763-1815), 1821: 9 Feb.
Foster, Augustus (1780-1848), 1821: 1 Nov.
Francis I, emperor of Austria (1767-1835), 1821: 5 Jul., 29 Sep.
Frankfurt, 1822: 20 Jun.
Frascati, 1821: 1 May
  Abbazia di San Nilo, Grottaferrata, 1821: 1 May
Frauenlob, Heinrich (c. 1250-1318), 1822: 21 Jun.
Frederike Luise Wilhelmine, queen of the Netherlands (1774-1837), 1822: 25 Jun.
Friedrich Wilhelm III, king of Prussia (1770-1840), 1822: 25 Jun.
Frimont, General Johann (1759-1831), 1821: 6 Mar.

Galilei, Alessandro (1690-1737), 1820: 24 Dec.
Galilei, Galileo (1564-1642), 1820: 24 Dec.
Gall, Franz (1758-1828), 1821: 29 Jan.
Garda, 1822: 28 May
  Lago di Garda, Sirmione [Catullus's Villa], 1822: 28 May
Gell, Sir William (1777-1836), 1821: 31 Jan., 26 May
Geneva, 1821: 24 Aug.
Genoa, 1821: 17-19 Oct.
  Palazzo Brignole [Palazzo Rosso], 1821: 18 Oct.
  Palazzo Ducale, 1821: 18 Oct.
  Palazzo Durazzo [Palazzo Doria], 1821: 18 Oct.
Giambologna, Jean de Boulogne (1529-1608), 1820: 20 Dec.

Giessbach, 1821: 6 Aug.
Giordano, Luca (1634-1705), 1821: 2 Jan., 26 Jun.
Giorgione, Giorgio Barbarelli (c. 1477-1510), 1821: 25 Jun.
Giulio Romano (1499-1546), 1821: 22 Jan.
Giustiniani, Cardinal Alessandro (1778-1843), 1821: 31 May
Giustiniani, Vincenzo, 6th Prince (1762-1826), 1821: 15 Dec.
Godoy de Faria, Manuel (1767-1851) see Alcudia, 1st duke of
Gordon, Colonel Charles (1790-1835), 1822: 26 Feb.
Gradwell, Richard (1777-1823), 1821: 18 Jan.
Grafenort, 1821: 2 Aug.
Greenough, George (1778-1855), 1821: 24 Jan.
Greville, Harriet Catherine (1803-1866), 1822: 14 Jun.
Grindelwald, 1821: 7 Aug.
Grosvenor, Lady Eleanor (later marchioness of Westminster) (1770-1846), 1822: 25 Jul.
Grosvenor, Robert, 2nd Earl (later marquess of Westminster) (1767-1845), 1822: 6 Jul.
Guarini, Giovanni (1538-1612), 1822: 17 May
Guercino, Giovanni Francesco Barbieri (1591-1666), 1821: 17 Jan., 18 Oct.
Guérin, Pierre-Narcise (1774-1833), 1822: 17 Jun.

Hamilton, Alexander Douglas-Hamilton, 10th duke of (1767-1852), 1821: 10 Jan.
Hamilton, Susan Euphemia Beckford, duchess of (1786-1859), 1821: 9 Jun.
Hamilton, Lady Emma (1765-1815), 1821: 28 Jun.
Hammersley, Hugh (1774-1840), 1821: 8 Oct.
Haugwitz, General Eugen (1777-1857), 1821: 6 Nov.
Hawtry, Edward (1789-1862), 1822: 14 Jul.
Heidelberg, 1822: 18 Jun.
Hentsch, Henri (1761-1835), 1821: 9 Sep.
Hesse, Philip, prince of (1779-1846), 1821: 13 May
Hitroff [Khitrovo], Countess Elise (1783-1839), 1820: 10 Dec.
Hoche, General Louis (1768-1797), 1822: 23 Jun.
Hofer, Andreas (1767-1810), 1821, 5 Jul.
Hope, Thomas (1769-1830), 1821: 30 Mar.
Hopwood, Edward (1810-1891), 1822: 13 Jul.
Hornby, Edmund (1773-1857), 1821: 14 Mar.
Hornby, Edmund George (1799-1865), 1820: 10 Dec.; 1822: 23 Jul.
Hornby, Revd James (1777-1855)
Hornby, Admiral Phipps (1785-1867), 1821: 9 Apr.; 1822: 6 Jul.
Horner, Francis (1778-1817), 1820: 29 Dec.
Howard, Lady Elizabeth (1803-1845), 1822: 27 Feb.

Il Pordenone, Giovanni Antonio de' Sacchis (1484-1539), 1822: 20 May
Innsbruck, 1821: 3 Jul., 1822: 31 Jun.
Interlaken, 1821: 9 Aug.
Isola Bella, 1821: 16 Sep.

Jetzer, Captain August von (1789-1859), 1821: 21 Nov.
Jordan, Dorothy (1761-1828), 1821: 31 Jan.
Joseph II, Holy Roman Emperor (1741-1791), 1822: 21 Jun.

Karlsruhe [Carlsruhe], 1822: 15, 18 Jun.
  Palace, 1822: 15 Jun.
Keate, John (1773-1852), 1822: 14 Jul.
Kemble, John Philip (1757-1823), 1821: 9 Aug.
Kemble, Priscilla (1756-1845), 1821: 9 Aug.
Kinnaird, Charles, 8th Baron (1780-1826), 1821: 6
  Feb., 1 Oct.
Kinnaird, Elizabeth FitzGerald, Baroness (1787-
  1858), 1821: 1 Oct.
Knowsley, Lancs., 1822: 19 Jul.
Knowsley Hall: 1821: 8 Nov.
Koblenz [Coblenz], 1822: 23 Jun.
Koch, Christoph von (1737-1771), 1822: 17 Jun.

L'Aquila, 1822: 5, 6 May
  Lago di Fucino, 1822: 5, 6 May
La Neuveville, 1821: 17 Aug.
La Spezia, 1821: 21 Oct.
Labouchere, Henry (1798-1869), 1822: 1 Oct.
Lansdowne, Henry Fitzmaurice, 3rd marquis of
  (1780-1863), 1822: 15 Jul.
Lascelles, Edwin (1799-1865), 1822: 14 Jun.
Lascelles, Henry (1797-1857), 1822: 14 Jun.
Lausanne, 1821: 19, 24 Aug.
Laveno-Mombello, 1821: 15, 17 Sep.
Lecco, 1821: 27 Sep.
Leeds, Charlotte, duchess of (1776-1856), 1821: 9
  Sept.
Leeds, George Osborne, 6th duke of (1775-1838),
  1821: 2 Sept.
Lemon, Lady Charlotte (1785-1851), 1822: 28 Jul.
Leopold of Saxe-Coburg, Prince (later King Leopold
  I of Belgium) (1790-1865), 1821: 16 Dec.
Leveson-Gower, Lord Francis (later 1st earl of
  Ellesmere) (1800-1857), 1822: 14 Jun.
Licenza, 1821: 12 Apr.
  Horace's Villa, 1821: 12 Apr.
Liechtenstein, Johann, prince of (1760-1836), 1821:
  16 Dec.
Liège, 1822: 25 Jun.
Lindau, 1821: 18 Jul.
Lindsay, Lady Charlotte (1770-1849), 1821: 2 Mar.
Livorno [Leghorn], 1820: 29 Dec.
Lodi, duke of (1753-1816), 1821 25 Sep.
Lombardo, Girolamo (1506-1590), 1821: 19 Jun.
London, 1822: 6-14 Jul.
Longhena, Baldessare (1598-1682), 1821: 26 Jun.
Loreto, 1821: 19 Jun.
Lucca, 1820: 26 Dec.
Lucca, Filippo Sardi, archbishop of, 1820: 27 Dec.
Lucerne [Luzern], 1821: 28 Jul.
Lugano, 1821: 20 Sep.
Lushington, Sir Henry (1775-1863), 1821: 28 Oct.

Macerata, 1821: 18 Jun.; 1822: 10 May
Mack von Leiberich, General Karl (1752-1828),
  1822: 12 Jun.
Mainz, 1822: 21 May
Mannheim, 1822: 19 Jun.
Marceau, General François (1769-1796), 1822: 23
  Jun.
Maria Isabella of Spain (1789-1848), 1821: 19 Nov.
Marini, Antonio Maria (1668-1725), 1822: 20 May
Masséna, André, marshal of the French Empire
  (1758-1817), 1821: 28 Jun.

Mathias, Thomas (1754-1835), 1821: 21 Nov.
Maximilian, Holy Roman Emperor (1459-1519),
  1821: 4 Jul.
Meiringen, 1821: 5 Aug.
Melzi, Francesco (1753-1816) see Lodi, duke of
Memmingen, 1821: 17 Jul.
Mestre, 1821: 24 Jun.
Milan, 1821: 28 Sep. to 16 Oct.
  Brera Museum [Gallery], 1821: 29 Sep.
  Castello Sforzesco, 1821: 29 Sep.
  Duomo, 1821: 29 Sep.
  La Scala, 1821: 29 Sep.
  S. Maria della Grazie, 1821: 29 Sep.
Motte, Nicholas de la (1758-1826), 1821: 25 Oct.
Munich, 1821: 11-14 Jul.; 1822: 3-11 Jun.
  Gallery, 1821: 13-14 Jul.; 1822: 3, 9 Jun.
  Residenz, 1821: 12 Jul.
  Schliessheim, 1822: 4 Jun.
Murat, Caroline, queen consort of Naples (1782-
  1839), 1821: 12 May
Murat, General Joachim, king of Naples (1767-
  1815), 1821: 5 May

Namur, 1822: 25 Jun.
Naples, 1821: 4 May to 14 Jun., 5 Nov. to 1822: 22
  Feb.
  Accademia Reale, 1821: 10 May
  Baiae, 1821: 17 May
  Castel dell'Ovo, 1821: 5 May
  Certosa di San Martino, 1821: 9 Jun.
  Duomo di San Gennaro, 1821: 5 May
  Herculaneum, 1821: 16 May
  Teatro di San Carlo, 1821: 13 May, 19, 25
    Nov.
  Vesuvius, Mount, 1821: 10-11 May
Narni, 1821: 9 Jan.
  Bridge of Augustus, 1822: 8 Jan.
  Mount Soracte [Monte Soratte], 1822: 8 Jan.
Neuchâtel, 1821: 16-17 Aug.
Newburgh, 'de jure' 6th earl of (1762-1826) see
  Giustiniani, Vincenzo, 6th Prince
Nibby, Antonio (1792-1839), 1821: 21 Jan., 14, 23
  Mar.
Novi Ligure, 1821: 16 Oct.

Ohmacht, Landolin (1760-1834), 1822: 17 Jun.
Osborne, Lady Charlotte (1801-1836), 1821: 9 Sep.
Oscar, prince of Sweden (later King Oscar I)
  (1799-1859), 1822: 25 Jun.

Pacca, Cardinal Bartolomeo (1756-1844), 1821: 9
  Mar.; 1822: 7 Apr.
Padua, 1821: 22 May; 1822: 18, 25 May
Paestum, 1821: 20 May
  Temples, 1821: 20 May
Palazzo della Ragione, 1821: 22 May
Palladio, Andrea (1508-1580), 1821: 24 Jun.
Palma il Giovane, Jacopo Negretti (1548-1628),
  1821: 25 Jun.
Palma il Vecchio, Jacopo Negretti (1480-1528), 1821:
  26 Jun.
Parr, Samuel (1747-1825), 1821: 9 Sep.
Paulet, William, Lord (1804-1893), 1822: 7 Jan.
Pavia, 1821: 16 Oct.
  Certosa di Pavia, 1821: 16 Oct.

Palestrina [Praeneste], 1821: 6 Apr.
Temple of Fortuna, 1821: 6 Apr.
Pallanza, 1821: 16 Sep.
Parma, Marie-Louise, duchess of (and archduchess of Austria) (1791-1847), 1821: 8 Jan., 26 Jun.
Pavia, 1821: 16 Oct.
Pergami, Bartolomeo (1783/4-1842), 1821: 15 Sep.
Perugia, 1821: 4 Jan.
Perugino, Pietro (1446-1523), 1821: 8 Jan.
Pesaro, 1821: 19 Jun.
Pestalozzi, Johann (1746-1826), 1821: 18 Aug.
Pfyffer, Franz (1716-1802), 1821: 30 Jul.
Pigott, William (1773-1838), 1820: 17 Dec.
Pino, General Domenico (1760-1826), 1821: 22 Sep.
Piola, Domenico (1627-1703), 1821: 19 Oct.
Piombino, Maddalena Odescalchi, princess of (1782-1846), 1821: 25 Jan.
Pisa, 1820: 29 Dec.
Pius VII, Pope (1742-1823), 1821: 18 Jan.; 1822: 7 Apr.
Pliny the Younger (61-114), 1821: 25 Sep.
Ponte Tresa, 1821: 20 Sep.
Porro-Lambertenghi, Luigi (1780-1860), 1821: 25 Sep.
Porta, Giovanni Battista della (1535-1615), 1821: 27 Feb.
Portella, 1822: 15 Jan.
Portici, 1822: 22 Jan.
Poussin, Nicolas (1594-1665), 1820: 27 Dec.
Prato, 1821: 21 Oct.
Primolano, 1821: 1 Jul.
Pyrker, Ladislaus, patriarch of Venice (1772-1847), 1821: 25 Jun.

Quin, Lady Caroline (later countess of Dunraven) (1789-1870) 1821: 20 Aug.
Quin, Lady Charlotte (1794-1823), 1821: 26 Feb.
Quin, George, Lord (1792-1888), 1821: 26 Feb.
Quin, Windham Henry, Lord (later 2nd earl of Dunraven) (1782-1850), 1821: 20 Aug.

Raphael (1483-1520), 1821: 8 Jan.
Rembrandt van Rijn (1606-69), 1821: 25 Jun.
Reni, Guido (1575-1642), 1821: 22 Jan.
Rezzonico, 1821: 26 Sep.
Ribera, Jusepe de (1591-1652), 1821: 6 Jun.
Rice, Thomas Spring (later 1st Baron Monteagle) (1790-1866), 1821: 13 Oct.
Rieti, 1822: 6 May
Rocca di Mezzo, 1822: 5 May
Rome, 1821: 10 Jan. to 30 Apr., 16 Jun., 1-3 Nov.; 1822: 23 Feb. to 2 May
Accademia di San Luca, 1821: 24 Jan.
Baths of Caracalla, 1821: 27 Jan.
Canova's Studio, 1821: 16 Jan., 10 Feb.
Capitol, 1821: 15, 21 Jan., 23 Mar.
Capitoline Museum, 1821: 21, 25 Jan.
Carnival on the Corso, 1821: 24-28 Feb., 4 Mar.
Castel San Angelo, 1821: 3 Feb.
Colosseum, 1822: 12 Jan.
Farnesina, 1821: 23 Jan.
Forum, 1822: 12, 25 Jan.
Galleria Borghese, 1821: 22, 30 Jan., 20 Feb.
Palazzo Braschi, 1821: 1 Feb.

Palazzo Colonna, 1821: 16 Mar.
Palazzo Corsini, 1821: 23 Jan., 20 Feb.
Palazzo del Quirinale, 1821: 9 Feb.
Palazzo Doria [Pamphilj], 1821: 19 Jan.
Palazzo Farnese, 1821: 23 Jan.
Palazzo Sciarra, 1821: 17 Jan.
Palazzo Spada, 1821: 23 Jan.
Palazzo Torlonia, 1821: 9 Feb.
Pantheon, 1821: 16 Jan.
Ponte Molle [Milvian Bridge], 1821, 6, 22 Feb.
San Giovanni in Laterano, 1822: 22 Jan.
San Pietro in Vinculi, 1821: 12 Feb.
St Peter's Basilica, 1821: 11-12, 18, 28 Jan., 1 Feb.
Thorvaldsen's studio, 1821: 1 Feb.
Vatican, 1821: 14, 28 Jan., 4, 7 Feb.
Villa Doria Pamphilj, 1821: 23 Jan., 7 Feb.
Villa Mattei [now Villa Celimontana], 1821: 1 Apr.
Villa Paolina, 1821: 27 Jan.
Romilly, Joseph (1791-1864), 1821: 28 Oct.
Rosehill, William Carnegie, Lord (later 8th earl of Northesk) (1794-1874), 1821: 12 Dec.
Ross, General Robert (1766-1814), 1821: 1 Oct.
Rossini, Gioachino (1792-1868), 1821: 16 May, 6 Jun.
Rudolph, Cardinal, archduke of Austria (1788-1831), 1821: 7 Apr.
Russell, William, Lord (1767-1840), 1821: 22 Jan.
Ruthven, James, 6th Baron (1777-1853), 1821: 10 Mar.

Salerno, Leopold, prince of (1790-1851), 1821: 24 May
Sant'Agata, 1821: 4 Nov.; 1822: 14 Jan.
Sankt Goar, 1822: 22 Jun.
St Johann in Tirol, 1821: 6 Jul.
St John, The Hon. Ferdinand (1804-65), 1822: 28 Feb.
Saint-Maurice, 1821: 22 Aug., 12 Sep.
Salvator Rosa (1615-1673), 1821: 19 Jan., 9 Jul.
Salzburg, 1821: 7 Jul.
Salt mines, Hallein: 7 Jul. 1821
Sampieri, Francesco (1790-1863), 1821: 25 Nov.
Sandwich, Lady Louisa, countess of (1781-1862), 1821: 25 Feb.
Sapieha, Eustachy Kajetan, Prince (1797-1860), 1822: 14 Apr., 21 May
Sarto, Andrea del (1486-1530), 1820: 29 Dec.; 1821: 19 Oct.
Saxe, Maurice, marshal de (1696-1750), 1822: 17 Jun.
Scamozzi, Vincenzo (1548-1616), 1821: 24 Jun.
Schaffhausen, 1821: 20 Jul.
Schömberg, Friedrich Hermann von Schönberg, 1st duke of (1615-90), 1822: 22 Jun.
Schöpflin, Johann (1694-1771), 1822: 17 Jun.
Schwarzenberg, Bishop Ernst (1773-1821), 1821: 8 Jul.
Schwarzenberg, Karl Philipp, prince of (1771-1820), 1821: 8 Jul.
Sestri Levante, 1821: 20 Oct.
Seymour, Edward (1775-1855), 1822: 14 Jul.
Siddons, Cecilia (1794-1868), 1821: 9 Aug.
Siddons, Sarah (1755-1831), 1821: 9 Aug.
Siena, Duomo, 1821: 1 Nov.

Simplon Pass, 1821: 14-15 Sep.
Sion, 1821: 13 Sep.
Sirani, Elisabetta (1638-65), 1821: 21 Jun.
Smollett, Tobias (1721-1771), 1820: 29 Dec.
Sneyd, Ralph (1793-1870), 1821: 7 Oct.
Snyders, Frans (1579-1657), 1821: 13 Jul.
Sombeval *see* Sonceboz
Sommariva, Count Giovanni Battista (1760-1826), 1821: 1, 14 Feb., 25 Sep.
Sonceboz, 1821: 16 Aug.
Spagnoletto *see* Ribera, Jusepe de
Spina, Cardinal Giuseppe (1756-1828), 1822: 13 May
Spoleto, 1821: 7 Jan., 17 Jun.
Spurzheim, Johann (1776-1832), 1821: 29 Jan.
Stackelberg, Count Ernst von (1766-1850), 1822: 19 Mar.
Staanstad, 1821: 1 Aug.
Staël, Anne Louise, Madame de (1766-1817), 1821: 24 Aug.
Standish, Frank Hall (1799-1840), 1821: 19 Aug., 13 Oct.
Stanley, Charles James Fox (1808-1884), 1820: 23 Dec.; 1822: 13 Jul.
Stanley, Charlotte Elizabeth (1801-1853), 1820: 10 Jan.; 1821: 26 Jan.
Stanley, Ellinor Mary (1807-1887), 1821: 7 Feb.
Stanley, Henry (1803-1875), 1820: 23 Dec.; 1821: 24 Feb.
Stanley, Louisa Emily (1805-1825), 1821: 26 Feb.
Stanley, Lady Lucy (1751-1833), 1822: 23 Jul.
Stanley, Lady Mary, countess of Wilton (1801-1858), 1821: 10 Jan.
Stechelberg, 1821: 9 Aug.
Stockbridge, Hants., 1822: 27 Jul.
Stonyhurst, Lancs., 1822: 27 Jul.
Strasbourg, 1822: 16 Jun.
Stuttgart, 1822: 13-15 Jun.
    Ludwigsburg Palace, 1822: 14 Jun.
Subiaco, 1821: 10 Apr.
Suvorov [Suwarrow], General Alexander (1729-1800), 1821: 27 Jul.

Talbot, Sir George (1761-1850), 1821: 23 Jan.
Tasso, Torquato (1544-1595), 1822: 17 May
Teniers the Younger, David (1610-1690), 1821: 13 Jul.
Terni, 1822: 7 May
Terracina, 1821: 2 Feb., 15 Jun.; 1822: 15 Jan.
Thellusson, William (later 3rd Baron Rendlesham) (1798-1839), 1820: 20 Dec.
Thonon-les-Bains, 1821: 12 Sep.
Thorvaldsen, Bertel, 1821: 1 Feb.
Thrasimene, battle of, 1821: 6 Jan.
Thun, 1821: 11 Aug.
Thurn and Taxis, Karl Alexander of (1770-1827), 1821: 9 Dec.
Tiesenhausen, Catherine von (1803-1888), 1821: 12 Jan., 13 Jun., 7 Nov.
Tiesenhausen, Dorothea 'Dolly' von (1804-1863), 1821: 15 Jan.
Tintoretto, Jacopo Robusti (1518-1594), 1821: 26 Jun.
Titian, Tiziano Vecellio (c. 1488/90-1576), 1821: 25 Jun.

Tivoli, 1821: 7, 13 Apr.; 1822: 2 May
Torella, Prince Giuseppe (1787-1856), 1821: 14 Nov.
Torno, 1821: 25 Sep.
Trasimeno, 1821: 6 Jan.
Trento [Trent], 1821: 1 Jul.; 1822: 29 May
    Opera House, 1822: 29 May
Trevor, Arthur Hill (later 3rd Viscount Dungannon) (1798-1862), 1821: 27 Oct.
Tuscany, Maria-Luisa, archduchess of (1798-1857), 1821: 22 Aug.
Twiss, Francis (1759-1827), 1821: 22 Sep.
Twiss, Richard (1747-1821), 1821: 22 Sep.

Ulm, 1822: 12 Jun.

Valganna, 1821: 20 Sep.
Varese, 1821: 21 Sep.
Velletri, 1821: 2 May, 3 Nov.
Venice, 1821: 24-30 May; 1822: 19-25 May
    Arsenale, 1821: 28 May
    Basilica di San Marco, 1821: 29 May; 1822: 21 May
    Chiesa della Salute, 1821: 26 May
    Galleria dell'Accademia, 1821: 26 May; 1822: 20 May
    Galleria Manfrin, 1821: 25 May; 1822: 23 May
    Palazzo Barbarigo, 1821: 27 May; 1822: 22 May
    Palazzo Ducale, 1821: 29 May; 1822: 21 May
    Palazzo Pisani, 1821: 27 May
    Piazza San Marco, 1822: 21 May
    Prisons of the Inquisition, 1822: 21 May
Verona, 1822: 26-27 May
    Chiesa di S. Giorgio: 1822: 27 May
    Colosseum [Arena]: 1822: 27 May
Veronese, Paolo Caliari (1528-1588), 1821: 23, 26 Jun.; 1822: 27 May
Vicenza, 1822: 27 May
    Teatro Olimpico: 1822: 27 May
Vicovaro, 1821: 9, 11 Apr., 1822: 3 May
Voltaire (1694-1770), 1821: 9 Sep.
Vyvyan, Sir Richard (1800-1879), 1821: 20 Jan.

Wallersee, 1822: 1 Jun.
Wassen, 1821: 3 Aug.
Wasserburg am Inn, 1821: 10 Jul.
Werff, Adriaen van der (1659-1722), 1821: 13 Jun.
Weymouth, Thomas Thynne, Viscount (1796-1837), 1821: 13 Oct.
Weymouth, Harriet Robbins, Viscountess (1796-1873), 1821: 13 Oct.
Wilkie, Sir David (1785-1841), 1822: 5 May
Wilton, Thomas Grosvenor Egerton, 2nd earl of (1799-1882), 1821: 22, 23 Nov.; 1822: 19, 25 Jul.
Wood, Matthew (1768-1848), 1821: 25 Jun.
Württemburg, King Willhelm of (1771-1864), 1822: 14 Jun.

Ypres, 1822: 2 Jul.
Yverdon-les-Bains, 1821: 18 Aug.

Zug, 1821: 25, 28 Jul.
Zurich, 1821: 22 Jul.